SURPRISED BY HOPE

SURPRISED BY HOPE

Rethinking Heaven,
the Resurrection,
and the Mission of the Church

N. T. WRIGHT

HarperOne
An Imprint of HarperCollinsPublishers

HarperOne

HarperCollins books may be purchased for educational, business, or sales promotional use. For information please write: Special Markets Department, HarperCollins Publishers, 10 East 53rd Street, New York, NY 10022.

HarperCollins Web site: http://www.harpercollins.com

HarperCollins®, 📖®, and HarperOne™ are trademarks of Harper-Collins Publishers

BOOK DESIGN: Claudia Smelser

FIRST EDITION

Library of Congress Cataloging-in-Publication Data is available.

ISBN: 978–0–06–155182–6

09 10 11 12 RRD(H) 10 9

In grateful memory
of Stephen Neill, George Caird, and Charlie Moule
teachers, scholars, pastors, and friends
in the sure and certain hope of the resurrection of the dead

CONTENTS

14. Reshaping the Church for Mission (1): Biblical Roots

15. Reshaping the Church for Mission (2): Living the Future

PREFACE

What are we waiting for? And what are we going to do about it in the meantime?

Those two questions shape this book. First, it is about the ultimate future hope held out in the Christian gospel: the hope, that is, for salvation, resurrection, eternal life, and the cluster of other things that go with them. Second, it is about the discovery of hope within the present world: about the practical ways in which hope can come alive for communities and individuals who for whatever reason may lack it. And it is about the ways in which embracing the first can and should generate and sustain the second.

Most people, in my experience—including many Christians—don't know what the ultimate Christian hope really is. Most people—again, sadly, including many Christians—don't expect Christians to have much to say about hope within the present world. Most people don't imagine that these two could have anything to do with each other. Hence the title of the book: hope comes as a surprise, at several levels at once.

At the first level, the book is obviously about death and about what can be said from a Christian perspective about what lies beyond it. I am not going to attempt a physical or medical analysis of death and its aftermath or a psychological or anthropological description of beliefs and practices having to do with death. There are plenty of books about such things. Rather, I approach the question as a biblical theologian, drawing on other disciplines but hoping to supply what they usually lack and what I believe the church needs to recapture: the classic Christian answer to the question of death and beyond, which these days is not so much disbelieved (in world and church alike) as simply not known. A survey of beliefs about life after death conducted in Britain in 1995 indicated that though most people believed in some kind of continuing life, only a tiny minority, even among churchgoers, believed in the classic Christian position, that of a future bodily resurrection. Indeed, I often find that though Christians still use the word *resurrection,* they treat it as a synonym for "life after death" or "going to heaven" and that, when pressed, they often share the confusion of the wider world on the subject. And some Christian writers on the subject of death manage to marginalize resurrection and all that goes with it without apparently supposing that any great harm is thereby done.

I should say, as a kind of disclaimer, that at one level I am not well qualified to speak on the subject of death. Now in my late fifties, I am the least bereaved middle-aged person I know. My life has been remarkably free from tragedy; almost all my relatives have lived to a good age. I am surprised and grateful for this, and I certainly don't take it for granted. Moreover, though I have been ordained for over thirty years, the fact that my vocation has led me into universities, on the one hand, and into cathedral and diocesan work, on the other, means that I have conducted fewer funerals and memorial services than most clergy manage in their first two or three years. Seldom have I stood at a deathbed. But, whereas I obviously have a lot to learn firsthand about all these matters, I think I have made up for it by soaking myself, in a way that many don't have the chance to do, in the life and thought of the early Christians.[1] As I do that I regularly return with a sense that their voice has not been disbelieved but simply not heard at all. My aim in this book is to bring their beliefs to light, and I hope to life, again in the conviction that they offer not only the best hope but also the best-*grounded* hope that we have and, what's more, a hope that joins up, as I have said, with the hope that ought to energize our work for God's kingdom in the present world.

At the second level, then, the book is about the groundwork of practical and even political theology—of, that is, Christian reflection on the nature of the task we face as we seek to bring God's kingdom to bear on the real and painful world in which we live. (I apologize to librarians that this may cause confusion: is the book to be cataloged with "eschatology"—death, judgment, heaven, and hell—or "politics"?) Here too a disclaimer is in order. I am not a politician, though it is true that by virtue of my office I am a member of the British House of Lords. I have neither run for public office nor campaigned actively—in terms of the sheer hard work of speaking, writing, marching, cajoling—for many of the causes in which I believe. I have tried to put my shoulder to the wheel by other means. But the subjects in which I have specialized, and the pastoral situations I now face every day in a diocese several parts of which suffer severely from the faceless cruelties of the last fifty years, have forced me to think through some of what a Christian should be saying and thinking about rediscovering hope in the public and political world. As I have done so, I have found these two themes of hope, again and again, joining themselves together. I freely hand to potential critics these two disclaimers, my inexperience in both grief and politics and my hope that nevertheless the surprise of the Christian hope in both areas will reenergize and refresh those who work, more than I have been able to do, with both the dying and the dispossessed.

One more general word of introduction. All language about the future, as any economist or politician will tell you, is simply a set of signposts pointing into a fog. We see through a glass darkly, says St. Paul as he peers toward what lies ahead. All our language about future states of the world and of ourselves consists of complex pictures that may or may not correspond very well to the ultimate reality. But that doesn't mean it's anybody's guess or that every opinion is as good as every other one. And—supposing someone came forward out of the fog to meet us? That, of course, is the central though often ignored Christian belief.

This book grew out of lectures that were originally given in Westminster Abbey during the course of 2001. Some of these were reworked as the Stephenson Lectures in Sheffield, England, in spring 2003; some were given in Holy Trinity Church, Guildford, also in spring 2003; some were reworked again into the Didsbury Lectures at the Nazarene College in Manchester in October 2005; others found their way into church study days in St. Andrew's Church, Charleston, South Carolina, in January 2005; in St. Mark's Episcopal Church, Jacksonville, Florida, in March 2005; in City Church, Newcastle, England, also in 2005; in St. Mark's Theological Centre, Canberra, Australia, in April 2006; in a consortium of churches in Roanoke, Virginia, in March 2007, and (in the form of the Faraday Lecture) in Cambridge in May 2007. I am extremely grateful to all those who invited, welcomed, and hosted me on all these occasions and particularly to those who by their questions and acute comments helped me think through the issues further and avoid at least some mistakes. I am grateful to the Ship of Fools Web site for commissioning the piece included at the end and for permission to republish a lightly emended version of it here. My thanks too to Dr. Nick Perrin, who during his time at Westminster Abbey worked over the text as it then was and made all kinds of helpful suggestions. And my thanks, as ever and always, to Simon Kingston, Joanna Moriarty, and the energetic and watchful staff at SPCK, and their counterparts, not least Mickey Maudlin, at HarperOne.

N. T. Wright
Auckland Castle
Feast of the Ascension 2007

PART I

SETTING THE SCENE

1. ALL DRESSED UP AND NO PLACE TO GO?

INTRODUCTION

Five snapshots set the scene for the two questions this book addresses.

In autumn 1997 much of the world was plunged into a week of national mourning for Princess Diana, reaching its climax in the extraordinary funeral service in Westminster Abbey. People brought flowers, teddy bears, and other objects to churches, cathedrals, and town halls and stood in line for hours to write touching if sometimes tacky messages in books of condolence. Similar if somewhat smaller occasions of public grief took place following such incidents as the Oklahoma City bombing in 1995. They showed a rich confusion of belief, half belief, sentiment, and superstition about the fate of the dead. The reaction of the churches showed how far we had come from what might once have been traditional Christian teaching on the subject.

The second scene was farce, with a serious undertone. Early in 1999 I awoke one morning to hear on the radio that a public figure had been sacked for heretical statements about the afterlife. I listened eagerly. Was this perhaps a radical bishop or theologian, exposed at last? Back came the answer, incredible but true: no, it was a soccer coach. Glen Hoddle, the manager of the England team, declared his belief in a particular version of reincarnation, according to which sins committed in one life are punished by disabilities in the next. Groups representing disabled people objected strongly, and Hoddle was dismissed. It was commented at the time, however, that reincarnation had become remarkably popular in our society and that it would be very odd if Hindus (many of whom hold similar beliefs) were automatically banned from coaching a national sports team.

The third scene is not a single moment, but the snapshot will be familiar. Twenty or thirty people arrive in slow-moving cars at a shabby building on the edge of town. A tinny electronic organ plays supermarket music. A few words, the press of a button, a solemn look from the undertaker, and they file out again, go home for a cup of tea, and wonder what it was all about. Cremation, almost unknown in the Western world a hundred years ago, is now the preference, actual or assumed, of the great majority. It both reflects and causes subtle but far-reaching shifts in attitudes to death and to whatever hope lies beyond.

I initially wrote those opening descriptions in early 2001. By the end of that year, of course, we had witnessed a fourth moment, too well known but also too horrible to describe or discuss in much detail. The events of September 11 of that year are etched in global memory; the thousands who died and the tens of thousands who were bereaved evoke our love and prayers. I shall not say much more about that day, but for many people it raised once more, very sharply, the questions this book seeks to discuss—as did, in their different ways, the three massive so-called natural disasters of 2004 and 2005: the Asian tsunami of Boxing Day 2004; the hurricanes on the Gulf Coast of North America of August 2005, bringing long-lasting devastation to New Orleans in particular; and the horrifying earthquake in Pakistan and Kashmir in October of that same year.

The fifth scene is a graveyard of a different sort. If you go to the historic village of Easington in County Durham, England, and walk down the hill toward the sea, you come to the town called Easington Colliery. The town still bears that name, but there is no colliery there anymore. Where the pit head once stood, with thousands of people working to produce more coal faster and more efficiently than at most other pits, there is smooth and level grass. Empty to the eye, but pregnant with bereavement. All around, despite the heroic efforts of local leaders, there are the signs of postindustrial blight, with all the human fallout of other people's power games. And that sight stands in my mind as a symbol, or rather a symbolic question, every bit as relevant to similar communities in America and elsewhere in the world as they are to my home territory. What hope is there for communities that have lost their way, their way of life, their coherence, their *hope?*[1]

This book addresses two questions that have often been dealt with entirely separately but that, I passionately believe, belong tightly together. First, what is the ultimate Christian hope? Second, what hope is there for change, rescue, transformation, new possibilities within the world in the present? And the main answer can be put like this. As long as we see Christian hope in terms of "going to heaven," of a salvation that is essentially *away from* this world, the two questions are bound to appear as unrelated. Indeed, some insist angrily that to ask the second one at all is to ignore the first one, which is the really important one. This in turn makes some others get angry when people talk of resurrection, as if this might draw attention away from the really important and pressing matters of contemporary social concern. But if the Christian hope is for *God's new creation,* for "new heavens and new earth," and if that hope has already come to life in Jesus of Nazareth, then there is every reason to join the two questions together. And if that is so, we find that answering the one is also answering the other. I find that to many— not least, many Christians—all this comes as a surprise: both that the Christian hope is surprisingly different from what they had assumed and that this same hope offers a coherent and energizing basis for work in today's world.

In this first chapter I want to set the scene and open up the questions by looking at the contemporary confusion in our world—the wider world, beyond the churches—about life after death. Then, in the second chapter, I shall look at the churches themselves, where there seems to me a worryingly similar uncertainty. This will highlight the key questions that have to be asked and suggest a framework for how we go about answering them.

I am convinced that most people, including most practicing Christians, are muddled and misguided on this topic and that this muddle produces quite serious mistakes in our thinking, our praying, our liturgies, our practice, and perhaps particularly our mission to the world. What's more, as the examples at the start of this chapter indicate, the non-Christian world, not least within the contemporary West, is confused about what to believe on its own account, and it is confused too about what Christians are supposed to believe. Often people assume that Christians are simply committed to a belief in "life after death" in the most general terms and have no idea how the more specific notions of resurrection, judgment, the second coming of Jesus, and so on fit together and make any sense—let alone how they relate to the urgent concerns of today's real world.

Nor is this a matter simply of sorting out what to believe about someone who has died or about one's own probable postmortem destiny, important though both of those are. It's a matter of thinking straight about God and his purposes for the cosmos and about what God is doing right now, already, as part of those purposes. From Plato to Hegel and beyond, some of the greatest philosophers declared that what you think about death, and life beyond it, is the key to thinking seriously about everything else—and, indeed, that it provides one of the main reasons for thinking seriously about anything at all. This is something a Christian theologian should heartily endorse.

So, without further delay, we plunge into the confusion on this topic that exists in the wider world, the world outside the church door.

Beliefs about death and what lies beyond come in all shapes and sorts and sizes. Even a quick glance at the classic views of the major religious traditions gives the lie to the old idea that all religions are basically the same. There is a world of difference between the Muslim who believes that a Palestinian boy killed by Israeli soldiers goes straight to heaven and the Hindu for whom the rigorous outworking of karma means that one must return in a different body to pursue the next stage of one's destiny. There is a world of difference between the Orthodox Jew who believes that all the righteous will be raised to new individual bodily life in the resurrection and the Buddhist who hopes after death to disappear like a drop in the ocean, losing one's own identity in the great nameless and formless Beyond.[2] And there are of course major variations between different branches or schools of thought in these great religions.

So too there are wide varieties of beliefs about what the dead are up to right now. In many parts of Africa the ancestors still play a large role in communal and family life, and there are widespread and complex systems for seeking their help or at least preventing them from making mischief. Nor are these beliefs—as Western secularists might arrogantly assume—confined to so-called primitive peoples. The anthropologist Nigel Barley tells how he met a highly trained Japanese colleague who had worked near him in Chad. Barley had been fascinated by "the complicated form of ancestor-worship involving bones and the destruction of the skull and all sorts of exchanges between the dead and the living." His Japanese friend had found all this quite dull. Barley comments:

> He was, of course, a Buddhist who had a shrine to his departed parents in his living room, on which regular offerings were made. . . . He had taken to Africa some bone from his dead father's leg, carefully wrapped in white cloth, to ensure protection during his fieldwork.

For me [Barley comments], ancestor worship was something to be described and analysed. For him, it would be the *absence* of such links between the living and the dead that would require special explanation.[3]

Coming closer to home, we have seen in our own day and culture a bewildering variety not only of stated beliefs but also of telltale practices associated with death and life afterward. I suspect there was never a period when Christian orthodoxy on the subject was the belief of even the majority of people in Britain. Certainly, already by the time of the Victorians there was a wide variety of belief as people wrestled with questions of faith and doubt. This variety of belief toward the end of the nineteenth century was closely reflected, as we shall see, in the hymns and prayers of the church.

Moving forward toward our own time, the First World War produced not only a great deal of sudden death but also much reflection on its meaning. Some historians have suggested that belief in hell, already under attack from theologians in the nineteenth century, was one of the major casualties of the Great War. There had been so much hell on earth that people couldn't believe that God would create such a place hereafter as well. So much death affected so many at that time, and again less than a generation later in World War II, that my own reading of our twentieth-century British attitudes to death is that there was simply too much to cope with. I grew up in a culture of near silence about death; children in the 1950s were insulated from it. I didn't attend a funeral until I was nearly twenty. This may have been, I suspect, a reaction against perceived melodramatic Victorian deathbed and funeral practices. It may also have been a strategy whereby adults might protect themselves from their own enormous and still-buried grief, which could all too clearly be reflected in and brought to the surface by the innocent reactions of a child.

But if death, and life beyond, was the great unmentionable in the 1950s, it certainly is not today. Films, plays, and novels explore it from all kinds of angles. Films like *Four Weddings and a Funeral* and *Perchance to Dream* reflect the interest, even the fascination, of a new generation with the question they had not asked and to which they knew no satisfying answers. The darker end of the market wallows in death, not only in screened violence but also in snuff movies, where death becomes the ultimate thrill. The nihilism to which secularism has given birth leaves many with no reason for living, and death is once again in the cultural air.

The most brilliant play I saw when we lived in London was the Pulitzer Prize–winning play *Wit* by Margaret Edson, a schoolteacher from Atlanta, Georgia.[4] The heroine, Vivian Bearing, is a renowned specialist in the *Holy Sonnets* of John Donne, and the entire play takes place in the cancer ward, where she is herself dying, reflecting as she does so on Donne's great sonnet "Death Be Not Proud," to which I shall presently return. The play was more successful in New York than in London; perhaps Britain is not yet as ready for a full exploration of midlife death as are our American cousins. But the questions are around us all the time, and people are increasingly curious about possible answers.

Where does all this leave us? What *do* people believe in when they talk about life after death?

VARIETIES OF BELIEF

The main beliefs that emerge in the present climate seem to me of three types, none of which corresponds to Christian orthodoxy. There are still attempts at restating a more traditional view; I think, for instance, of William Golding's dark but stunning *Pincher Martin*. But in general the mood is that traditional beliefs, both in judgment and hell and in resurrection, are actually offensive to modern sensibilities.[5]

First, some believe in complete annihilation; that is at least clean and tidy, however unsatisfying it may be as an account of human destiny. This, presumably, is what lies underneath Dylan Thomas's angry outburst at the death of his father:

> Do not go gentle into that good night.
> Rage, rage, against the dying of the light.[6]

But not many can sustain complete denial of any future life. Look at the religion section of the average bookshop, and you will find that more and more people today seem to believe in some form of reincarnation. This is not confined to practicing Hindus and half converts like Glen Hoddle. In the gruesome but fascinating novel by Will Self, *How the Dead Live,* his central character, a grumpy London woman recently deceased and living in a ghostly parody of London, discovers that she will be condemned to regular reincarnation unless she manages to grasp at what her underworld guide calls "the hooks and eyes of grace," through which, it seems, she will be able to escape the continual circle:

> Still one last chance to get off the go-round, girl. Still time to attach you to the hooks and eyes of grace. If you want it. If you can just— even for a few instants—achieve a one-pointedness of thought.[7]

But she doesn't and is reborn—as an unhappy baby, destined to a short and brutal life. Will Self seems to envisage a kind of Hinduism, where the mental achievement of brief, focused thought, replacing the wandering and distracted mind or soul, is the key to escaping the cycle, the ever-rotating wheel, of death and birth. A different twist on reincarnation is provided by the many for whom— again to judge from the literature available—it has become a way of pursuing psychoanalysis by other means, discovering aspects of your personality that come from who you were or what happened to you in a previous life. It thus flows into the larger New Age culture in which bits and pieces of esoteric beliefs are mixed with dreams of self-help and self-fulfillment.

Also on the fringe of New Age ideas is a revival of the views we discovered in Shelley, a sort of low-grade, popular nature religion with elements of Buddhism. At death one is absorbed into the wider world, into the wind and the trees. The anonymous poem left, in case of his death, by a soldier going to Northern Ireland expresses it well:

Do not stand at my grave and weep;
I am not there. I do not sleep.
I am a thousand winds that blow.
I am the diamond glints on snow.
I am the sunlight on ripened grain.
I am the gentle autumn rain.
. . . .
Do not stand at my grave and cry;
I am not there. I do not die.[8]

After Diana's death one message left in London spoke as in the princess's own voice: "I did not leave you at all. I am still with you. I am in the sun and in the wind. I am even in the rain. I did not die, I am with you all."[9] Many funerals, memorial services, and even funerary inscriptions now give voice to this kind of belief. Many would-be Christians try to persuade themselves and others that this kind of ongoing life is really what is meant by traditional teaching either about the immortality of the soul or the resurrection of the dead. Others, however, like the highly successful children's writer Philip Pullman, who takes something like this line, make it pretty clear that he is thereby attacking and deconstructing traditional Christian belief and offering something else instead.[10]

The funeral practices that have grown up, or reappeared, in our own day exhibit the same kind of confusion. The practice of putting objects in coffins along with the dead to comfort or help them in the life to come was until recently described by students of culture as an interesting practice now abandoned in the modern West; but gifts for the dead are making a comeback, with photographs, jewelry, teddy bears, and the like being placed in coffins.[11] Nigel Barley relates stories, told by a crematorium official, of widows placing in the coffin a packet of digestive biscuits or the deceased's spare glasses and false teeth. On one occasion a widow put into her husband's coffin two cans of the spray adhesive that the dead man had used to paste on his toupee, causing an explosion that bent the furnace door.[12] What sort of belief, if any, does all this reflect?

Finally, at the popular level, belief in ghosts and the possibility of spiritualistic contact with the dead has resisted all the inroads of a century of secularism. When I first delivered in Westminster Abbey the series of lectures that became this book, the Abbey's weekly newsletter advertising the first lecture also announced that one of the Abbey's very own seventeenth-century ghosts might make his annual appearance around the same time. And there are of course numerous popular phenomena on both sides of the Atlantic, such as the continuing Elvis cult in the United States, that need categories of their own to be described.

I take it that I am describing a world my readers will recognize. My aim is not to catalog it exhaustively but to draw attention to certain features of it as well as to the striking fact that not only is it quite unlike anything that can be called orthodox Christian belief but also, so far as I can tell, *most people simply don't know what orthodox Christian belief is*. It is assumed that Christians believe in life after death, as opposed to denying any survival after death, and that every sort of life after death must therefore be the same kind of (Christian) thing. The idea that "life after death" might include variations embodying significantly different beliefs about God and the world, and significantly different agendas for how people might live in the present, has simply never occurred to most modern Western people. In particular, most people have little or no idea what the word *resurrection* actually means or why Christians say they believe it.

What is more worrying, this multiple ignorance seems often to be true in the churches as well. This is the subject of the next chapter.

2. PUZZLED ABOUT PARADISE?

CHRISTIAN CONFUSION ABOUT HOPE

One of the most frequently quoted Anglican sermons of the twentieth century is also, alas, one of the most misleading. In a widely used guide to arranging secular funerals, words by Canon Henry Scott Holland of St. Paul's are quoted as the preface, and thousands of people request that they be read at funerals and memorial services:

> Death is nothing at all. It does not count. I have only slipped away into the next room. Nothing has happened. Everything remains exactly as it was. I am I and you are you, and the old life we lived so fondly together is untouched, unchanged. Whatever we were to each other, that we still are. Call me by the old familiar name. Speak of me in the easy way which you always used. Put no difference into your tone. Wear no forced air of solemnity or sorrow. . . . Life means all that it ever meant. It is the same as it ever was. There is absolute and unbroken continuity. What is this death but a negligible accident? Why should I be out of mind because I am out of sight? I am waiting for you, for an interval, somewhere very near, just around the corner. All is well. Nothing is hurt; nothing is lost. One brief moment and all will be as it was before. How we shall laugh at the trouble of parting when we meet again![1]

What nobody usually points out is that this was not the view that Scott Holland himself was advocating. It was simply what, he suggested, came to mind as we "look down upon the quiet face" of "one who has been very near and dear to us." Elsewhere in the same sermon, preached in 1910 upon the death of King Edward VII, he spoke of the other feelings that also are raised by death, which seems "so inexplicable, so ruthless, so blundering . . . the cruel ambush into which we are snared . . . It makes its horrible breach in our gladness with careless and inhuman disregard of us. . . . Beyond the darkness hides its impenetrable secret. . . . Dumb as the night, that terrifying silence!"

Scott Holland went on to attempt something of a reconciliation between these two views of death. The Christian has, according to the New Testament, "already passed from death to life" so that the further transition of actual death ought not to be as terrifying as it appears. In addition, we should (he suggests) think of the life beyond death in terms of a continuation of the growth in the knowledge of God and in personal holiness that has already begun here. That raises questions we cannot address at this stage of the book, but it is already clear that to take the paragraph so frequently quoted out of the context of the sermon in which it was originally spoken does serious violence to the author's intention. We can only wonder at the extraordinary denial that is going on when this is done. It amounts to a resolute refusal to tell the truth about the real and savage break, the horrible denial of the goodness of human life, that every death involves. I would love to think that one of the effects of the present book would be to challenge the use of the Scott Holland piece in Christian funerals. It offers hollow comfort. By itself, without comment, it simply tells lies. It is not even a parody of Christian hope. Instead, it simply denies that there is any problem, any need for hope in the first place.

Contrast with that well-known piece the robust attitude of a classic Christian theology, stated by the sometime dean of St. Paul's, John Donne:

Death be not proud, though some have call'd thee
    Mighty and dreadful, for thou art not so;
    For those who thou think'st thou dost overthrow
Die not, poor Death, nor yet canst thou kill me.
From rest and sleep, which but thy pictures be,
    Much pleasure—then, from thee much more must flow;
    And soonest our best men with thee do go,
Rest of their bones, and soul's delivery.
Thou'rt slave to fate, chance, kings, and desperate men,
    And dost with poison, war, and sickness dwell,
    And poppy or charms can make us sleep as well,
And better than thy stroke. Why swell'st thou then?
    One short sleep past, we wake eternally,
    And death shall be no more. Death, thou shalt die.[2]

At first sight this might seem rather close to Scott Holland. Death is nothing at all? Death is not after all mighty and dreadful? But no, the last two lines say it all. Death is a great enemy, but it has been conquered and will at the last be conquered fully. "One short sleep past, we wake eternally, / And death shall be no more. Death, thou shalt die." In the Scott Holland passage, there is nothing to be conquered. For John Donne, death is important; it is an enemy, but for the Christian, it is a *beaten* enemy. In line with much classic Christian thought, Donne sees life after death in two stages: first, a short sleep, then an eternal waking.[3] *And death shall be no more.* Donne grasped what we shall discover to be the central New Testament belief: that at the last, death will be not simply redefined but defeated. God's intention is not to let death have its way with us. If the promised final future is simply that immortal souls leave behind their mortal bodies, then death still rules—since that is a description not of the *defeat* of death but simply of death itself, seen from one angle.[4]

But I am running too far ahead of myself. The classic Christian position is stated in the early creeds, themselves dependent on the

New Testament in ways we shall explore later in the book. In my church we declare every day and every week that we believe in "the resurrection of the body." But do we? Many Christian teachers and theologians in recent decades have questioned the appropriateness of this language. One recent lavishly illustrated coffee-table book on the subject of death and the afterlife, devoting a bare four pages to the apparently odd idea of resurrection, declares blandly that "current orthodox Christianity no longer holds to the belief in physical resurrection, preferring the concept of the eternal existence of the soul, although some creeds still cling to the old ideas."[5] Let us again be quite clear. If this is true, then death is not conquered but redescribed: no longer an enemy, it is simply the means by which, as in *Hamlet,* the immortal soul shuffles off its mortal coil.[6]

EXPLORING THE OPTIONS

There has been, in fact, an oscillation between two poles, which you can see by walking around any old church and looking at the monuments. Some envisage death as a horrid enemy, stalking its prey. This is often combined with the firm proclamation that, though an enemy, death will finally be defeated. Until at least the late eighteenth century, many tombstones and memorials were inscribed with the Latin word *resurgam,* which means "I shall arise," indicating that the now-dead person believed in an intermediate sleep to be followed by a new bodily life at some future point. That was why people were buried facing east, so as to rise to meet the Lord at his coming. We shall come back to this in the tenth chapter.

The other pole of belief is represented by St. Francis's hymn, "All Creatures of Our God and King," with its remarkable invocation of "And thou, most dear and kindly death, waiting to hush our latest breath." Many hymns, prayers, and sermons have tried to soften the blow by presenting death as a friend coming to take us to a better place; this was a familiar theme in the nineteenth century and has its secular echo in the modern movements toward voluntary euthanasia. Thus Christian thought has oscillated between seeing death as a vile enemy and a welcome friend.

Traditionally, of course, we suppose that Christianity teaches about a heaven above, to which the saved or blessed go, and a hell below, for the wicked and impenitent. This is still assumed by many both inside and outside the church as the official line, which they may or may not accept.

A remarkable example arrived in the mail not long ago: a book, apparently a best-seller, by Maria Shriver, the present first lady of California, who is married to Arnold Schwarzenegger and whose uncle was John F. Kennedy. The book is called *What's Heaven?*[7] and is aimed at children, with lots of large pictures of fluffy clouds in blue skies. Each page of text has one sentence in extra large type, making the basic message of the book crystal clear. Heaven, says Shriver,

is somewhere you believe in. . . . It's a beautiful place where you can sit on soft clouds and talk to other people who are there. At night you can sit next to the stars, which are the brightest of anywhere in the universe. . . . If you're good throughout your life, then you get to go to heaven. . . . When your life is finished here on earth, God sends angels down to take you up to Heaven to be with him. . . . [And Grandma is] alive in me. . . . Most important, she taught me to believe in myself. . . . She's in a safe place, with the stars, with God and the angels. . . . She is watching over us from up there. . . .

"I want you to know [says the heroine to her great-grandma] that even though you are no longer here, your spirit will always be alive in me."[8]

This is more or less exactly what millions of people in the Western world have come to believe, to accept as truth, and to teach to their children. The book was sent me by a friend who works with grieving children and who described this as "one of the worst books for children" and said, "I hope you find this awful book helpful in what not to say"! It is indeed a prime example of that genre. The truth of what the Bible teaches is very, very different at several levels.

It comes as something of a shock, in fact, when people are told what is in fact the case: that there is very little in the Bible about "going to heaven when you die" and not a lot about a postmortem hell either. The medieval pictures of heaven and hell, boosted though not created by Dante's classic work, have exercised a huge influence on Western Christian imagination. Many Christians grow up assuming that whenever the New Testament speaks of heaven it refers to the place to which the saved will go after death. In Matthew's gospel, Jesus's sayings in the other gospels about the "kingdom of God" are rendered as "kingdom of heaven"; since many read Matthew first, when they find Jesus talking about "entering the kingdom of heaven," they have their assumptions confirmed and suppose that he is indeed talking about how to go to heaven when you die, which is certainly not what either Jesus or Matthew had in mind. Many mental pictures have grown up around this and are now assumed to be what the Bible teaches or what Christians believe.[9]

But the language of heaven in the New Testament doesn't work that way. "God's kingdom" in the preaching of Jesus refers not to postmortem destiny, not to our escape from this world into another one, but to God's sovereign rule coming "on earth as it is in heaven."[10] The roots of the misunderstanding go very deep, not least into the residual Platonism that has infected whole swaths of Christian thinking and has misled people into supposing that Christians are meant to devalue this present world and our present bodies and regard them as shabby or shameful.

Likewise, the pictures of heaven in the book of Revelation have been much misunderstood. The wonderful description in Revelation 4 and 5 of the twenty-four elders casting their crowns before the throne of God and the lamb, beside the sea of glass, is not, despite one of Charles Wesley's great hymns, a picture of the last day, with all the redeemed in heaven at last.[11] It is a picture of *present* reality, the heavenly dimension of our present life. Heaven, in the Bible, is not a future destiny but the other, hidden, dimension of our ordinary life—God's dimension, if you like. God made heaven and earth; at the last he will remake both and join them together forever. And when we come to the picture of the actual end in Revelation 21–22, we find not ransomed souls making their way to a disembodied heaven but rather the new Jerusalem coming down from heaven to earth, uniting the two in a lasting embrace.[12]

Most Christians today, I fear, never think about this from one year to the next. They remain satisfied with what is at best a truncated and distorted version of the great biblical hope. Indeed, the popular picture is reinforced again and again in hymns, prayers, monuments, and even quite serious works of theology and history. It is simply assumed that the word *heaven* is the appropriate term for the ultimate destination, the final home, and that the language of resurrection, and of the new earth as well as the new heavens, must somehow be fitted into that.[13]

What we see in today's church is, I think, a confused combination of several things. For one, the old heaven-and-hell view has been under attack. Many now refuse to believe in hell at all, but we find over the last century, as this denial developed, that paradoxically it has led to a diminution of the promise of heaven since if everybody is on the same track it would seem unfair to allow some to go directly to the destination rather than continue the long postmortem journey. The idea of such a journey after death is itself now frequent, though again it has virtually no warrant in the Bible or early Christian thought. We see too the rehabilitation of a modern, sanitized, version of the old theory of purgatory: since at death we are all still quite unready to meet our Maker, we will need (it is suggested) a period of refinement, of growing toward the light. (People who think like this tend to prefer to put it that way rather than emphasizing purging or other uncomfortable things.)[14] Many embrace a universalism in which God will endlessly offer to the unrepentant the choice of faith until at last all succumb to the wooing of divine love.[15] Some declare that heaven as traditionally pictured looks insufferably boring—sitting on clouds playing harps all the time—and that they either don't believe it or don't want to go there. Others declare, rather sniffily, that a God who simply wants people to adore him all the time is not a figure they would respect. Those of us who protest that the orthodox picture is of a vibrant and active human life, reflecting God's image in the new heavens and new earth, are sometimes accused of projecting our go-getting contemporary life onto the screen of the future.

THE EFFECTS OF CONFUSION

This many-sided confusion plays out in the hymns we sing, in the way we celebrate the Christian year, and in the type of funerals or cremations we have. A few words about each of these will show what I mean.

First, hymns. A glance through the average hymnbook reveals that a good many references to the future life beyond death are closer to Tennyson, or even to Shelley, than they are to orthodox Christianity:

Till in the ocean of thy love
We lose ourselves in heaven above.

The words are those of the devout John Keble, but it was he who was for a moment lost not in Christianity but in a drop-in-the-ocean Buddhist eschatology.[16] And what about his Oxford movement colleague, John Henry Newman, with his almost-Gnostic line?

So long thy power hath blest me, sure it still
Will lead me on,
O'er moor and fen, o'er crag and torrent, till

The night is gone.
And with the morn those angel faces smile
Which I have loved long since, and lost awhile.

Did Newman *really* believe that he had a previous life with the angels, whether before his conception or in early childhood, and that he would return there in due course? And—though of course the idea of the lonely pilgrim following the "kindly light" across the moors and fens is a powerful, romantic idea—did he really think that the present world and the present life could be described simply as "night"?[17]

Or what about the blatant Platonism of the hymn "Abide with Me," still a favorite in some circles?

Heaven's morning breaks, and earth's vain shadows flee.

There are entire hymns and anthems that embody this train of thought. In a quick flip through the hymnbook, I noted dozens of other examples, not all explicable by the process of selection at a time when the prevailing theology wanted to say that sort of thing.

Or what about the Christmas hymn "It Came upon the Midnight Clear," which declares in the final verse that

For lo! the days are hastening on
By prophet bards foretold,
When, with the ever-circling years
Comes round the age of gold.
When peace shall over all the earth
Its ancient splendors fling,
And the whole world give back the song
Which now the angels sing.

It's a well-loved Christmas carol, but the idea of cycles of history eventually returning to a golden age is neither Christian nor Jewish but decidedly pagan. While we're on Christmas carols, consider "Away in a Manger," which prays, "and fit us for heaven, to live with thee there." No resurrection, no new creation, no marriage of heaven and earth.

Some of the hymns in the revivalist and charismatic traditions slip into the easy mistake, cognate as we shall see with misleading views of the "second coming," of suggesting that Jesus will return to take his people away from earth and "home" to heaven. Thus that wonderful hymn, "How Great thou Art," in its final stanza, declares:

> When Christ shall come, with shout of acclamation,
> And take me home, what joy shall fill my heart.

The second line (to anticipate our later argument) might better read, "And heal this world, what joy shall fill my heart." Actually, the original Swedish version of the hymn doesn't talk about Christ coming to take me home; that was the translator's adaptation. Rather, it speaks of the veils of time falling, faith being changed into clear sight, and the bells of eternity summoning us to our Sabbath rest, all of which has a lot more to recommend it.[18]

Some hymns, of course, stand out against this trend. "Jerusalem the Golden" draws attention to the decisive final chapters of Revelation. A few hymns speak of being "woken by the last dread call" or of "rising glorious at the last day." One great hymn speaks of God working his purpose out so that "the earth shall be filled with the glory of God as the waters cover the sea." But, towering over all these, is the great All Saints' Day hymn, "For All the Saints," whose sequence of thought catches the New Testament emphasis exactly right. After celebrating the life of the saints in the opening verses, our communion with them in the fourth, and their strengthening of us in the fifth, the sixth verse speaks of our joining them in their present abode, which is *not* the final resting place but rather the intermediate place of rest, joy, and refreshment, for which one name is paradise:

The golden evening brightens in the west;
Soon, soon to faithful warriors comes their rest;
Sweet is the calm of paradise the blest.
Alleluia, Alleluia!

Only *after* that does the resurrection occur:

But lo! there breaks a yet more glorious day;
The saints triumphant rise in bright array;
The King of glory passes on His way.
Alleluia, Alleluia!

Which leads in to the triumphant final verse, arriving at last in the new Jerusalem.[19]

If our hymns reveal the confusion we have got ourselves into, the way many mainstream Christians keep the Christian year shows much the same thing. I have written elsewhere about the sheer muddle that has, in recent years, allowed a two-day festival, if you can call it that, of All Saints and All Souls, preceded yet more confusingly by Halloween.[20]

What's more, Christmas itself has now far outstripped Easter in popular culture as the real celebratory center of the Christian year—a move that completely reverses the New Testament's emphasis. We sometimes try, in hymns, prayers, and sermons, to build a whole theology on Christmas, but it can't in fact sustain such a thing. We then keep Lent, Holy Week, and Good Friday so thoroughly that we have hardly any energy left for Easter except for the first night and day. Easter, however, should be the center. Take that away and there is, almost literally, nothing left.

The same confusions are apparent in the ways we do funerals. Many new funeral rites have been penned and published in recent years, often after lengthy debates. But before we get to them, a word about the implicit theology held by many of those who opt for cremation rather than burial. Reasons of hygiene and overcrowding led reformers toward the end of the last century to propose this step, which, as not all Western Christians know, is still firmly opposed by the Eastern Orthodox (despite the shortage of land in Greece at least) as well as by Orthodox Jews and Muslims. But cremation tends, classically, to belong with a Hindu or Buddhist theology, and at a low-grade and popular level, as we have already seen, that is the direction toward which our culture is rapidly moving. When people ask for their ashes to be scattered on a favorite hillside or in a well-loved river or along a shoreline, we can sympathize with the feeling (though not, perhaps, with denying the bereaved a specific spot to visit in their grief). But the underlying implication, of a desire simply to be merged back into the created world, without any affirmation of a future life of new embodiment, flies in the face of classic Christian theology.

I am not of course saying that cremation is heretical. I shall speak in due course about its relation to the resurrection body. I am merely noting that the huge swing toward it in the last century reflects at least in part some of the confusions, both in the church and in the world, that we have observed. I also note in passing that a ceremony in a building that is used for nothing else is a very different event from a funeral, whether or not followed by cremation, in a building that is used daily and weekly for prayer, Eucharist, celebration, for baptisms and weddings, for the whole worshipping life of a community. Or, to look at it another way, there is something wonderful and profound about entering church through the churchyard, where are buried those who worshipped there in centuries past. But all that too is another story.

When it comes to funerals themselves, the confusion elsewhere is reflected quite faithfully (if that's the right word). So much goes on in different churches that I can only comment selectively and in relation to my own church (the Church of England). Spot checks elsewhere indicate that it is not untypical. Resurrection itself has not disappeared entirely, but again and again it is pushed to the margins, and the underlying story told in the service about the recently deceased is not (as it would be were it in line with the New Testament) about their resting peacefully in anticipation of the final renewal of all things but about their going on a journey to end up in "God's kingdom." One could put it like this: if someone came to these funeral services with no idea of the classic Jewish and Christian teaching on the subject, the funeral services would do little to enlighten them and plenty to mislead them or confirm them in their existing muddle. I hope that those who take seriously the argument of this present book will examine the current practice of the church, from its official liturgies to all the unofficial bits and pieces that surround them, and try to discover fresh ways of expressing, embodying, and teaching what the New Testament actually teaches rather than the mangled, half-understood, and vaguely held theories and opinions we are meeting in these first two chapters. Frankly, what we have at the moment isn't, as the old liturgies used to say, "the sure and certain hope of the resurrection of the dead" but the vague and fuzzy optimism that somehow things may work out in the end.

As the argument of this book develops, it will become clear that we cannot simply regard this as a problem at which we simply shrug our shoulders and say, "Well, there are different views on these topics." What we say about death and resurrection gives shape and color to everything else. If we are not careful, we will offer merely a "hope" that is no longer a surprise, no longer able to transform lives and communities in the present, no longer generated by the resurrection of Jesus himself and looking forward to the promised new heavens and new earth.

Hymns, the Christian year, and ceremonies of death all tell a similar story. Perhaps equally important is the larger theology, and the wider worldview, accompanying the contemporary muddle.

WIDER IMPLICATIONS OF CONFUSION

What role does a belief in life beyond the grave play within the larger issues that face us in Christian life and thought?

Karl Marx famously spoke of religion as the opium of the people. He supposed that oppressive rulers would use the promise of a joyful future life to try to stop the masses from rising in revolt. That has indeed often been the case. But my impression is that religion is an 'opium' when the religion in question includes the Platonic downgrading of bodies and of the created order in general, regarding them as the "vain shadows" of earth, which we happily leave behind at death. Why try to improve the present prison if release is at hand? Why oil the wheels of a machine that will soon plunge over a cliff? That is precisely the effect created to this day by some devout Christians who genuinely believe that "salvation" has nothing to do with the way the present world is ordered.

By contrast, it has often been observed that the robust Jewish and Christian doctrine of the resurrection, as part of God's new creation, gives more value, not less, to the present world and to our present bodies. What these doctrines give, both in classic Judaism and in classic Christianity, is a sense of continuity as well as discontinuity between the present world (and the present state), and the future, whatever it shall be, with the result that what we do in the present matters enormously. Paul speaks of the future resurrection as a major motive for treating our bodies properly in the present time (1 Corinthians 6:14), and as the reason not for sitting back and waiting for it all to happen but for working hard in the present, knowing that nothing done in the Lord, in the power of the Spirit, in the present time will be wasted in God's future (1 Corinthians 15:58). To this we shall return.

The classic Christian doctrine, therefore, is actually far more powerful and revolutionary than the Platonic one. It was people who believed robustly in the resurrection, not people who compromised and went in for a mere spiritualized survival, who stood up against Caesar in the first centuries of the Christian era. A piety that sees death as the moment of "going home at last," the time when we are "called to God's eternal peace," has no quarrel with powermongers who want to carve up the world to suit their own ends.

SURPRISED BY HOPE

Resurrection, by contrast, has always gone with a strong view of God's justice and of God as the good creator. Those twin beliefs give rise not to a meek acquiescence to injustice in the world but to a robust determination to oppose it. English evangelicals gave up believing in the urgent imperative to improve society (such as we find with Wilberforce in the late eighteenth and early nineteenth centuries) about the same time that they gave up believing robustly in resurrection and settled for a disembodied heaven instead. It would take a longer study than this one to see whether the same shift happened at the same time in the United States and elsewhere, but I would not be surprised to find that it did. We shall come back to this crucial theme toward the end of the book.

THE KEY QUESTIONS

I hope the brief survey offered in these first two chapters is enough to give at least a flavor of the confusing picture that meets us at every turn today in world and church alike. We must now list the key questions that underlie the whole book and glance ahead to the discussions, and indeed to the solutions, that I shall offer in the coming chapters.

The first two questions are presupposed throughout without having a particular chapter devoted to them. First, how do we know about all this? My own church, the Church of England, part of the worldwide Anglican Communion, declares that it finds its doctrine in scripture, tradition, and reason, taken together in their proper blend.[21] I suggest that a good deal of our current view of death and the life beyond has come from none of these but rather from impulses in the culture that created, at best, semi-Christian informal traditions that now need to be reexamined in the clear light of scripture. Scripture, in fact, teaches things about the future life that most Christians, and almost all non-Christians, have never heard of. Of course, the evidence of parapsychology and similar studies and of so-called near-death experiences is not unimportant, but such evidence quite easily blends with the accumulation of folk wisdom. What we are here concerned with is going beyond that and investigating the often forgotten riches of the Christian tradition itself, with scripture at its heart.

Second, do we have immortal souls, and if so, what are they? Again, much Christian and sub-Christian tradition has assumed that we all do indeed have souls that need saving and that the soul, if saved, will be the part of us that goes to heaven when we die. All this, however, finds minimal support in the New Testament, including the teaching of Jesus, where the word *soul,* though rare, reflects when it does occur underlying Hebrew or Aramaic words referring not to a disembodied entity hidden within the outer shell of the disposable body but rather to what we would call the whole person or personality, seen as being confronted by God. As to immortality, 1 Timothy 6:16 declares that only God himself has immortality, and 2 Timothy 1:10 declares that immortality has only come to light, and hence is presumably only available, through the gospel. In other words, the idea that every human possesses an immortal soul, which is the "real" part of them, finds little support in the Bible.

Third, the starting point for all Christian thinking about this topic must be Jesus's own resurrection. But to understand Jesus's resurrection and what it meant to the first disciples and why they drew from it the conclusions they did, we must look at issues of life after death in Jesus's own world, the world of first-century Judaism, with its Old Testament roots and its context in Greece and Rome. So the third chapter will examine what the ancient world believed about life after death and the radical and revolutionary nature of the Jewish belief in resurrection, which flourished at Jesus's time; and the fourth chapter will ask, in that context, what can we say about the resurrection of Jesus himself?

This will project us forward into the second and central part of the book, in which I shall ask, what then is the ultimate Christian hope for the whole world and for ourselves? This divides into three separate topics, each with its own further divisions: First, what can we say about the future of the whole cosmos? Second, what do we mean when we speak of Jesus "coming again to judge the living and the dead"? And, third, what should we mean by, and what should we believe about, "the resurrection of the body and the life everlasting"? A further question goes with all this, but I believed it was so important that I turned it into a separate small book on its own:[22] Where are the dead now, especially the Christian dead? What can we say in the present time about them? Should we pray for them, or even *to* them? Is any contact permissible? What is the "communion of saints"? And, not least, how can Christians grieve appropriately? In the present book I summarize these topics in a single chapter, together with a section on the prospect of final loss.

Then, in the third and final part of the book, we come back from the past (part 1) and the future (part 2) to the present and ask, how can we appropriately celebrate and live by this very specific hope in our own day and culture? What will it mean, in particular, in terms of the church's mission and work in the world? What might "hope" look like, not just in the ultimate future, but nearer at hand? What surprises might there be in store there?

The whole book thus attempts to reflect the Lord's Prayer itself when it says, "Thy kingdom come, on earth as in heaven." That remains one of the most powerful and revolutionary sentences we can ever say. As I see it, the prayer was powerfully answered at the first Easter and will finally be answered fully when heaven and earth are joined in the new Jerusalem. Easter was when Hope in person surprised the whole world by coming forward from the future into the present. The ultimate future hope remains a surprise, partly because we don't know when it will arrive and partly because at present we have only images and metaphors for it, leaving us to guess that the reality will be far greater, and more surprising, still. And the intermediate hope—the things that happen in the present time to implement Easter and anticipate the final day—are always surprising because, left to ourselves, we lapse into a kind of collusion with entropy, acquiescing in the general belief that things may be getting worse but that there's nothing much we can do about them. And we are wrong. Our task in the present—of which this book, God willing, may form part—is to live as resurrection people in between Easter and the final day, with our Christian life, corporate and individual, in both worship and mission, as a sign of the first and a foretaste of the second.

3. EARLY CHRISTIAN HOPE IN ITS HISTORICAL SETTING

INTRODUCTION

On Friday, October 25, 1946, at 8:30 p.m., in a large room in King's College, Cambridge, two of the greatest philosophers of the twentieth century came face to face for the first and last time. It was not a happy occasion. Afterward, when those present compared notes, they could not quite agree on what exactly had happened.

The two philosophers were Ludwig Wittgenstein and Karl Popper. Wittgenstein had already established a reputation for brilliance; many were under the spell of his revolutionary ideas. He was the chairman of the Cambridge Moral Science Club (in Cambridge, moral science means philosophy). Many other philosophers, though, including Popper, regarded him with deep distrust. Popper was just making his name, having recently published the English translation of his masterpiece, *The Open Society and Its Enemies.*[1] Both men had been brought up, as assimilated Jews, in prewar Vienna: Wittgenstein in a wealthy family with the world at his feet, Popper in a much more ordinary setting. Popper had longed for a chance to demonstrate the folly of Wittgenstein's ways, and now here it was. He had come to Cambridge to give a paper in which he would attack the great man head-on. It was a chilly evening; the fire was lit in the grate; and Wittgenstein was sitting beside it. Many of those present were, or would become, household names in philosophy: Bertrand

Russell, Peter Geach, Stephen Toulmin, Richard Braithwaite. Others went into other professions, such as law. Many of them are still alive and remember the occasion well. Or so they say.

Popper did not know that Wittgenstein was not in the habit of listening to papers all the way through or that he had a reputation for arrogance and rudeness or that he frequently left meetings well before the end. Before long, that evening—and this is where the accounts start to diverge—Wittgenstein had interrupted Popper, and the two men had begun a brief, acrimonious exchange. At one point Wittgenstein picked up the poker from the fireplace and waved it around. Shortly after that he left the room and did not return.

Within a short time rumors went literally around the world. Popper got a letter from New Zealand asking if it was true that Wittgenstein had threatened him with a red-hot poker. From that day to this the great minds present cannot agree on what precisely happened. Some say the poker was red-hot, others that it was cool. Some say Wittgenstein waved it around to make his point (which wouldn't have been unusual); others, including Popper, say he seemed to threaten his opponent with it. Some say that Wittgenstein left after an angry exchange with Russell and that after he'd gone Popper gave, as an example of an obvious moral principle, "Not to threaten visiting speakers with pokers." Others, including Popper, say that he left when Popper said that to his face. Some say he slammed the door, others that he left quietly. It's a fascinating story and has recently been written up as an enterprising book.[2] The main conclusion the book draws is that Wittgenstein probably left before Popper's remark. Popper's memory probably played him false; he had so much at stake, personally and professionally, that he badly wanted to tell the story as the story of his famous victory over Wittgenstein. So, quite soon, he did; and so, before too long, he believed his own account.

Everybody disagrees on the precise details. But nobody doubts that the meeting took place. Nobody doubts that Wittgenstein and Popper were the two main adversaries, with Russell as a kind of senior umpire. Nobody doubts that Wittgenstein did at least wave a poker around and that he left quite abruptly.

I begin with this story for an obvious reason. It is a commonplace among lawyers that eyewitnesses disagree but that this doesn't mean nothing happened. It is more remarkable that disagreement happens when the witnesses are all extremely erudite and professionally concerned with knowledge and truth. But there it is. And the Christian gospel affirms, as the central fact without which there would be no gospel at all, that something happened, perhaps fifty years before our most detailed records of it, about which those records don't exactly agree. Some have said that this casts doubt on whether anything happened at all on the first Easter Day. We have in the four gospels, together with Acts and Paul, a first-century equivalent of the varying accounts of Wittgenstein's poker, and my question now is clear: What sort of an event was it? Just how empty was the tomb on Easter morning?

With this we dive, of course, right into the middle of one of the debates that has bothered the mainstream Western church for well over a century. William Temple, who later became Archbishop of Canterbury, did not get ordained until he had made up his mind that he really did believe in the bodily resurrection of Jesus. Subsequent clergy, including many bishops, have not taken the same line, and David Jenkins famously whipped up a storm of controversy with his remarks about the empty tomb, Jesus's bones, and conjuring tricks—though his words, like the exchange between Popper and Wittgenstein, have had an interesting subsequent career in oral and written tradition. What should we believe about Jesus's resurrection, and why?

This question has been muddled up with several other related but distinct questions, and now it's often difficult to clear people's minds sufficiently to concentrate on the real issues. The issue is not whether the Bible is true or not. The issue is not whether miracles occur or not. The issue is not whether we believe in something called the supernatural or not. The issue is not whether Jesus is alive today and we can get to know him for ourselves. If we treat the question of Easter simply as a test case in any of those discussions, we are missing the point.

Nor can we say, though many have tried to, that because we know the laws of nature, whereas first-century people didn't, we now know that Jesus can't have risen from the dead. As I have shown in considerable detail elsewhere, the ancient world—with the exception of the Jews—was adamant that dead people did not rise again; and the Jews did not believe that anyone *had* done so or that anyone *would* do so all by themselves in advance of the general resurrection.[3] But even when we've cleared away those misunderstandings, deep questions remain. What precisely was it that the early Christians believed? Why did they use the language of resurrection to express that belief? Is it possible to mount a historical case for or against the empty tomb and the bodily resurrection, or will it always be a take-it-or-leave-it matter? How far can history take us, what role does faith have, and how do they work together? The question is not simply *what* we can know but also *how* we can know, and at this point all our knowing is called into question.

Edmonds and Eidinow advance their investigation of the Popper-Wittgenstein encounter by two principal methods. First, they interrogate the eyewitnesses to make sure the firsthand evidence is on the table. Second, they painstakingly reconstruct the background to the meeting in terms of the complex lives and agendas of the two main characters. They then draw their conclusions in terms of a connected historical narrative, claiming not that it is absolutely true but that it is the most likely way of reconciling the various claims.

We must do something similar in looking at the empty tomb and at the event of Easter itself. The eyewitnesses—if that is what they were—are well known. We have them in front of us in the New Testament. We can reconstruct the background quite fully in terms of Jewish beliefs and expectations and of Jesus's own public career and his followers' beliefs and hopes. But there is a third element, without a real parallel in the 1946 Cambridge debate. The philosophical issues there discussed, and the heat they generated, were of their time and have passed away. Popper is increasingly old hat; Wittgenstein's more brilliant legacy is deeply ambiguous. We can't tell, by looking at subsequent philosophy, who if anybody won the debate that evening. Even if one or the other man's achievement was now seen as superior, that might well have nothing to do with ten minutes of heated Cambridge rhetoric. But with Easter it's different. What happened then, whatever it was, generated something quite new: something that grew and developed in particular ways but always with this moment as its supposed point of origin. A major part of our inquiry, then, must be to look at the emerging Christian movement and to ask: what caused it? Even if our eyewitnesses disagree in detail, something must have happened.

Since I have written about this extensively elsewhere, we can now cut straight to the heart of the issue. In the present chapter I shall locate the early Christian beliefs about life beyond death on the map of ancient views, both pagan and Jewish. The striking results of this will send us back, in the next chapter, to the Easter narratives themselves to investigate afresh their character and provenance and to reflect on the options open to the historian.

RESURRECTION AND LIFE AFTER DEATH IN ANCIENT PAGANISM AND JUDAISM

To begin with, then, what did the ancient world believe about life beyond the grave? I am here summarizing the mass of evidence I have set out elsewhere.

As far as the ancient pagan world was concerned, the road to the underworld ran only one way. Death was all-powerful; one could neither escape it in the first place nor break its power once it had come. Everybody knew there was in fact no answer to death. The ancient pagan world then divided broadly into those who, like Homer's shades, might have wanted a new body but knew they couldn't have one and those who, like Plato's philosophers, didn't want one because being a disembodied soul was far better.

Within this world, the word *resurrection* in its Greek, Latin, or other equivalents was never used to mean life after death. *Resurrection* was used to denote new bodily life *after* whatever sort of life after death there might be. When the ancients spoke of resurrection, whether to deny it (as all pagans did) or to affirm it (as some Jews did), they were referring to a two-step narrative in which resurrection, meaning new bodily life, would be preceded by an interim period of bodily death. *Resurrection* wasn't, then, a dramatic or vivid way of talking about the state people went into immediately after death. It denoted something that might happen (though almost everyone thought it wouldn't) sometime *after* that. This meaning is constant throughout the ancient world until the post-Christian coinages of second-century Gnosticism. Most of the ancients believed in life after death; some of them developed complex and fascinating beliefs about it, which we have only just touched on; but outside Judaism and Christianity (and perhaps Zoroastrianism, though the dating of that is controversial), they did not believe in resurrection.

In content, *resurrection* referred specifically to something that happened to the body; hence the later debates about how God would do this—whether he would start with the existing bones or make new ones or whatever. One would have debates like that only if it was quite clear that what you ended up with was something tangible and physical. Everybody knew about ghosts, spirits, visions, hallucinations, and so on. Most people in the ancient world believed in some such things. They were quite clear that that wasn't what they meant by *resurrection*. While Herod reportedly thought Jesus might be John the Baptist raised from the dead, he didn't think he was a ghost.[4] Resurrection meant bodies. We cannot emphasize this too strongly, not least because much modern writing continues, most misleadingly, to use the word *resurrection* as a virtual synonym for *life after death* in the popular sense.

An important conclusion follows from all this, before we look at the Jewish material. When the early Christians said that Jesus had risen from the dead, they knew they were saying that something had happened to him that had happened to nobody else and that nobody had expected to happen. They were not talking about Jesus's soul going into heavenly bliss. Nor were they saying, confusedly, that Jesus had now become divine. That is simply not what the words meant; there was no implicit connection for either Jews or pagans between resurrection and divinization. While the ancient Romans declared that the recently departed emperor had gone to heaven and become divine, nobody dreamed of saying that he had been raised from the dead. The exception proves the rule: those who believed that Nero had come back to life (a group, we may suppose, not unlike those who think Elvis has come back to life, despite his well-known and much-visited grave) precisely did *not* think that he was now in heaven.

What then about the ancient *Jewish* world? Some Jews agreed with those pagans who denied any kind of future life, especially a reembodied one. The Sadducees are famous for taking this position. Others agreed with those pagans who thought in terms of a glorious though disembodied future for the soul. Here the obvious example is the philosopher Philo. But most Jews of the day believed in an eventual resurrection—that is, that God would look after the soul after death until, at the last day, God would give his people new bodies when he judged and remade the whole world. That is what Martha assumed Jesus was talking about in their conversation beside the tomb of Lazarus: "I know he will rise again in the resurrection on the last day."[5] That is what *resurrection* meant.[6]

Jesus's own teaching during his brief public career simply reinforced the Jewish picture. He redefined a lot of ideas that were current at the time—notably, of course, *kingdom of God* itself, explaining in many coded parables and symbolic actions that God's sovereign, saving rule *was* now breaking in, even though it didn't look like what his contemporaries had imagined and wanted. But he hardly even tried to redefine the notion of resurrection. When he did, briefly and cryptically, his closest followers, as we shall see presently, didn't have a clue what he was talking about.

In the one head-on discussion of the topic—the time when the Sadducees asked him a trick question designed to make the idea of resurrection look silly—he answered in quite a traditional fashion, doing better with the question than the Pharisees would have done but not moving significantly beyond the then-standard Jewish view.[7] He spoke of "the resurrection" as a complete event in the future when all the righteous would be raised, and he seems to have indicated that in this resurrection state certain things would be different so that there would be no problem about who had been married to whom in the present life—the point on which the Sadducees had tried to nail him down. (Contrary to what people sometimes suggest, by the way, he didn't say that in the resurrection God's people would *become* angels; he said that they would in certain respects be *like* angels [Matthew, Mark] or *equal to* angels [Luke].) Apart from this discussion, almost the only reference to "the resurrection" as a whole within the gospels occurs in Matthew 13:43, when Jesus declares that on the last day the righteous will shine like the sun in the kingdom of their father. The echo of Daniel 12:3 ensured that this would be taken as a reference to the resurrection. When Jesus speaks of the reward awaiting God's people, he can simply refer to "the resurrection of the righteous" in the normal Jewish way (Luke 14:14). In one isolated Johannine saying (John 5:29) he speaks of a coming resurrection of both the righteous and the wicked. Thus far he is exactly on the map of first-century Jewish belief. Unlike his redefining of kingdom and messiahship, on the question of resurrection he seems to have little or nothing new to say.

Except that he then begins to tell his followers that he himself is going to be killed and then raised again three days later. Many scholars have thought, of course, that these are pseudoprophecies, put in Jesus's mouth by the later church. I have argued at length for the opposite view: that someone doing what Jesus was doing, thinking as he must have been thinking, was highly likely to fore-see his own death, to speak of it in apocalyptic imagery and meta-phor, and to invest it, as the Maccabean martyrs were thought to have done with respect to their own deaths, with some kind of sav-ing significance. In that world, someone thinking that sort of thing would be almost bound to say, in addition: "And God will vindicate me after my death." And the kind of vindication they would have expected, as 2 Maccabees again bears witness, would of course be resurrection.

But the disciples, as the gospels insist over and over, simply couldn't understand what Jesus was saying. His dark saying was in any case couched in the apocalyptic metaphor about the son of man, and they clearly thought they were meant to decode it but didn't know how. The last thing they imagined was that this king-dom bringer, this Jesus they were coming to believe might be God's Messiah, would actually die at the hands of the pagan occupying forces. At no point do we get even a hint of anyone saying, "Well, that's all right—he's got to go and die to save us, and then he'll rise again soon after." Thus the one time that Jesus really does seem to have been trying to redefine the Jewish belief in resurrection, by hinting that it was going to happen to him in the first place, they had no idea what he was talking about. When he told them not to breathe a word about the transfiguration "until the son of man is raised from the dead," they discussed among themselves, in some puzzlement, what this "rising from the dead" might mean.[8] It wasn't that they didn't know about resurrection. It was rather that they had never thought—despite Herod's supposed remark about John the Baptist—that, as Jesus seemed to be implying, it was something that would happen to one person ahead of everybody else. This scenario is completely credible both for Jesus and for the disciples. It fits with everything else we know about their context, their understanding, and their motivations.

And it shows, of course, that the crucifixion of Jesus was the end of all their hopes. Nobody dreamed of saying, "Oh, that's all right—

he'll be back again in a few days."[9] Nor did anybody say, "Well, at least he's now in heaven with God." They were not looking for that sort of kingdom. After all, Jesus himself had taught them to pray that God's kingdom would come "on earth as in heaven." What they said—and again this has the ring of first-century truth— was, "We had hoped that he was the one who would redeem Israel" (Luke 24:21), with the implication, "but they crucified him, so he can't have been." The cross, we note, already had a symbolic meaning throughout the Roman world, long before it had a new one for the Christians. It meant: we Romans run this place, and if you get in our way we'll obliterate you—and do it pretty nastily too. Crucifixion meant that the kingdom hadn't come, not that it had. Crucifixion of a would-be Messiah meant that he wasn't the Messiah, not that he was. When Jesus was crucified, every single disciple knew what it meant: we backed the wrong horse. The game is over. Whatever their expectations, and however Jesus had been trying to redefine those expectations, as far as they were concerned hope had crumbled into ashes. They knew they were lucky to escape with their own lives.

That is the world within which early Christianity burst upon the scene as a new thing, and yet not new. What happens when we locate this sudden movement on the map of ancient Judaism, within its wider pagan context?

THE SURPRISING CHARACTER
OF EARLY CHRISTIAN HOPE

The answer, put simply, is that the early Christian belief in hope beyond death belongs demonstrably on the Jewish, not the pagan, map but that in seven significant ways this Jewish hope underwent remarkable modifications, which can be plotted with remarkable consistency in writers from Paul in the middle of the first century to Tertullian and Origen at the end of the second and beyond.

SURPRISED BY HOPE

To begin with, then, the early Christian future hope centered firmly on resurrection. The first Christians did not simply believe in life after death; they virtually never spoke simply of going to heaven when they died. (As I have often said, alluding to the title of a good popular book on this subject, heaven is important but it's not the end of the world.)[10] When they did speak of heaven as a postmortem destination, they seemed to regard this heavenly life as a temporary stage on the way to the eventual resurrection of the body. When Jesus tells the brigand that he will join him in paradise that very day, paradise clearly cannot be their ultimate destination, as Luke's next chapter makes clear. Paradise is, rather, the blissful garden where God's people rest prior to the resurrection. When Jesus declares that there are many dwelling places in his father's house, the word for dwelling place is *monē,* which denotes a temporary lodging. When Paul says that his desire is "to depart and be with Christ, which is far better," he is indeed thinking of a blissful life with his Lord immediately after death, but this is only the prelude to the resurrection itself.[11] In terms of the discussion in the previous chapter, the early Christians hold firmly to a two-step belief about the future: first, death and whatever lies immediately beyond; second, a new bodily existence in a newly remade world.

There is nothing remotely like this in paganism. This belief is as Jewish as you can get. But within this Jewish belief, early Christians made seven modifications, each of which crops us in writers as diverse as Paul and John the Seer, as Luke and Justin Martyr, as Matthew and Irenaeus. This is highly significant because what people believe about life beyond death tends to be very conservative. Faced with bereavement, people lurch back to the safety of what they heard or learned before. But the early Christians all articulate a belief that is in these seven ways quite new, and the historian has to ask, why?

1. The first of these modifications is that within early Christianity there is virtually no spectrum of belief about life beyond death. What people believe about life beyond death, and the social and cultural

ways in which these beliefs find expression, is notoriously one of the most conservative features of a culture. Yet whereas the early Christians were drawn from many strands of Judaism and from widely differing backgrounds within paganism, and hence from circles that must have held very different beliefs about life beyond death, they all modified that belief to focus on one point on the spectrum. Christianity looks, to this extent, like a variety of Pharisaic Judaism. There is no trace of a Sadducean view or of that of Philo.

The Corinthian group, muddled ex-pagans that they were, apparently included some people who denied the resurrection; well, they would, but that didn't last long.[12] Two teachers mentioned in the pastorals claim that the resurrection is past already.[13] That was a misunderstanding likely to occur, anticipating perhaps the later Gnostic rethinking of the whole question, but it doesn't alter the overwhelming impression of unanimity. And, to anticipate a later argument, let us not imagine, as some do today, that the reason for the apparent unanimity is that the heavy-handed orthodox obliterated all trace of a more polymorphous early period. We have plenty of evidence of debates about all sorts of things, and the virtual unanimity on resurrection stands out. Only in the late second century, a good 150 years after the time of Jesus, do we find people using the word *resurrection* to mean something quite different from what it meant in Judaism and early Christianity, namely, a spiritual experience in the present leading to a disembodied hope in the future.[14] For almost all of the first two centuries, resurrection in the traditional sense holds not just center stage but the whole stage.

2. This leads to the second mutation. In second-Temple Judaism, resurrection is important but not that important. There are lots of lengthy works that never mention the question, let alone this answer. It is still difficult to be sure what the authors of the Dead Sea Scrolls thought on the topic. Apart from occasional highlights like 2 Maccabees 7, resurrection is a peripheral topic. But in early Christianity resurrection moved from the circumference to the center.

You can't imagine Paul's thought without it. You shouldn't imagine John's thought without it, though some have tried. It is enormously important in Clement and Ignatius, in Justin and Irenaeus. It is one of the key beliefs that infuriated the pagans in Lyons in A.D. 177 and drove them to butcher several Christians, including the bishop who preceded the great Irenaeus. Belief in bodily resurrection was one of the two central things that the pagan doctor Galen noted about the Christians (the other being their remarkable sexual restraint). Take away the stories of Jesus's birth, and you lose only two chapters of Matthew and two of Luke. Take away the resurrection, and you lose the entire New Testament and most of the second-century fathers as well.

These first two mutations have to do with the new position that resurrection assumed within early Christianity, as opposed to the place it held within its native Judaism. The next mutation has to do with something more organic about what precisely resurrection *means*.

3. In Judaism it is almost always left quite vague as to what sort of a body the resurrected will possess. The Maccabean martyrs assume it will be a body more or less exactly like the present one. Most of the Jewish texts that glance at the question have little to say beyond this apart from occasional references to "glory," perhaps in the sense of light. But from the start within early Christianity it was built in as part of the belief in resurrection that the new body, though it will certainly be a body in the sense of a physical object occupying space and time, will be a *transformed* body, a body whose material, created from the old material, will have new properties. There has been a dramatic sharpening up of what resurrection itself actually entailed.

It is of course Paul, in a much misunderstood passage in 1 Corinthians 15, who sets this out most clearly and to whom many, though not all, subsequent writers look back. He speaks of two sorts of body, the present one and the future one. He uses two key adjectives to describe these two bodies. Unfortunately, many translations get him radically wrong at this point, leading to the widespread supposition that for Paul the new body would be a spiritual body in the sense of a nonmaterial body, a body that in Jesus's case wouldn't have left an empty tomb behind it. It can be demonstrated in great detail, philologically and exegetically, that this is precisely not what Paul meant. The contrast he is making is not between what we would mean by a present physical body and what we would mean by a future spiritual one, but between a present body animated by the normal human soul and a future body animated by God's spirit.[15]

And the point about the future body is that it will be incorruptible. The present flesh and blood is corruptible, doomed to decay and die. That's why Paul says, "Flesh and blood cannot inherit God's kingdom." The new body will be incorruptible. The entire chapter, one of Paul's longest sustained discussions and the vital climax of the whole letter, is about new creation, about the creator God remaking the creation, not abandoning it as Platonists of all sorts, including Gnostics, would have wanted.

But this transformed physicality (or, as I have called it elsewhere, "transphysicality") does not involve being transformed into luminosity. Here again many go wrong, misunderstanding the word *glory* to imply a physical shining rather than a status within God's world. This is the more remarkable in that the best-known of the biblical resurrection texts, Daniel 12, speaks of the resurrected righteous shining like stars. Surprisingly, this text is never quoted in the New Testament about the resurrection body except in the interpretation of one parable.[16] When we do find it, it is used metaphorically of present Christian witness in the world.[17] What we find, then, throughout early Christian resurrection belief is the view that the new body, when it is given, will possess a transformed physicality, but not transformed in the one way the central biblical text might have suggested.

4. The fourth surprising mutation evidenced by the early Christian resurrection belief is that the resurrection, as an event, has split into

two. 1 Corinthians 15 is again central for this, but it is assumed right across the first two centuries. No first-century Jew prior to Easter expected the resurrection to be anything other than a large-scale event happening to all God's people, or perhaps to the entire human race, as part of the sudden event in which God's kingdom would finally come on earth as in heaven. There is no suggestion that one person would rise from the dead in advance of all the rest. The exceptions sometimes quoted (Enoch and Elijah) do not count precisely because (a) they were held not to have died and so resurrection (new life after bodily death) would not be relevant and (b) they were in heaven, not in a new body on earth.[18] Resurrection, we must never cease to remind ourselves, did not mean going to heaven or escaping death or having a glorious and noble postmortem existence but rather coming to bodily life again after bodily death. This is why, when after the transfiguration Jesus tells the disciples not to mention the vision until the son of man has been raised from the dead, they are (as we saw a few moments ago) puzzled and wonder what this "rising from the dead" can mean—if it is to be an event that will leave them in a position to be telling people about details of Jesus's life rather than an event in which God's whole new world will be born.

Of course, other Jewish movements roughly contemporary with early Christianity also held some kind of inaugurated eschatology (that is, the belief that "the end" had already in some sense begun). The Essenes, as represented in the Dead Sea Scrolls, believed that the covenant had been secretly reestablished with them, in advance of the final denouement. But we never find outside Christianity what becomes a central feature within it: the belief that the mode of this inauguration consisted in the resurrection itself happening to one person in the middle of history in advance of its great, final occurrence, anticipating and guaranteeing the final resurrection of God's people at the end of history.

5. I am indebted to Dominic Crossan for highlighting what I now list as the fifth mutation in Jewish resurrection belief. In a public

debate in New Orleans in March 2005, Crossan designated this mutation as "collaborative eschatology." My understanding of this, in line with what I believe Crossan intended, is this. Because the early Christians believed that resurrection had begun with Jesus and would be completed in the great final resurrection on the last day, they believed that God had called them to work with him, in the power of the Spirit, to implement the achievement of Jesus and thereby to anticipate the final resurrection, in personal and political life, in mission and holiness. It was not merely that God had inaugurated the "end"; if Jesus, the Messiah, was the End in person, God's-future-arrived-in-the-present, then those who belonged to Jesus and followed him and were empowered by his Spirit were charged with transforming the present, as far as they were able, in the light of that future.

6. The sixth remarkable mutation within the Jewish belief is the quite different metaphorical use of *resurrection*. Within Judaism resurrection could function both as metaphor and as metonymy for the return from exile. For Ezekiel himself, in chapter 37, it is pretty clearly metaphor; by the time the rabbis come to the idea, and indeed already in 2 Maccabees, 4 Ezra, and elsewhere, and also in the gospels,[19] it is metonymy, one part of the great eschatological picture standing for the whole. And the concrete referent of this Jewish metaphor is the national, ethnic, geographical restoration of Israel. So when *resurrection* is used metaphorically in Judaism, it refers to the restoration of Israel; but from the earliest days of Christianity, all the more remarkably when we consider how it began as a Jewish messianic movement, this meaning has disappeared, making perhaps its only fleeting appearance in the disciples' puzzled question at the start of Acts ("Lord, will you at this time restore the kingdom to Israel?").[20]

In its place, equally remarkably, we have a new metaphorical meaning of resurrection, which has already taken firm root by the time of Paul: resurrection as referring metaphorically to baptism (a dying and rising with Christ), and resurrection as referring to the new life of strenuous ethical obedience, enabled by the Holy Spirit, to which the believer is committed. We should note that these metaphorical meanings are regularly found right alongside passages in which the literal meaning, of a future actual bodily resurrection, is also emphasized, as for instance in Romans; in other words, this is not the beginning of a slide into a nonphysical meaning. And we should also note that this metaphorical meaning still has a concrete referent—baptism and ethics—rather than the abstract or "spiritual" one beloved of the later Gnostics.

This, then, is the sixth modification of the Jewish belief: resurrection, while still being embraced as literal language about a future embodied existence, has shed its powerful earlier meaning as a metaphor for the renewal of ethnic Israel and has acquired a new one, about the renewal of human beings in general. In fact, within early Christianity we begin to discover the language of return from exile, of the ethnic and territorial renewal of Israel, now itself used metaphorically to refer both to the present renewal of human beings and to their eventual bodily resurrection. Once more, all these meanings make sense only within the Jewish world of thought; no pagan ever dreamed of anything like this; but until Christianity no Jew either had come this route. We are faced with a further remarkable mutation from within.

7. The seventh and last mutation of the Jewish resurrection belief was its association with messiahship. Nobody in Judaism had expected the Messiah to die, and therefore naturally nobody had imagined the Messiah rising from the dead. This leads to a remarkable modification not just of resurrection belief but of messianic belief itself. Where messianic speculations existed (again, by no means all Jewish texts spoke of a Messiah, but the notion became central in early Christianity), the Messiah was supposed to fight God's victorious battle against the wicked pagans; to rebuild or cleanse the Temple; and to bring God's justice to the world. Jesus, it appeared,

had done none of these things. He had suffered the typical injustice of the world; he had mounted a strange and apparently ineffectual demonstration in the Temple; and he had died at the hands of the pagans rather than defeating them gloriously in battle. No Jew with any idea of how the language of messiahship worked could have possibly imagined, after his crucifixion, that Jesus of Nazareth was indeed the Lord's anointed. But from very early on, as witnessed by what may be pre-Pauline fragments of early creedal belief, the Christians affirmed that Jesus was indeed the Messiah, precisely because of his resurrection.

We may note at this point, as an aside but an important one, how impossible is it to account for the early Christian belief in Jesus as Messiah without the resurrection. We have evidence of several other Jewish movements—messianic movements, prophetic movements—during the one or two centuries on either side of Jesus's public career. Routinely they ended with the violent death of the central figure. Members of the movement (assuming they got away with their own skins) then faced a choice: either give up the struggle or find a new Messiah. Had the early Christians wanted to go the latter route, they had an obvious candidate: James, the Lord's brother, a great and devout teacher, the central figure in the early Jerusalem church. But nobody ever imagined that James might be the Messiah. Josephus describes him, somewhat contemptuously but echoing the language people must have used of him, as "the brother of the so-called Messiah."[21]

This means we can already rule out the revisionist positions on Jesus's resurrection that have been offered by so many writers in recent years. Many suggest that the early disciples were so overwhelmed with grief at Jesus's death that they picked up the idea of resurrection from their surrounding culture and clung to it, persuading themselves that Jesus had been raised from the dead, though of course they knew he hadn't been. Some suggest that the earliest Christians believed that Jesus after his death had been exalted to heaven or that they had a strange sense that his mission, to bring in God's kingdom, was now going ahead in a new way and that this kind of belief led them to say he'd been raised from the dead.

But would this make any sense? We can test it out with a little thought experiment. In A.D. 70 the Romans conquered Jerusalem, and they led back to Rome thousands of captive Jews, including the man they regarded as the leader of the Jewish revolt, "the king of the Jews," a man called Simon bar Giora. He was led into Rome at the back of the triumphal procession, and the end of the spectacle was Simon being flogged and then killed.[22]

Now, suppose we imagine a few Jewish revolutionaries, three days or three weeks later. The first one says, "You know, I think Simon really was the Messiah—and he still is!"

The others would be puzzled. Of course he isn't; the Romans got him, as they always do. If you want a Messiah, you'd better find another one.

"Ah," says the first, "but I believe he's been raised from the dead."

"What d'you mean?" his friends ask. "He's dead and buried."

"Oh, no," replies the first, "I believe he's been exalted to heaven."

The others look puzzled. All the righteous martyrs are with God, everybody knows that; their souls are in God's hand; that doesn't mean they've *already* been raised from the dead. Anyway, the resurrection will happen to us all at the end of time, not to one person in the middle of continuing history.

"No," replies the first, "you don't understand. I've had a strong sense of God's love surrounding me. I have felt God forgiving me—forgiving us all. I've had my heart strangely warmed. What's more, last night I saw Simon; he was there with me. . . ."

The others interrupt, now angry. We can all have visions. Plenty of people dream about recently dead friends. Sometimes it's very vivid. That doesn't mean they've been raised from the dead. It certainly doesn't mean that one of them is the Messiah. And if your heart has been warmed, then sing a psalm, don't make wild claims about Simon.

That is what they would have said to anyone offering the kind of statement that, according to the revisionists, someone must have come up with as the beginning of the idea of Jesus's resurrection. But this solution isn't just incredible, it's impossible. Had anyone said what the revisionists suggest, some such conversation as the above would have ensued. A little bit of disciplined historical imagination is all it takes to blow away enormous piles of so-called historical criticism.

What is more (to round off this final mutation from within the Jewish belief), because of the early Christian belief in Jesus as Messiah, we find the development of the very early belief that Jesus is Lord and that therefore Caesar is not. This is a whole other topic for another occasion. But already in Paul the resurrection, both of Jesus and then in the future of his people, is the foundation of the Christian stance of allegiance to a different king, a different Lord.[23] Death is the last weapon of the tyrant, and the point of the resurrection, despite much misunderstanding, is that death has been defeated. Resurrection is not the redescription of death; it is its overthrow and, with that, the overthrow of those whose power depends on it. Despite the sneers and slurs of some contemporary scholars, it was those who believed in the bodily resurrection who were burned at the stake and thrown to the lions. Resurrection was never a way of settling down and becoming respectable; the Pharisees could have told you that. It was the Gnostics, who translated the language of resurrection into a private spirituality and a dualistic cosmology, thereby more or less altering its meaning into its opposite, who escaped persecution. Which emperor would have sleepless nights worrying that his subjects were reading the Gospel of Thomas? Resurrection was always bound to get you into trouble, and it regularly did.[24]

We have thus noted seven major mutations of the Jewish resurrection belief, each of which became central within the Christianity of the first two centuries. The early Christian belief in resurrection remains emphatically on the map of first-century Judaism rather than paganism, but from within the Jewish theology of monotheism, election, and eschatology, it opened up a whole new way of seeing history, hope, and hermeneutics. *And this demands a historical explanation.* Why did the early Christians modify the Jewish resurrection language in these seven ways, and do it with such consistency? When we ask them, they of course reply that they did it because of what they believed had happened to Jesus on the third day after he died. This projects us on into the next chapter, to ask, what then must we say about the very strange stories they tell as they describe the events of that first Easter Day?

4. THE STRANGE STORY OF EASTER

STORIES WITHOUT PRECEDENT

When we plunge in to the stories of the first Easter Day—the accounts we find in the closing chapters of the four canonical gospels—we find ourselves back with Wittgenstein's poker. Notoriously, the accounts of Easter do not fit snugly together.[1] How many women went to the tomb, and how many angels or men did they meet there? Did the disciples meet Jesus in Jerusalem or Galilee or both? And so on. But, as with Cambridge in 1946, so with Jerusalem in A.D. 30 (or whenever it was): surface discrepancies do not mean that nothing happened. Indeed, they are a reasonable indication that something remarkable happened, so remarkable that the first witnesses were bewildered into telling different stories about it.

As part of the larger argument that I have advanced elsewhere, I here draw attention to four strange features shared by the accounts in the four canonical gospels. These features, I suggest, compel us to take them seriously as very early accounts, not, as is often suggested, later inventions.[2]

First, we note the strange silence of the Bible in the stories. Up to this point, all four evangelists have drawn heavily upon biblical quotation, allusion, and echo to make it clear that Jesus's death was "according to the scriptures." Even the burial narrative has biblical echoes. But the resurrection narratives are almost entirely innocent of them, with only a couple of small exceptions. This is all the more remarkable when we note that from as early as Paul, the common creedal formula declared that the resurrection too was "according to the scriptures," and Paul himself joins the rest of the early church in ransacking psalms and prophets to find texts to explain what just happened and set it within, and as the climax to, the long story of God and Israel. Why do the gospel resurrection narratives not do the same? It would be easy for Matthew to refer to one or two scriptural prophecies that were being fulfilled, but he doesn't. John tells us that the disciples didn't yet know the scriptural teaching that the Messiah would rise again, but he doesn't quote the texts he has in mind.

We could say, of course, that whoever wrote the stories in the form we now have them went through, cunningly, and took material out *to make them look as if they were very old,* rather like someone deliberately taking all the electric fittings out of a house to make it look like it might have done a century or more ago. The normal assumption among many scholars, that the stories grew up in the second generation, as late (say) as the 80s or 90s, would require us to say that, though they interestingly embody (as we shall see) the theology of Paul, they have carefully extracted from that theology all the biblical allusions that are already so plentiful in a passage like 1 Corinthians 15.

That might be marginally plausible if we had just one account or if the four accounts were obviously derived from one another. We don't, and they aren't.[3] You either have to imagine four very different writers each deciding to write up an Easter narrative based on the theology of the early church but removing all the biblical echoes, and managing to do so in four very different though theologically consistent ways, or you have to say, which I think is infinitely more probable, that the stories, even if they were written down a lot later, go back to very, very early oral tradition, which was formed and set firmly in the memory of different storytellers before there was any time for biblical reflection.

SURPRISED BY HOPE

The second strange feature of the stories is more often remarked upon: the presence of the women as the principal witnesses. Whether we like it or not, women were not regarded as credible witnesses in the ancient world. When the tradition had time to sort itself out and acquire the fixed form we already find in Paul's quotation of it in 1 Corinthians 15, the women were quietly dropped; they were apologetically embarrassing. But there they are in all four gospel stories, front and center, the first witnesses, the first apostles. Nobody would have made them up. Had the tradition started in the male-only form we find in 1 Corinthians 15, it would never have developed, in such different ways as well, into the female-first stories we find in the gospels.

The third strange feature is the portrait of Jesus himself. If, as many revisionists have tried to make out, the gospel stories developed either from people mulling over the scriptures or from an experience of inner subjective illumination, the one thing you would expect to find is the risen Jesus shining like a star. That's what Daniel says will happen; that's what an experience of inner illumination might have generated. We have such an account in the transfiguration. But none of the gospels say this about Jesus at Easter. Indeed, he appears as a human being with a body that in some ways is quite normal and can be mistaken for a gardener or a fellow traveler on the road. Yet the stories also contain—and this marks them out as among the most mysterious stories ever written—definite signs that this body has been transformed. It is clearly physical: it uses up (so to speak) the matter of the crucified body; hence the empty tomb. But, equally, it comes and goes through locked doors; it is not always recognized; and in the end it disappears into God's space, that is, "heaven," through the thin curtain that in much Jewish thought separates God's space from human space. This kind of account is without precedent. No biblical texts predict that the resurrection will involve this kind of body. No speculative theology had laid this trail for the evangelists to follow—and to follow, we note once more, in interestingly different ways.

In particular, this should put a stop to the old nonsense that Luke's and John's accounts, which are the most apparently "physical," were written late in the first century in an attempt to combat Docetism (the view that Jesus wasn't a real human being but only seemed to be so).[4] Granted, if all you had was Jesus eating broiled fish (Luke) and inviting Thomas to touch him (John), such an account might have some initial plausibility. But if Luke and John were simply constructing narratives to combat Docetism, they surely shot themselves in the foot with both barrels when they spoke of the risen Jesus appearing through locked doors, disappearing again, sometimes being recognized, sometimes not, and finally ascending into heaven.

The fourth strange feature of the resurrection accounts is the fact that they never mention the future Christian hope. Almost everywhere else in the New Testament, the resurrection of Jesus is spoken of in connection with the final hope that those who belong to Jesus will one day be raised as he has been, adding that this must be anticipated in the present in baptism and behavior. Despite a thousand Easter hymns and a million Easter sermons, the resurrection narratives in the gospels never, ever say anything like, "Jesus is raised, therefore there is a life after death," let alone, "Jesus is raised, therefore we shall go to heaven when we die." Nor even, in a more authentic first-century Christian way, do they say, "Jesus is raised, therefore we shall be raised from the dead after the sleep of death." No. Insofar as the event is interpreted, Easter has a very this-worldly, present-age meaning: Jesus is raised, so he is the Messiah, and therefore he is the world's true Lord; Jesus is raised, so God's new creation has begun—and we, his followers, have a job to do! Jesus is raised, so we must act as his heralds, announcing his lordship to the entire world, making his kingdom come on earth as in heaven! To be sure, as early as Paul the resurrection of Jesus is firmly linked to the final resurrection of all God's people. Had the stories been invented toward the end of the first century, they would certainly have included a mention of the final resurrection of all God's people. They don't, because they weren't.

There is much more to say about the gospel resurrection narratives. But I conclude this first section of the chapter with the proposal that it is far, far easier to believe that the stories are essentially very early, pre-Pauline, and have not been substantially altered except for light personal polishing, in subsequent transmission or editing. Yes, they show signs of the theological interests of the different evangelists: Matthew's story of the resurrection emphasizes typically Matthean themes, and so on. But this is like what you get when different artists paint portraits of the same person. This painting is certainly a Rembrandt; that is indubitably a Holbein. The touch of the individual artist is unmistakable. And yet the sitter is fully recognizable. The artists have not changed the color of her hair, the shape of his nose, the particular half smile. And when we ask why such stories, so different in many ways and yet so interestingly consistent in these and other features, could have come into existence so early, all the early Christians give the obvious answer: something like this is what happened, even though it was hard to describe at the time and remains mind-boggling thereafter. The stories, though lightly edited and written down later, are basically very, very early. They are not, as has so often been suggested, legends written up much later to give a pseudohistorical basis for what essentially was a private, interior experience.

This, then, is the more or less universal witness of the early Christians: that they are who they are, they do what they do, they tell the stories they tell not because of a new religious experience or insight but because of something that happened; something that happened to the crucified Jesus; something that they at once interpreted as meaning that he was after all the Messiah, that God's new age had after all broken into the present time, and that they were charged with a new commission; something that made them reaffirm the Jewish belief in resurrection, not swap it for a pagan alternative, but introduce several distinctive but consistent modifications within it. It is now time to ask, in the second section of this chapter: what can the historian say about all this?

I begin with what I regard as fixed historical points. The only way we can explain the phenomena we have been examining is by proposing a two-pronged hypothesis: first, Jesus's tomb really was empty; second, the disciples really did encounter him in ways that convinced them that he was not simply a ghost or hallucination. A brief word about each of these.

If the disciples simply saw, or thought they saw, someone they took to be Jesus, that would not by itself have generated the stories we have. Everyone in the ancient world took it for granted that people sometimes had strange experiences involving encounters with the dead, particularly the recently dead. They knew at least as much as we do about such visions, about ghosts and dreams—and the fact that such things often occurred within the context of bereavement or grief. They had language for this, and it wasn't *resurrection*. However many such visions they'd had, they wouldn't have said Jesus was raised from the dead; they weren't expecting such a resurrection.

In any case—a point people often ignore or conveniently forget—Jesus was buried according to a particular Jewish tradition, which was designed to occur in two stages. First, you carefully wrapped up the body with spices and linen and placed it on a shelf in a cave. Then, when the flesh had decomposed—hence the spices, because of the smell, since the cave would be used for more than one corpse—you would collect the bones, fold them up reverently, and store them in a bone box (an ossuary). If Jesus had not been raised, then sooner or later someone would have had to go and collect his bones, fold them up, and store them. If anyone suggested that he had been raised from the dead, the bones in the tomb would be enough to disprove the suggestion. Nobody in the Jewish world would have spoken of such a person being already raised from the dead.

Thus, without the empty tomb, the disciples would have been as quick to say "hallucination" as we would. Apparent meetings with Jesus would have been dismissed: you've obviously seen a ghost.

Equally, an empty tomb by itself proves almost nothing. It might (as many have suggested) have been the wrong tomb, though a quick check would have sorted that one out. Someone—the soldiers, the gardeners, the chief priests, other disciples, or someone else—might have taken away the body for some reason or other. Grave robbery was well known. That was the conclusion Mary drew in John's gospel: they've taken him away—and perhaps it was the gardener that did it. That was the conclusion the Jewish leaders broadcast, according to Matthew: his disciples took him away. All sorts of similar explanations could have been offered, and would have been, had not the empty tomb been accompanied by sightings of, and meetings with, Jesus himself. No: in order to explain historically how all the early Christians came to the belief they held, that Jesus had been raised, we have to say at least this: that the tomb was empty, except for some graveclothes, and that they really did see and talk with someone who gave every appearance of being a solidly physical Jesus, though a Jesus who was strangely changed, more strangely than they were able fully to describe.

Both the meetings and the empty tomb are therefore necessary if we are to explain the rise of the belief and the writing of the stories as we have them. Neither by itself was sufficient; put them together, though, and they provide a complete and coherent explanation for the rise of the early Christian belief.

Is there an alternative explanation, one that would get us off the hook of saying that the ancient pagan view (resurrection is impossible), along with its modern equivalents, was wrong? No. Like everything else in this chapter, the answer could be spelled out at much greater length, but we must at least note that the main alternative accounts, the revisionist proposals, lack all explanatory power.

Take the phenomenon of cognitive dissonance, about which much has been written in the last half century or so. Cognitive dissonance is what happens when people who badly want something to be true but are faced with strong evidence to the contrary manage to leap over the data that point the wrong way and become even more strident in announcing their claims. This theory has some initial plausibility. There are some interesting examples of people behaving in this way. But theories like this will not serve as an explanation of the early Christian phenomena. In fact, the research on which the theory was originally based was already deeply flawed, as I have shown elsewhere.[5]

But, more particularly, it simply doesn't fit the state of affairs at Easter. The disciples were emphatically not expecting Jesus to be raised from the dead, all by himself in the middle of history. The fact that they were second-Temple Jews and that resurrection was, as some have said, an idea that was in the air, simply won't account for the radical modifications they made in the Jewish belief or for the astonishing features of the Easter stories themselves.

In the same way, some have suggested that the early disciples had a new experience of grace, that they felt forgiven in a new way, that they had come to a new faith in the power of God, a new conviction that God's kingdom project was still going ahead despite Jesus's death.[6] But this too simply won't work. As we saw earlier, to say that one had a new experience of grace doesn't take you one step nearer to saying that the leader you followed had been raised from the dead. The resurrection did indeed function as metaphor, but not as metaphor for a new religious experience. Judaism already had a rich language for that. Saying "he's been raised from the dead" if he wasn't is simply inexplicable historically. I am reminded of John Updike's trenchant poem:

> Let us not mock God with metaphor,
> analogy, sidestepping, transcendence;
> making of the event a parable, a sign painted in the

faded credulity of earlier ages:
let us walk through the door.

. . . .

Let us not seek to make it less monstrous,
for our own convenience, our own sense of beauty,
lest, awakened in one unthinkable hour, we are
embarrassed by the miracle,
and crushed by remonstrance.[7]

Many smaller arguments might be brought in at this point that
we can only summarize. To begin with, here are other proposals regularly advanced as rival explanations to the early Christian one:

1. Jesus didn't really die; someone gave him a drug that made him
   look like dead, and he revived in the tomb. Answer: Roman soldiers knew how to kill people, and no disciple would have been
   fooled by a half-drugged, beat-up Jesus into thinking he'd defeated death and inaugurated the kingdom.

2. When the women went to the tomb they met someone else (perhaps James, Jesus's brother, who looked like him), and in the half
   light they thought it was Jesus himself. Answer: they would have
   noticed soon enough.

3. Jesus only appeared to people who believed in him. Answer: the
   accounts make it clear that Thomas and Paul do not belong to
   this category; and actually none of Jesus's followers believed, after his death, that he really was the Messiah, let alone that he was
   in any sense divine.

4. The accounts we have are biased. Answer: so is all history, all
   journalism. Every photo is taken by somebody from some
   angle.

5. They began by saying, "He will be raised," as people had done of the martyrs, and this quickly passed into saying, "He has been raised," which was functionally equivalent. Answer: no, it wasn't.[8]

6. Lots of people have visions of someone they love who has just died; this was what happened to the disciples. Answer: they knew perfectly well about things like that, and they had language for it; they would say, "It's his angel" or "It's his spirit" or "his ghost."[9] They wouldn't say, "He's been raised from the dead."

7. Perhaps the most popular: what actually happened was that they had some kind of rich "spiritual" experience, which they interpreted through Jewish categories. Jesus after all really was alive, spiritually, and they were still in touch with him. Answer: that is simply a description of a noble death followed by a Platonic immortality. Resurrection was and is the *defeat* of death, not simply a nicer *description* of it; and it's something that happens some while *after* the moment of death, not immediately.

Equally, we may just notice three of the many small-scale arguments that are often, and quite rightly, advanced to support the belief that Jesus did indeed rise from the dead:

1. Jewish tombs, especially those of martyrs, were venerated and often became shrines. There is no sign whatever of that having happened with Jesus's grave.

2. The early church's emphasis on the first day of the week as their special day is very hard to explain unless something striking really did happen then. A gradual or even sudden dawning of faith is hardly sufficient to explain it.

3. The disciples were hardly likely to go out and suffer and die for a belief that wasn't firmly anchored in fact. This is an important

point though subject to the weakness that they might have been genuinely mistaken: they believed the resurrection of Jesus to be a fact, and they acted on that belief, but we know (so it would be said) that they were wrong.

All this brings us face-to-face with the ultimate question. The empty tomb and the meetings with Jesus are as well established, by the arguments I have advanced, as any historical data could expect to be. They are, in combination, the only possible explanation for the stories and beliefs that grew up so quickly among Jesus's followers. How, in turn, do we explain *them?*

In any other historical inquiry, the answer would be so obvious that it would hardly need saying. Here, of course, this obvious answer ("well, it actually happened") is so shocking, so earth shattering, that we rightly pause before leaping into the unknown. And here indeed, as some skeptical friends have cheerfully pointed out to me, it is always possible for anyone to follow the argument so far and to say simply, "I don't have a good explanation for what happened to cause the empty tomb and the appearances, but I choose to maintain my belief that dead people don't rise and therefore conclude that something else must have happened, even though we can't tell what it was." That is fine; I respect that position; but I simply note that it is indeed then a matter of choice, not a matter of saying that something called scientific historiography forces us to take that route.

But at this moment in the argument all the signposts are pointing in one direction. I and others have studied quite extensively all the alternative explanations, ancient and modern, for the rise of the early church and the shape of its belief.[10] Far and away the best historical explanation is that Jesus of Nazareth, having been thoroughly dead and buried, really was raised to life on the third day with a renewed body (not a mere "resuscitated corpse," as people sometimes dismissively say), a new *kind* of physical body, which left an empty tomb behind it because it had used up the material of Jesus's original body and which possessed new properties that nobody had expected or imagined but that generated significant mutations in the thinking of those who encountered it. If something like this happened, it would perfectly explain why Christianity began and why it took the shape it did.

But this is where I want to heed carefully the warnings of theologians who caution against any attempt to stand on the ground of rationalism and try to prove in a mathematical fashion something that, if it happened, ought to be regarded as the center not only of history but also of epistemology, not only of *what* we know but also of *how* we know it. I do not claim, in other words, that I have hereby proved the resurrection in terms of some neutral standpoint. I am offering, rather, a historical challenge to other explanations and to the worldviews within which they gain their meaning. Precisely because at this point we are faced with worldview-level issues, there is no neutral ground, no island in the middle of the epistemological ocean as yet uncolonized by any of the warring continents. Historical argument alone cannot force anyone to believe that Jesus was raised from the dead, but historical argument is remarkably good at clearing away the undergrowth behind which skepticisms of various sorts have long been hiding. The proposal that Jesus was bodily raised from the dead possesses unrivaled power to explain the historical data at the heart of early Christianity. The obvious fact that this remains hugely challenging at the personal and corporate level ought not to put us off from taking it seriously. Or were we only playing when we entertained the question in the first place?

There are, after all, different types of knowing. Science studies the repeatable; history studies the unrepeatable. Caesar only crossed the Rubicon once, and if he'd crossed it again it would have meant something different the second time. There was, and could be, only one first landing on the moon. The fall of the second Jerusalem Temple took place in A.D. 70 and never happened again. Historians don't of course see this as a problem and are usually not shy about declaring that these events certainly took place, even though we can't repeat them in the laboratory.

But when people say, "But that can't have happened because we know that *that sort of thing* doesn't actually happen," they are appealing to a would-be scientific principle of history, namely, the principle of *analogy*. The problem with analogy is that it never quite gets you far enough. History is full of unlikely things that happened once and once only, with the result that the analogies are often at best partial. In any case, if someone declares that certain kinds of events "don't normally happen," that merely invites the retort, "Who says?" And indeed, in the case in point, we should note as an obvious but often overlooked point the fact that the early Christians did *not* think that Jesus's resurrection was one instance of something that happened from time to time elsewhere. Granted, they saw it as the first, advance instance of something that would eventually happen to everyone else. But they didn't employ that future hope as an analogy from which to argue backward that it had happened already in this one instance ("It's going to happen to everyone eventually, so that shows it's all right for it to have happened this once in advance").

So how does the historian work when the evidence points toward things that we do not normally expect? The resurrection is such a prime example of this that it's hard to produce, at this meta-level, analogies for the question itself. But sooner or later questions of worldview begin to loom in the background, and the question of what kinds of material the historian will allow onstage is inevitably affected by the worldview within which he or she lives. And at that point we are back to the question of the scientist who, faced with the thoroughly repeatable experiment of what happens to dead bodies—what has always, it seems, happened and what seems likely always to go on happening—declares that the evidence is so massive that it is impossible to believe in the resurrection without ceasing to be a scientist altogether.

But how far does that "scientific" position go? When we ask what a scientist can believe about something, we are asking a two-level question. First, we are asking about what sort of things the scientific method can explore and how it can know or believe certain things. Second, we are asking about the kind of commitment someone wedded to scientific knowing is expected to have in all other areas of his or her life. Is a scientist, for example, expected to have a scientific approach to listening to music? To watching a football game? To falling in love? The question of whether a scientist can believe in Jesus's resurrection assumes, I think, that the resurrection, and perhaps particularly the resurrection of Jesus, is something that might be expected to impinge on the scientist's area of concern, somewhat as if one were to ask, "Can a scientist believe that the sun could rise twice in a day?" or "Can a scientist believe that a moth could fly to the moon?"[11] This is different, in other words, from asking, "Can a scientist believe that Schubert's music is beautiful?" or "Can a scientist believe that her husband loves her?" There are those, of course, who by redefining the resurrection as simply a spiritual experience in the inner hearts and minds of the disciples pull the question toward the latter pair and away from the former. But that is ruled out by what, as we shall see, all first-century users of the language of resurrection meant by the word. *Resurrection* in the first century meant someone physically, thoroughly dead becoming physically, thoroughly alive again, not simply surviving or entering a "purely spiritual" world, whatever that might be. *Resurrection* therefore necessarily impinges on the public world.

But at this point we meet a third element in knowing, a puzzling area beyond science (which "knows" what in principle can be repeated in a laboratory) and the kind of history that claims to "know" what makes sense by analogy with our own experience. Sometimes human beings—individuals or communities—are confronted with something that they must reject outright or that, if they accept it, will demand the remaking of their worldview.

To make this point, I once imagined a fantasy Oxbridge scenario. A rich old member gives to a college a wonderful, glorious painting that simply won't fit any of the spaces available in the college and that is so magnificent that eventually the college decides to pull itself down and rebuild itself around this great and unexpected gift, discovering as it does so that all the best things about the college are thereby enhanced within the new structure and all the problems of which people had been aware are thereby dealt with. And the key thing about that illustration, inadequate though it is, is that there must be some point at which the painting is received by the existing college, some epistemological point of overlap to enable the college officers to make their momentous decision. The donor doesn't just come along, blow up the college unasked, present the painting, and then say, "Now figure out what to do." My point is that the resurrection of Jesus, presenting itself as the obvious answer to the question "How do you explain the rise of early Christianity?" has that kind of purchase on serious historical inquiry and therefore poses that kind of challenge to the larger worldview of both the historian and the scientist.

The challenge is in fact the challenge of *new creation*. To put it at its most basic: the resurrection of Jesus offers itself, to the student of history or science no less than the Christian or the theologian, not as an odd event within the world as it is but as the utterly characteristic, prototypical, and foundational event within the world as it has begun to be. It is not an absurd event within the old world but the symbol and starting point of the new world.[12] The claim advanced in Christianity is of that magnitude: Jesus of Nazareth ushers in not simply a new religious possibility, not simply a new ethic or a new way of salvation, but a new creation.

Now that might seem to be an epistemological as well as a theological preemptive strike. If a new creation is really on the loose, the historian wouldn't have any analogies for it, and the scientist wouldn't be able to consider its characteristic events in the light of other events that might otherwise have been open to inspection. What are we to do?

History alone, certainly as conceived within the modern Western world and placed on the Procrustean bed of science, which (rightly) observes the world as it is, appears to leave us like the Children of

Israel waiting in fear on the shore of the Red Sea. Behind are the forces of skepticism: Pharaoh's hordes, mocking and shouting that they're coming to get us. Ahead is the sea, representing chaos and death, forces that nobody else has ever claimed were beaten. What are we to do? There is no way back. No other explanations have been offered, in two thousand years of sneering skepticism toward the Christian witness, that can satisfactorily account for how the tomb came to be empty, how the disciples came to see Jesus, and how their lives and worldviews were transformed. The alternative accounts are actually remarkably thin; I've read most of the current ones, and many of them are laughable. History appears to leave us shivering on the shore. It can press the question to which Christian faith is the answer. But, if someone chooses to stay between Pharaoh and the deep sea, history itself cannot force them further.[13]

Everything then depends on the context within which the history is considered. The most important decisions we make in life are not made by post-Enlightenment left-brain rationality alone. I do not suggest that one can argue right up to the central truth of Christian faith by pure human reason building on simple observation of the world. Indeed, it is should be obvious that that is impossible. Equally, I would not suggest that historical investigation of this sort has therefore no part to play and that all that is required is a blind leap of faith. God has given us minds to think; the question has been appropriately raised; Christianity appeals to history, and to history it must go. And the question of Jesus's resurrection, though it may in some senses burst the boundaries of history, also remains within them; that is precisely why it is so important, so disturbing, so life-and-death. We could cope—the world could cope—with a Jesus who ultimately remains a wonderful idea inside his disciples' minds and hearts. The world cannot cope with a Jesus who comes out of the tomb, who inaugurates God's new creation right in the middle of the old one.

That is why, for a complete approach to the question, we need to locate our study of history within a larger complex of human, both personal and corporate, contexts. This of course forms a challenge not only to the historian and not only to the scientist but also to all humans in whatever worldview they habitually live. Worldview issues are at stake here and cannot be dealt with by the old liberal strategy of pretending (as some reviewers of my earlier work have suggested) that to believe in the resurrection of Jesus is impossible for those who accept what one writer has called "current paradigms of reality." If this means capitulating before the worldview of Hume and other Enlightenment thinkers, I reply that precisely now, in the early twenty-first century, there are all kinds of reasons for questioning current paradigms. In any case, it is, as we have seen, wrong to imply that the choice is between an ancient worldview and a modern (or even a postmodern) one. The ancient worldview of Homer, Plato, Cicero, and the rest had no room for resurrection either. What is at stake is the clash between a worldview that allows for a God of creation and justice and worldviews that don't.

I am aware that many people still today assume that faith lives in a private sphere, shutting itself off from history lest history make unwelcome inroads. Meanwhile, many others view history as a closed chain of visible cause and effect, which is never open to anything new happening. What the Easter stories do—and what, I argue, the whole existence of the church does, from the very first days onward—is to pose a huge question. We need to set our asking of that question, ultimately, in dialogue at least with the life of the community that believes the gospel and seeks by its life to live out its truth. We need to set it within the reading of the scriptures, which by their whole narrative lay out the worldview within which it makes sense. We need to think it through within a context of personal openness to the God of whom the Bible speaks—the creator of the world, not simply a divine presence within it, the God of justice and truth. These are not substitutes for historical inquiry or lame supplements to it. They are ways of opening the windows of mind and heart to see what really, after all, might be possible in God's world, the world not only of creation as it is but also of new creation. History, I believe, brings us to the point where we are bound to say: there really was an empty tomb, and there really were sightings of Jesus, the same and yet transformed. History then says: so how do you explain that?

It offers us no easy escapes at that point, no quick side exits to the question. They've all been tried, and none of them work. History poses the question. And when Christian faith answers it, a sober, humble, questioning history (as opposed to an arrogant rationalism that has decided the issue in advance) may find itself saying, "That sounds good to me."

The story of Thomas in John 20 will serve as a parable for this. Thomas, like a good historian, wants to see and touch. Jesus presents himself to his sight and invites him to touch, but Thomas doesn't. He transcends the type of knowing he had intended to use and passes into a higher and richer one. In the image I used before, of Israel at the Red Sea, this is how it looks, in words from the *Easter Oratorio.*[14] Thomas begins with doubt:

> The sea is too deep
> The heaven's too high
> I cannot swim
> I cannot fly;
> I must stay here
> I must stay here
> Here where I know
> How I can know
> Here where I know
> What I can know.

Jesus then reappears and invites Thomas to see and touch. Suddenly the new, giddying possibility appears before him:

> The sea has parted. Pharaoh's hosts—
> Despair, and doubt, and fear, and pride—
> No longer frighten us. We must

Cross over to the other side.
The heaven bows down. With wounded hands
Our exiled God, our Lord of shame
Before us, living, breathing, stands;
The Word is near, and calls our name.
New knowing for the doubting mind,
New seeing out of blindness grows;
New trusting may the sceptic find
New hope through that which faith now knows.

And with that, Thomas takes a deep breath and brings history and faith together in a rush. "My Lord," he says, "and my God."

That is not an antihistorical statement. The "Lord" in question is precisely the one who is the climax of Israel's history and the launch of a new history. Once you grasp the resurrection, you see that Israel's history is full of partial and preparatory analogies for this moment. The epistemological weight is borne not simply by the promise of ultimate resurrection and new creation but also by the narrative of God's mighty actions in the past.

Nor is it an antiscientific statement. The world of new creation is precisely the world of new *creation;* as such, it is open to, and indeed eager for, the work of human beings—not to manipulate it with magic tricks nor to be subservient to it as though the world of creation were itself divine but to be its stewards. And stewards need to pay close, minute attention to that of which they are stewards, in order the better to serve it and to enable it to attain its intended fruitfulness.

What I am suggesting is that faith in Jesus risen from the dead *transcends but includes* what we call history and what we call science. Faith of this sort is not blind belief, which rejects all history and science. Nor is it simply—which would be much safer!—a belief that inhabits a totally different sphere, discontinuous from either, in a separate watertight compartment. Rather, this kind of faith, which like all modes of knowledge is defined by the nature of its object, is faith in the creator God, the God who promised to put all things to rights at the last, the God who (as the sharp point where those two come together) raised Jesus from the dead *within* history, leaving evidence that demands an explanation from the scientist as well as anybody else. Insofar as I understand scientific method, when something turns up that doesn't fit the paradigm you're working with, one option at least, perhaps when all others have failed, is to change the paradigm—not to exclude everything you've known to that point but to include it within a larger whole. That is, if you like, the Thomas challenge.

If Thomas represents an epistemology of faith, which transcends but also includes historical and scientific knowing, we might suggest that Paul represents at this point an epistemology of hope. In 1 Corinthians 15 he sketches his argument that there will be a future resurrection as part of God's new creation, the redemption of the entire cosmos as in Romans 8. Hope, for the Christian, is not wishful thinking or mere blind optimism. It is a mode of knowing, a mode within which new things are possible, options are not shut down, new creation can happen. There is more to be said about this, but not here.

All of which brings us to Peter. Epistemologies of faith and hope, both transcending and including historical and scientific knowing, point on to an epistemology of love—an idea I first met in Bernard Lonergan but that was hardly new with him. The story of John 21 sharpens it up. Peter, famously, has denied Jesus. He has chosen to live within the normal world, where the tyrants win in the end and where it's better to dissociate yourself from people who get on the wrong side of them. But now, with Easter, Peter is called to live in a new and different world. Where Thomas is called to a new kind of faith and Paul to a radically renewed hope, Peter is called to a new kind of love.[15]

Here I go back to Wittgenstein once more, not now for a poker but for a famous and haunting aphorism: "It is *love* that believes the resurrection."[16] "Simon, son of John," says Jesus, "do you love me?"

There is a whole world in that question, a world of personal invitation and challenge, of the remaking of a human being after disloyalty and disaster, of the refashioning of epistemology itself, the question of how we know things, to correspond to the new ontology, the question of what reality consists of. The reality that is the resurrection cannot simply be "known" from within the old world of decay and denial, of tyrants and torture, of disobedience and death. But that's the point. To repeat: the resurrection is not, as it were, a highly peculiar event within the *present* world (though it is that as well); it is, principally, the defining event of the *new* creation, the world that is being born with Jesus. If we are even to glimpse this new world, let alone enter it, we will need a different kind of knowing, a knowing that involves us in new ways, an epistemology that draws out from us not just the cool appraisal of detached quasi-scientific research but also that whole-person engagement and involvement for which the best shorthand is "love," in the full Johannine sense of *agapē*. My sense, from talking to some scientific colleagues, is that, though it's hard to describe, something like this is already at work when the scientist devotes himself or herself to the subject matter so completely that the birth of new hypotheses comes about not so much through an abstract brain (a computer made of meat?) crunching data but through a soft and mysterious symbiosis of knower and known, of lover and beloved.[17]

The skeptic will at once suggest that this is a way of collapsing the truth of Easter once more into mere subjectivism. Not so. Just because it takes *agapē* to believe the resurrection, that doesn't mean that all that happened was that Peter and the others felt their hearts strangely warmed. Precisely because it is *love* we are talking about, it must have a correlative reality in the world outside the lover. Love is the deepest mode of knowing because it is love that, while completely engaging with reality other than itself, affirms and celebrates that other-than-self reality. This is the point at which much modernist epistemology breaks down. The sterile antithesis of "objective" and "subjective," where we say that things are either objectively true (and can be perceived as such by a dispassionate observer) or subjectively true (and so of no use as an account of the real, public world), is overcome by the epistemology of love, which is called into being as the necessary mode of knowing for those who will live in the new public world, the world launched at Easter, the world in which Jesus is Lord and Caesar isn't.

That is why, though the historical arguments for Jesus's bodily resurrection are truly strong, we must never suppose that they will do more than bring people to the questions faced by Thomas, Paul, and Peter, the questions of faith, hope, and love. We cannot use a supposedly objective historical epistemology as the ultimate ground for the truth of Easter. To do so would be like lighting a candle to see whether the sun had risen. What the candles of historical scholarship will do is to show that the room has been disturbed, that it doesn't look like it did last night, and that would-be normal explanations for this won't do. Maybe, we think after the historical arguments have done their work, maybe morning has come and the world has woken up. But to investigate whether this is so, we must take the risk and open the curtains to the rising sun. When we do so, we won't rely on the candles anymore, not because we don't believe in evidence and argument but because they will have been overtaken by the larger reality from which they borrow, to which they point, and in which they will find a new and larger home. All knowing is a gift from God, historical and scientific knowing no less than that of faith, hope, and love; but the greatest of these is love.

CONCLUSION

One final note. I am convinced that the climate of skepticism, which for the last two hundred years has made it unfashionable and even embarrassing to suggest that Jesus's resurrection really happened, was never and is not now itself a neutral thing, sociologically or po-litically. The intellectual coup d'état by which the Enlightenment convinced so many that "we now know that dead people don't rise," as though this was a modern discovery rather than simply the re-affirmation of what Homer and Aeschylus had taken for granted, goes hand in hand with the Enlightenment's other proposals, not least that we have now come of age, that God can be kicked upstairs, that we can get on with running the world however we want to, carving it up to our advantage without outside interference. To that extent, the totalitarianisms of the last century were simply among the varied manifestations of a larger totalitarianism of thought and culture against which postmodernity has now, and rightly in my view, rebelled. Who, after all, was it who didn't want the dead to be raised? Not simply the intellectually timid or the rationalists. It was, and is, those in power, the social and intellectual tyrants and bullies; the Caesars who would be threatened by a Lord of the world who had defeated the tyrant's last weapon, death itself; the Herods who would be horrified at the postmortem validation of the true King of the Jews.[18] *And this is the point where believing in the resurrection of Jesus suddenly ceases to be a matter of inquiring about an odd event in the first century and becomes a matter of rediscovering hope in the twenty-first century.* Hope is what you get when you suddenly realize that a different worldview is possible, a worldview in which the rich, the powerful, and the unscrupulous do not after all have the last word. The same worldview shift that is demanded by the resurrec-tion of Jesus is the shift that will enable us to transform the world.

Think of Oscar Wilde's wonderful scene in his play *Salome,* when Herod hears reports that Jesus of Nazareth has been raising the dead. "I do not wish him to do that," says Herod. "I forbid him to do that. I allow no man to raise the dead. This man must be found and told that I forbid him to raise the dead."

There is the bluster of the tyrant who knows his power is threat-ened, and I hear the same tone of voice not just in the politicians who want to carve up the world to their advantage but also in the intellectual traditions that have gone along for the ride.

But Wilde's next, haunting line is the real crunch, for us as for Herod: "Where is this man?" demands Herod. "He is in every place, my lord," replies the courtier, "but it is hard to find him."[19]

PART II

GOD'S FUTURE PLAN

5. COSMIC FUTURE: PROGRESS OR DESPAIR?

INTRODUCTION

I suggested in the first part of the book that when we look at the contemporary world and church, we discover great confusion about future hope but that when we look at the early Christians, we find not just faith but a very precise and specific faith, both about Jesus and his resurrection and about the future life that God had promised to all his people.

This isn't a matter of ancient people being credulous and modern people being skeptical. There is a great deal of credulity in our present world, and there was a great deal of skepticism in the ancient world. It is rather something to do with the very specific worldview that was generated by the events concerning Jesus, and supremely the event of Easter itself.

The early Christians looked back with joy to that great event. But precisely because of their very Jewish belief in God as the creator and redeemer, and because they had seen this belief confirmed in the totally unexpected event of Jesus's resurrection, they also looked forward eagerly to an event yet to come in which what began at Easter would be completed. This larger picture of a still-future renewal is the subject of the present part of the book.

It would be possible at this point to jump right in and to speak of the personal hope that the gospel provides for each believer. What

God did for Jesus on the first Easter Day, he has promised to do for each one who is in Christ, each one indwelt by the Spirit of Christ. That is the biblical and historic Christian expectation in terms of ourselves as human beings. We shall come to this in due course.

But there are good reasons for not starting there. In the last two hundred years Western thought has overemphasized the individual at the expense of the larger picture of God's creation. What is more, in much Western piety, at least since the Middle Ages, the influence of Greek philosophy has been very marked, resulting in a future expectation that bears far more resemblance to Plato's vision of souls entering into disembodied bliss than to the biblical picture of new heavens and new earth. If we start with the future hope of the individual, there is always the risk that we will, at least by implication, understand that as the real center of everything and treat the hope of creation as mere embroidery around the edges. That has happened often enough. I am keen to rule it out by the structure of the argument as well as through the detailed exposition.

The order of the discussion is therefore determined by what seems to me the appropriate arrangement of the material. Instead of looking first at the promise to the individual and working up from that to the renewal of creation, we begin with the biblical vision of the future world—a vision of the present cosmos renewed from top to bottom by the God who is both creator and redeemer. That is the context within which we will then be able to speak of the second coming of Jesus and then of the bodily resurrection.[1]

We turn then to the large-scale hope of the whole cosmos, the great drama within which our little dramas are, as it were, the play within the play. What is God's purpose for the world as a whole?

To answer this, we must first look, in the present chapter, at two very popular options before, in the next chapter, exploring the alternative that (though you'd never know it from much contemporary Christianity) is the one offered by the New Testament itself.[2]

OPTION 1: EVOLUTIONARY OPTIMISM

At the risk of gross oversimplification, we suggest that there are two quite different ways of looking at the future of the world. Both of these ways are sometimes confused with the Christian hope, and indeed both make use of some elements of the Christian hope in telling their grand stories. But neither comes anywhere near the picture we have in the New Testament and, in flashes, in the Old. The Christian answer lies not so much halfway in between as in a biblical answer, which combines the strengths and eliminates the weaknesses of both.

The first position is the myth of progress. Many people, particularly politicians and secular commentators in the press and elsewhere, still live by this myth, appeal to it, and encourage us to believe it. Indeed (if I may digress for a moment), the demise of serious political discourse today consists not least in this, that the politicians are still trying to whip up enthusiasm for their versions of this myth—it's the only discourse they know, poor things—while the rest of us have moved on. They are, to that extent, like people trying to row a boat toward the shore while the strong tide pulls them further and further out to sea. Because they face the wrong way, they can't see that their efforts are in vain, and they call out to other boats to join them in their splendid, shore-bound voyage. That is why the relentlessly modernist and progressivist projects that the politicians feel obliged to offer us ("vote for us and things will get better!") have to be dressed up with the relentlessly postmodernist techniques of spin and hype: in the absence of real hope, all that is left is feelings. Persuasion will not work because we're never going to believe it. What we appear to need, and therefore what people give us, is entertainment. As a journalist said recently, our politicians demand to be treated like rock stars while our rock stars are pretending to be politicians. Sorting out this mess—which the Christian hope, despite current opinion, is well suited to do—should mean, among many other things, a renewal of genuine political discourse, which God knows we badly need.

But to return to our main theme. The myth of progress has deep roots in contemporary Western culture, and some of those roots are Christian.[3] The idea that the human project, and indeed the cosmic project, could and would continue to grow and develop, producing unlimited human improvement and marching toward a utopia, goes back to the Renaissance and was given its decisive push by the eighteenth-century European Enlightenment. The full flowering of this belief took place in Europe in the nineteenth century, when the combination of scientific and economic advances, on the one hand, and democratic freedoms and wider education, on the other, produced a strong sense that history was accelerating toward a wonderful goal. El Dorado was just around the corner, the millennium in which the world would live at peace. Prosperity would spread out from enlightened Europe and America and embrace the world. By no means all thinkers a hundred years ago fitted into this mold, but many, including some of enormous influence such as Hegel, did so enthusiastically. This, again, is precisely where some of our politicians still gain their inspiration.

This utopian dream is in fact a parody of the Christian vision. The kingdom of God and the kingdoms of the world come together to produce a vision of history moving forward toward its goal, a goal that will emerge from within rather than being a new gift from elsewhere. Humans can be made perfect and are indeed evolving inexorably toward that point. The world is ours to discover, exploit, and enjoy. Instead of dependence on God's grace, we will become what we have the potential to be by education and hard work. Instead of creation and new creation, science and technology will turn the raw material of this world into the stuff of utopia. Like the mythical Prometheus, defying the gods and trying to run the world his own way, liberal modernism supposes that the world can become everything we want it to be by working a bit harder and helping forward the great march into the glorious future.

I leave to one side in this brief sketch the role played by Charles Darwin, whose iconic figure continues to haunt several quite different contemporary discussions. One of the strange and perhaps poetically appropriate twists in that story is our increasing recognition that Darwin was himself not so much the great new thinker, coming from nowhere to his radical new idea, but rather the exact product of his times, one particular high-water mark in the onward rush of liberal modernist optimism, himself the product of a particular evolution in Western thought. The eagerness with which his ideas were embraced and reapplied not only in the narrow biological sphere in which they belonged but also in far wider areas such as society and politics indicates well enough the mood of the times. The world in general, and humankind in particular, was marching onward and upward in an immanent process that couldn't be stopped and that would result in the great future that lay just around the corner. Evolution, in this more general sense of progress, was already widely believed; it was a deeply convenient philosophy for those who wanted to justify their own massive industrial and imperial expansion; Darwin gave it some apparent scientific legitimacy, which was quickly seized upon and which, within half a century, had been used to justify everything from eugenics to war. The same could be said, of course, mutatis mutandis, of Karl Marx.[4]

Many Christian thinkers went along for the ride on this apparently incoming tide of progress. Many embraced Darwin's ideas as a way of solving (for instance) some of the problems they had felt about the Old Testament. Many eagerly expounded social Darwinism as the way forward for the world, with some even encouraging the pursuit of war as the proper way to test who in the human species were the fittest and hence the most deserving of survival. Many Christians embraced what they called the social gospel, trying to put into practice in society the promises of the Christian message. An enormous amount of good work was done by this means, though after a century of it we now all know that it isn't the full answer.

But the best-known Christian development of the myth of progress was that of Pierre Teilhard de Chardin. This French Jesuit, born in 1881, was a distinguished scientist of human origins and a fervent Christian mystic who believed that the presence of God was to be discovered anywhere and everywhere in the natural world. He believed that the living world disclosed itself as an all-encompassing "cosmic, christic and divine milieu"; despite the turmoil and suffering of the world, he believed that it was being "animated and drawn up towards God." The divine spirit, he believed, is involved in the evolutionary process at every stage so that "cosmic and human evolution are moving onwards to an ever fuller disclosure of the Spirit, culminating in 'Christ-Omega.'"[5] All history had been moving toward the Omega-point of the emergence of the Christ and was now moving toward the climax and goal in which all creation would find its fulfillment in him. Teilhard de Chardin's most famous book, *The Phenomenon of Man,* written before the Second World War but only published after his death in 1955, became a best-seller and influenced a whole generation of those who wanted to combine Christian spirituality with scientific thought. One recent enthusiastic writer suggests that "his powerful affirmation of the Incarnation and his vision of the universal, cosmic Christ within an evolutionary perspective" can now "reaffirm the core of the Christian faith for our scientific age."[6] The influence of Teilhard de Chardin may lie behind the recent popularity of a prayer that speaks of "all things returning to perfection through him from whom they took their origin."[7]

Teilhard de Chardin's thinking is many-sided and subtle, and this isn't the place to launch an exposition, let alone a critique. It is a caricature to say, as some have done, that he is simply an advance prophet of New Age spirituality. Likewise, though there appear to be pantheistic elements in his thought, Teilhard de Chardin was not himself a pantheist as such. However, he does share the weaknesses of the evolutionary optimism of his times, not least, as we shall see, an inability to factor into his thinking the fact of radical evil (it was, interestingly, an early work on original sin, or rather its absence, that first brought him critical attention in his own church). Teilhard and his supporters have appealed to the Pauline idea of the cosmic Christ, as in Colossians 1:15–20, but Paul's thinking there and elsewhere hardly supports the structure Teilhard wishes to erect. In the long run—and of course it was to the long run that he appealed— he may appear as one of the great flowerings, in Christian form, of that evolutionary optimism of which our postscientific age is now increasingly skeptical. But more of that anon.

The real problem with the myth of progress is, as I just hinted, that it cannot deal with evil. And when I say "deal with," I don't just mean intellectually, though that is true as well; I mean in practice. It can't develop a strategy that actually addresses the severe problems of evil in the world. This is why all the evolutionary optimism of the last two hundred years remains helpless before world war, drug crime, Auschwitz, apartheid, child pornography, and the other interesting sidelines that evolution has thrown up for our entertainment in the twentieth century. We can't explain them, given the myth of progress, and neither can we eradicate them. Marx's own agenda, not to explain the world but to change it, remains unfulfilled. Of course, the twentieth century provided a quite full answer to the myth of progress, as many people (such as Karl Barth) saw during the First World War, but it's remarkable how many others have continued to believe and propagate it nonetheless. Teilhard himself was a stretcher bearer during the Great War, and the experience was influential not in leading him away from evolution but in his attempt to factor human suffering into his equation. Part of the problem in our contemporary debates about asylum seekers or about the Middle East is that our politicians still want to present us with the dream of progress, the steady forward advance of the golden dream of freedom; and when the tide of human misery washes up on our beaches or when people in cultures very different from our own seem not to want the kind of freedom we had in mind, it is not just socially but ideologically untidy and inconvenient. It reminds the politicians that there is a gap in their thinking.

The world is in fact still a sad and wicked place, not a happy upward progress toward the light.[8]

The myth, then, cannot deal with evil, for three reasons. First, it can't stop it: if evolution gave us Hiroshima and the Gulag, it can't be all good. There is no observable reason in science, philosophy, art, or anywhere else to suppose that if we simply plow ahead with the enlightenment dream these glitches will be ironed out and we'll get to utopia eventually. What's more, today's cutting-edge science is quite clear that whatever may and may not be true about specifically biological evolution, the cosmos as a whole is simply not evolving toward a golden future. The world that began with the Big Bang is heading either for the Big Cool-Down, as energy gradually runs out and the universe expands into the cold dark beyond, or for the Big Crunch, as gravity reasserts itself and everything slows down, stops, and then rushes back together again. It is quite possible that before either of these worrying possibilities takes place, a giant meteorite such as likely wiped out the dinosaurs could strike the Earth with similar devastating effects. None of these scenarios makes any sense within the myth of progress.[9]

Second, even if "progress" brought us to utopia after all, that wouldn't address the *moral* problem of all the evil that's happened to date in the world. Suppose the golden age arrived tomorrow morning; what would that say to those who are being tortured to death today? How would that be a satisfactory solution to the huge and indescribable evils of the last century, let alone all of world history? If, akin to Teilhard de Chardin, we were to make God part of the process of it all, what sort of a god would it be who builds his kingdom on the bones and ashes of those who have suffered along the way? The picture reminds me of the story of the old Oxford don who, whenever the paper on his desk got quite out of control, would simply spread a copy of the *Times* over the lot and start again. After his death they found several layers, like an archaeologist's tell, of matters that had never been dealt with. And after the construction of an evolutionist's kingdom of God, God would be left with precisely the same problem. It was because of this that the ancient Jews began to speak of the resurrection.

The myth of progress fails because it doesn't in fact work; because it would never solve evil retrospectively; and because it underestimates the nature and power of evil itself and thus fails to see the vital importance of the cross, God's *no* to evil, which then opens the door to his *yes* to creation. Only in the Christian story itself—certainly not in the secular stories of modernity—do we find any sense that the problems of the world are solved not by a straightforward upward movement into the light but by the creator God going down into the dark to rescue humankind and the world from its plight.

The myth of progress, then, has been enormously powerful in our culture. In fact, it still is, not least as an implicit belief to which one can appeal to justify any and every "development" in a supposed liberalizing, humanizing, freedom-bringing direction. ("Don't you believe in *progress?*" people ask scornfully when someone objects to a new "moral" proposal. They used to say that when people objected to cutting down ancient trees to build a new road, but we have begun to realize that progress in that sense wasn't all it was cracked up to be.) Christians have often gone along with the general idea of progress, but though it sometimes runs on parallel lines to Christian hope, the myth of progress comes from a different origin and veers off toward a very different destination—just as the trains that run from London to Manchester coincide for a stretch with those that run from Southampton to Newcastle but start and finish somewhere very different. Politicians and the media plug into the myth constantly though the appliances they run off it frequently subvert it, like someone using a power drill to cut into the very socket where the tool is getting its electricity. No wonder we live in a world of flying sparks, of self-defeating energy. But before we look at the truly Christian alternative, we must briefly examine the other myth, the negative myth, the story that tells us the world is a wicked place and we'd do better to escape it altogether.

Plato remains the most influential thinker in the history of the Western world. For Plato, the present world of space, time, and matter is a world of illusion, of flickering shadows in a cave, and the most appropriate human task is to get in touch with the true reality, which is beyond space, time, and matter. For Plato, this was the reality of eternal Forms.

To oversimplify once more, we may say that Plato's picture was based on a rejection of the phenomena of matter and transience. The mess and muddle of the space-time-matter world was an offense to the tidy, clean philosophical mind, which dwelt upon eternal realities. It wasn't just evil that was wrong with the world; it was change and decay, the transitoriness of matter: the fact that spring and summer are followed by autumn and winter, that the sunset tails off into darkness, that human blossoming and flourishing are the prelude to suffering and death.

Here worldviews diverge radically. The optimist, the evolutionist, the myth-of-progress school all say that these are just the growing pains of something bigger and better. The Platonist, the Hindu, and, following Plato, the Gnostic, the Manichaean, and countless others within variants of the Christian and Jewish traditions all say that these are the signs that we are made for something quite different, a world not made of space, time, and matter, a world of pure spiritual existence where we shall happily have got rid of the shackles of mortality once and for all. And the way you get rid of mortality within this worldview is to get rid of the thing that can decay and die, namely our material selves.

The Platonic strain entered Christian thinking early on, not least with the phenomenon known as Gnosticism. Since the Gnostics have been making something of a comeback recently, a word about them is appropriate.[10] The Gnostics believed, like Plato, that the material world was an inferior and dark place, evil in its very existence, but that within this world could be found certain people who were meant for something else. These children of light were like fallen stars, tiny pinpricks of light currently hidden within a gross material body. Once they had realized who they were, though, this knowledge (Greek *gnosis*) would enable them to enter into a spiritual existence in which the material world would no longer count. Having entered upon that spiritual existence, they would then live by it, through death, and into the infinite world beyond space, time, and matter. "We are stardust," sang Joni Mitchell, plugging in to this millennia-old mythology, "we are golden; and we've got to get ourselves back to the garden."[11] The Gnostic myth often suggests that the way out of our mess is to return to our primeval state, before the creation of the world. In this view creation itself is the fall, producing matter, which is the real evil. I hope it is clear both how closely this view parodies some aspects of Christianity and how deeply and thoroughly it diverges from it.

Though most people in today's world have probably only a sketchy idea of Gnosticism, assuming they've heard of it at all, it has been argued with some plausibility that some elements of it—and Gnosticism is always an eclectic phenomenon—are found in some of the seminal thinkers and writers of the last two hundred years in our culture. The writer and playwright Stuart Holroyd, himself an unashamed apologist for Gnosticism, lists Blake, Goethe, Melville, Yeats, and Jung among others as representing this stream in the modern West, and though their insights have often been cross-fertilized with other types, he has a point that should not be ignored. Basically, if you move away from materialistic optimism but without embracing Judaism or Christianity, you are quite likely to end up with some kind of Gnosticism. It should be no surprise that certain elements of the Romantic movement, and some of their more recent heirs, have been prone to this.[12] The discovery of the Nag Hammadi scrolls (a library of Gnostic texts found in Upper Egypt) has in our day fueled a desire to reinterpret Christianity itself in terms of a supposedly original Gnostic spirituality that contrasts sharply with the concrete kingdom-of-God-on-Earth announced by the Jesus of the canonical gospels. Travel far enough down that road, and you will end up with the blatant and outrageous conspiracy theories of a book like *The Da Vinci Code.* But there are many who without going that far now assume that some kind of Gnosticism is what genuine Christianity was supposed to be about.

Most Western Christians—and most Western non-Christians, for that matter—in fact suppose that Christianity was committed to at least a soft version of Plato's position. A good many Christian hymns and poems wander off unthinkingly in the direction of Gnosticism. The "just passing through" spirituality (as in the spiritual "This world is not my home, / I'm just a'passin' through"), though it has some affinities with classical Christianity, encourages precisely a Gnostic attitude: the created world is at best irrelevant, at worst a dark, evil, gloomy place, and we immortal souls, who existed originally in a different sphere, are looking forward to returning to it as soon as we're allowed to. A massive assumption has been made in Western Christianity that the purpose of being a Christian is simply, or at least mainly, to "go to heaven when you die," and texts that don't say that but that mention heaven are read as if they did say it, and texts that say the opposite, like Romans 8:18–25 and Revelation 21–22, are simply screened out as if they didn't exist.[13]

The results are all around us in the Western church and in the worldviews that Western Christianity has generated. Secularists often criticize Christians for contributing to ecological disaster, and there's more than a grain of truth in the charge. I have heard it seriously argued in North America that since God intends to destroy the present space-time universe, and moreover since he intends to do so quite soon now, it really doesn't matter whether we emit twice as many greenhouse gases as we do now, whether we destroy the rain forests and the arctic tundra, whether we fill our skies with acid rain. That is a peculiarly modern form of would-be Christian negativity about the world, and of course its skin-deep "spiritual" viewpoint is entirely in thrall to the heart-deep materialism of the business inter-

SURPRISED BY HOPE

ests that will be served, in however short a term, by such hazardous practices.

I shall come to that sort of thing in more detail later on. My point for now is to notice that in many parts of the world an appeal to a Christian view of the future is taken to mean an appeal to the eventual demise of the created order and to a destiny that is purely "spiritual" in the sense of being completely nonmaterial. That remains the popular perception, both from inside and outside the church, of what we Christians are supposed to believe when we speak of heaven and when we talk of the hope that is ours in Christ.

Over against both these popular and mistaken views, the central Christian affirmation is that what the creator God has done in Jesus Christ, and supremely in his resurrection, is what he intends to do for the whole world—meaning, by *world,* the entire cosmos with all its history. It is to this hope that I turn in the next chapter.

6. WHAT THE WHOLE WORLD'S WAITING FOR

INTRODUCTION

The early Christians did not believe in progress. They did not think the world was getting better and better under its own steam—or even under the steady influence of God. They knew God had to do something fresh to put it to rights.

But neither did they believe that the world was getting worse and worse and that their task was to escape it altogether. They were not dualists.

Since most people who think about these things today tend toward one or other of those two points of view, it comes as something of a surprise to discover that the early Christians held a quite different view. They believed that God was going to do for the whole cosmos what he had done for Jesus at Easter. This is such a surprising belief, and so little reflected on even in Christian circles, still less outside the church, that we must set it out step by step and show how the different early writers developed different images that together add up to a stunning picture of a future for which, so they insisted, the whole world was waiting on tiptoe.

FUNDAMENTAL STRUCTURES OF HOPE

The clearest statements of the large-scale Christian hope are found in the New Testament, in Paul and in the book of Revelation. I want to explore these now, drawing out as we do so the ways in which they answer the two opposite views I have sketched. We need to notice, in particular, the way in which three themes emerge.

First, the *goodness of creation*. Granted the swirling currents of alternative worldviews available in the first century, it is a remarkable feature of the earliest Christianity known to us that it refused to lapse at any point into a cosmological dualism in which the created world is regarded as less than good and God-given. But it is good as *creation*, not as an independent or self-sufficient "nature." There is no suggestion of pantheism or even panentheism. God and the world are not the same thing, nor is everything simply held within something called "god." Within biblical theology it remains the case that the one living God created a world that is other than himself, not contained within himself. Creation was from the beginning an act of love, of affirming the goodness of the other. God saw all that he had made, and it was very good; but it was not itself divine. At its height, which according to Genesis 1 is the creation of humans, it was designed to *reflect* God, both to reflect God back to God in worship and to reflect God into the rest of creation in stewardship. But this image-bearing capacity of humankind is not in itself the same thing as divinity. Collapsing this distinction means taking a large step toward a pantheism within which there is no way of understanding, let alone addressing, the problem of evil.

Second, then, the *nature of evil*. Evil is real and powerful, within biblical theology, but it consists neither in the fact of being created nor in the fact of being other than God (since being loved into life by the one God is quite good enough!) nor yet in the fact that it's made of physical matter and belongs within space and time instead of being pure spirit in an eternal heaven. Nor—and this is crucial—does evil consist in being transient, made to decay. There is nothing wrong with the tree dropping its leaves in the autumn. There is nothing wrong with the sunset fading away into darkness. Evil consists in none of those things; indeed, it is precisely the transience of the good creation that serves as a pointer to its larger purpose. Creation was good, but it always had a forward look. Transience acts as a God-given signpost pointing not from the material world to a non-material world but from the world *as it is* to the world *as it is meant one day to be*—pointing, in other words, from the present to the future that God has in store. The human project of bringing wise order to the garden is not yet complete, and without transience we might the more easily be led into idolatry, treating the creature as though it was the creator—which, goodness knows, is all too easy as it is. This harks back to what I said in the first two chapters. What matters is eschatological duality (the present age and the age to come), not ontological dualism (an evil "earth" and a good "heaven").

Evil then consists not in being created but in the rebellious idolatry by which humans worship and honor elements of the natural world rather than the God who made them. The result is that the cosmos is out of joint. Instead of humans being God's wise vice-regents over creation, they ignore the creator and try to worship something less demanding, something that will give them a short-term fix of power or pleasure. The result is that death, which was always part of the natural transience of the good creation, gains a second dimension, which the Bible sometimes calls "spiritual death." In Genesis, and indeed for much of the Old Testament, the controlling image for death is exile. Adam and Eve were told that they would die on the day they ate the fruit; what actually happened was that they were expelled from the garden. Turning away from the worship of the living God is turning toward that which has no life in itself. Worship that which is transient, and it can only give you death. But when you do commit that idolatry, evil is unleashed into the world, setting off chain reactions with incalculable consequences. Mysteriously, this out-of-jointness seems to become entangled with the transience and decay necessary within the good-but-incomplete creation so that what we perhaps misleadingly call natural evil can be seen as, among other things, the advance signs of that final "shaking" of heaven and earth that the prophets understood to be necessary if God's eventual new world was to be born.[1]

Third, the *plan of redemption.* Precisely because creation is the work of God's love, redemption is not something alien to the creator but rather something he will undertake with delight and glad self-giving. Redemption doesn't mean scrapping what's there and starting again from a clean slate but rather liberating what has come to be enslaved. And because of the analysis of evil not as materiality but as rebellion, the slavery of humans and of the world does not consist in embodiment, redemption from which would mean the death of the body and the consequent release of the soul or spirit. The slavery consists, rather, in sin, redemption from which must ultimately involve not just goodness of soul or spirit but a newly embodied life.

This is the plan that throughout the Bible is articulated in terms of God's choice of Israel as the means of redemption and then, after the long and checkered story of God and Israel, God's sending of his son, Jesus. Incarnation—already adumbrated in the Jewish tradition in terms not least of the Temple as the place where God chooses to live on earth—is not a category mistake, as Platonists ancient and modern imagine. It is the center and fulfillment of the long-term plan of the good and wise creator.

If you tell this story from the point of view of the good creation, the coming of Jesus emerges as the moment all creation had been waiting for. Humans were made to be God's stewards over creation, so the one through whom all things were made, the eternal son, the eternal wisdom, becomes human so that he might truly become God's steward, ruler over all his world. Equally, if you tell the story from the point of view of human rebellion and the consequent sin and death that have engulfed the world, this again emerges as the moment all creation had been waiting for: the eternal expression of the father's love became the incarnate expression of the father's love so that by his self-giving to death, even the death of the cross, the whole creation can be reconciled to God. If you put these two ways of telling the story together and cast them into poetry, you will find you have rewritten Colossians 1:15–20. This is the real cosmic Christology of the New Testament: not a kind of pantheism, running under its own steam and cut off from the real Jesus, but a retelling of the Jewish story of wisdom in terms of Jesus himself, focusing on the cross as the act whereby the good creation is brought back into harmony with the wise creator.

The balance of the clauses in the poem in Colossians 1 shows the extent to which Paul insists on holding together creation and redemption.[2] Redemption is not simply making creation a bit better, as the optimistic evolutionist would try to suggest. Nor is it rescuing spirits and souls from an evil material world, as the Gnostic would want to say. It is the remaking of creation, having dealt with the evil that is defacing and distorting it. And it is accomplished by the same God, now known in Jesus Christ, through whom it was made in the first place. It is highly significant that in the passage just after the great poem of 1:15–20, Paul declares that the gospel has already been announced to every creature under heaven (1:23). What has happened in the death and resurrection of Jesus Christ, in other words, is by no means limited to its effects on those human beings who believe the gospel and thereby find new life here and hereafter. It resonates out, in ways that we can't fully see or understand, into the vast recesses of the universe.

Creation, evil, and the plan of redemption revealed in action in Jesus Christ: these are the constant themes that the New Testament writers, particularly Paul and the author of Revelation, struggle to express. I now want to explore the key New Testament texts that speak of the cosmic dimension of Christian hope. There are six main themes to be explored; several of these are themselves powerful images taken from the world of creation. If you're going to speak of God doing something new that nevertheless affirms the old, what better way than to speak of seedtime and harvest, of birth and new life, and of marriage? We begin with the first of these, seedtime and harvest.

In 1 Corinthians 15 Paul uses the image of the firstfruits.[3] This goes back to the Jewish festivals of Passover and Pentecost, which in their developed forms were both agricultural and salvation-historical festivals. Passover was the time when the first crop of barley was presented before the Lord. Pentecost, seven weeks later, was the time when the firstfruits of the wheat harvest were presented. The offering of the firstfruits signifies the great harvest still to come. At the salvation-historical level, of course, Passover commemorated Israel coming out of Egypt while Pentecost, seven weeks later, commemorated the arrival at Sinai and the giving of Torah. The two strands were woven together since part of God's promise in liberating Israel and giving it the law was that Israel would inherit the land and that the land would be fruitful.

Paul applies this Passover image to Jesus. He is the firstfruits, the first to rise from the dead. But this isn't an isolated instance. The point of the firstfruits is that there will be many, many more. Jesus's Passover, that is, Calvary and Easter, which occurred of course at Passover time and was from very early on interpreted in the light of that festival, indicated that the great slavemaster, the great Egypt, sin and death themselves, had been defeated when Jesus came through the Red Sea of death and out the other side. And Paul goes on later in the chapter to expound the nature of the Christian's resurrection body on the basis of the new body of Jesus. Please note, over against any move toward Gnosticism, how this imagery indicates continuity as well as discontinuity. Note too, over against any kind of evolutionary optimism, that moving from seed sown to crop harvested involves discontinuity as well as continuity and in particular that the Exodus from Egypt, symbolized by this story, could be seen only as an act of pure grace. Progress, left to itself, could never have brought it about.[4]

1 Corinthians then continues with a quite different image, one not so organically related to the natural order of creation but with many biblical antecedents: that of a king establishing his kingdom by subduing all possible enemies.

Paul is careful to stress both that Jesus will rule until every single power in the cosmos has been subjected to him and that God the Father is not included in that category. Whatever we say about the implied Christology of this passage, Paul is clearly articulating a theology of *new creation*. Every force, every authority in the whole cosmos, will be subjected to the Messiah, and finally death itself will give up its power. In other words, that which we are tempted to regard as the permanent state of the cosmos—entropy, threatening chaos, and dissolution—will be transformed by the Messiah acting as the agent of the creator God. If evolutionary optimism is squelched by, among other things, the sober estimates of the scientists that the universe as we know it today is running out of steam and cannot last forever, the gospel of Jesus Christ announces that what God did for Jesus at Easter he will do not only for all those who are "in Christ" but also for the entire cosmos. It will be an act of new creation, parallel to and derived from the act of new creation when God raised Jesus from the dead.

Here we find, coming into full view, one of the direct results of saying that Jesus was raised bodily from the dead rather than saying that upon his death he began to exist in a new, nonbodily mode. As I have argued elsewhere, if after his death he had gone into some kind of nonbodily existence, death would not be defeated. It would remain intact; it would merely be redescribed. Jesus, humankind, and the world itself could not look forward to any future within a created and embodied mode such as we now know. But this is precisely what Paul is denying. Death as we now know it is the last enemy, not a good part of the good creation; and therefore death must be defeated if the life-giving God is to be honored as the true lord of the world.[5] When this has happened, and only then, Jesus the Messiah, the Lord of the world, will hand over the rule of the kingdom to his father, and God will be all in all. We shall return to this presently.

CITIZENS OF HEAVEN, COLONIZING THE EARTH

Before we get to that, we look across to another royal image, found in Philippians 3:20–21. It is very close in theme to 1 Corinthians 15, quoting in fact at the crucial point from the same psalm (Psalm 8), emphasizing Jesus's authority over all other powers.

Philippi was a Roman colony. Augustus had settled his veterans there after the battles of Philippi (42 B.C.) and Actium (31 B.C.). Not all residents of Philippi were Roman citizens, but all knew what citizenship meant. The point of creating colonies was twofold. First, it was aimed at extending Roman influence around the Mediterranean world, creating cells and networks of people loyal to Caesar in the wider culture. Second, it was one way of avoiding the problems of overcrowding in the capital itself. The emperor certainly did not want retired soldiers, with time (and blood) on their hands, hanging around Rome ready to cause trouble. Much better for them to be establishing farms and businesses elsewhere.

So when Paul says, "We are citizens of heaven," he doesn't at all mean that when we're done with this life we'll be going off to live in heaven.[6] What he means is that the savior, the Lord, Jesus the King—all of those were of course imperial titles—will come *from* heaven *to* earth, to change the present situation and state of his people. The key word here is *transform:* "He will transform our present humble bodies to be like his glorious body." Jesus will not declare that present physicality is redundant and can be scrapped. Nor will he simply improve it, perhaps by speeding up its evolutionary cycle. In a great act of power—the same power that accomplished

Jesus's own resurrection, as Paul says in Ephesians 1:19–20—he will *change* the present body into the one that corresponds in kind to his own as part of his work of bringing all things into subjection to himself. Philippians 3, though it is primarily speaking of human resurrection, indicates that this will take place within the context of God's victorious transformation of the whole cosmos.[7]

GOD WILL BE ALL IN ALL

Turning back to 1 Corinthians 15, we find Paul declaring that as the goal of all history, God will be "everything in everything," or if you like, "all in all" (15:28). This is one of the clearest statements of the very center of the future-oriented New Testament worldview.

At this level, the problem with a Teilhardian evolutionary optimism, as well as with any form of pantheism, is that it collapses the entire future into the present and indeed into the past. God *will be* all in all. The tense is future. Until the final victory over evil, and particularly over death, this moment has not arrived. To suggest that it has is to collude with evil and with death itself.

How then can we think wisely about God's present relation to the created order? If God is indeed the creator of the world, it matters that creation is other than God. This is not a moral problem, as has sometimes been thought (if a good God makes something that is not himself, it must be less than good, and therefore he is not a good God for making it). Nor is it a logical one (if in the beginning God is all that there is, how can there be ontological room for anything or anyone else?). As we said earlier, if creation was a work of love, it must have involved the creation of something other than God. That same love then allows creation to be itself, sustaining it in providence and wisdom but not overpowering it. Logic cannot comprehend love; so much the worse for logic.

That, though, is not the end of the story. God intends in the end to fill all creation with his own presence and love. This is part of an answer to Jürgen Moltmann's proposal to revive the rabbinic doctrine of *zimzum,* in which God as it were retreats, creates space within himself, so that there is ontological space for there to be something else other than him.[8] If I am right, it works the other way around. God's creative love, precisely by being love, creates *new* space for there to be things that are genuinely other than God.

The New Testament develops the doctrine of the Spirit in just this direction, but the future glimpse is already provided in Isaiah. In chapter 11, anticipating the "new creation" passage in chapters 65 and 66, the prophet declares that "the earth will be full of the knowledge of the Lord as the waters cover the sea."[9] As it stands, that is a remarkable statement. How can the waters cover the sea? They *are* the sea. It looks as though God intends to flood the universe with himself, as though the universe, the entire cosmos, was designed as a receptacle for his love. We might even suggest, as part of a Christian aesthetic, that the world is beautiful not just because it hauntingly reminds us of its creator but also because it is pointing forward: it is designed to be filled, flooded, drenched in God, as a chalice is beautiful not least because of what we know it is designed to contain or as a violin is beautiful not least because we know the music of which it is capable. I shall return to this later.

The answer to the pantheism of the evolutionary or progressive optimist, on the one hand, and to the dualism of the Gnostic or Manichee, on the other, now begins to come into full view in the form of the cosmic eschatology offered in the New Testament. The world is created good *but incomplete.* One day, when all forces of rebellion have been defeated and the creation responds freely and gladly to the love of its creator, God will fill it with himself so that it will *both* remain an independent being, other than God, *and also* be flooded with God's own life. This is part of the paradox of love, in which love freely given creates a context for love to be freely returned, and so on in a cycle where complete freedom and complete union do not cancel each other out but rather celebrate each other and make one another whole.

This brings us to Romans 8, where we find a further image deeply embedded within the created order itself: that of new birth. This passage has routinely been marginalized for centuries by exegetes and theologians who have tried to turn Romans into a book simply about how individual sinners get individually saved. But it is in fact one of the great climaxes of the letter and indeed of all Paul's thought.

In this passage Paul again uses the imagery of the Exodus from Egypt but this time in relation not to Jesus, nor even to ourselves, but to creation as a whole. Creation, he says (verse 21) is in slavery at the moment, like the children of Israel. God's design was to rule creation in life-giving wisdom through his image-bearing human creatures. But this was always a promise for the future, a promise that one day the true human being, the image of God himself, God's incarnate son, would come to lead the human race into their true identity. Meanwhile, the creation was subjected to futility, to transience and decay, until the time when God's children are glorified, when what happened to Jesus at Easter happens to all Jesus's people. This is where Romans 8 dovetails with 1 Corinthians 15. The whole creation, as he says in verse 19, is on tiptoe with expectation, longing for the day when God's children are revealed, when their resurrection will herald its own new life.

Paul then uses the image of birth pangs—a well-known Jewish metaphor for the emergence of God's new age—not only of the church in verse 23 and of the Spirit a couple of verses later but also here in verse 22 of creation itself. Once again this highlights both continuity and discontinuity. This is no smooth evolutionary transition, in which creation simply moves up another gear into a higher mode of life. This is traumatic, involving convulsions and contractions and the radical discontinuity in which mother and child are parted and become not one being but two. But neither is this a dualistic rejection of physicality as though, because the present creation is transient and full of decay and death, God must throw it away and start again from scratch. The very metaphor Paul chooses for this decisive moment in his argument shows that what he has in mind is not the unmaking of creation or simply its steady development but the drastic and dramatic birth of new creation from the womb of the old.

THE MARRIAGE OF HEAVEN AND EARTH

We thus arrive at the last and perhaps the greatest image of new creation, of cosmic renewal, in the whole Bible. This scene, set out in Revelation 21–22, is not well enough known or pondered (perhaps because, in order to earn the right to read it, one should really read the rest of the Revelation of St. John first, which proves too daunting for many). This time the image is that of marriage. The New Jerusalem comes down out of heaven like a bride adorned for her husband.

We notice right away how drastically different this is from all those would-be Christian scenarios in which the end of the story is the Christian going off to heaven as a soul, naked and unadorned, to meet its maker in fear and trembling. As in Philippians 3, it is not we who go to heaven, it is heaven that comes to earth; indeed, it is the church itself, the heavenly Jerusalem,[10] that comes down to earth. This is the ultimate rejection of all types of Gnosticism, of every worldview that sees the final goal as the separation of the world from God, of the physical from the spiritual, of earth from heaven. It is the final answer to the Lord's Prayer, that God's kingdom will come and his will be done on earth as in heaven. It is what Paul is talking about in Ephesians 1:10, that God's design, and promise, was to sum up all things in Christ, things both in heaven and on earth. It is the final fulfillment, in richly symbolic imagery, of the promise of Genesis 1, that the creation of male and female would together reflect God's image in the world. And it is the final accomplishment of

God's great design, to defeat and abolish death forever—which can only mean the rescue of creation from its present plight of decay.

Heaven and earth, it seems, are not after all poles apart, needing to be separated forever when all the children of heaven have been rescued from this wicked earth. Nor are they simply different ways of looking at the same thing, as would be implied by some kinds of pantheism. No, they are different, radically different, but they are made for each other in the same way (Revelation is suggesting) as male and female. And when they finally come together, that will be cause for rejoicing in the same way that a wedding is: a creational sign that God's project is going forward; that opposite poles within creation are made for union, not competition; that love and not hate have the last word in the universe; that fruitfulness and not sterility is God's will for creation.

What is promised in this passage, then, is what Isaiah foresaw: a new heaven and a new earth replacing the old heaven and the old earth, which were bound to decay. This doesn't mean, as I have stressed throughout, that God will wipe the slate clean and start again. If that were so, there would be no celebration, no conquest of death, no long preparation now at last complete. As the chapter develops, the bride, the wife of the Lamb, is described lovingly: she is the new Jerusalem promised by the prophets of the Exile, especially Ezekiel. But unlike in Ezekiel's vision, where the rebuilt Temple takes eventual center stage, there is no Temple in this city (21:22). The Temple in Jerusalem was always designed, it seems, as a pointer to, and an advance symbol for, the presence of God himself. When the reality is there, the signpost is no longer necessary. As in Romans and 1 Corinthians, the living God will dwell with and among his people, filling the city with his life and love and pouring out grace and healing in the river of life that flows from the city out to the nations. There is a sign here of the future project that awaits the redeemed in God's eventual new world. So far from sitting on clouds playing harps, as people often imagine, the redeemed people of God in the new world will be the agents of his love going out in new ways, to accomplish new creative tasks, to celebrate and extend the glory of his love.

CONCLUSION

Of course, other passages in the New Testament speak of new creation. Ideally one would want to factor in the glorious picture of the city that is to come, at present in heaven but destined for earth, which we find in Hebrews 11 and 12. One would certainly want to discuss the famous passage in 2 Peter that, echoing Isaiah, speaks of waiting for new heavens and a new earth in which justice will dwell. I have discussed these, of course, in *The Resurrection of the Son of God*. We should certainly place here Ephesians 1:15–23, one of the grandest of all statements of the theme. But I come back, as I have often done over the years, to the great poem in Colossians 1. It has often been squashed into a shallow-level picture of a supposed cosmic Christ, legitimating a dehistoricized Jesus and an easygoing transition away from a Jewish creation theology and toward various soft versions of Teilhardian and similar thought. But it stands there as a rebuke to all such attempts, not least because if it is Jesus who is the key to the cosmos, it is of course the crucified and risen Jesus we are talking about:

> [15]He is the image of God, the invisible one,
> the firstborn of all creation.
> [16]For in him all things were created,
> in the heavens and here on the earth.
> Things we can see and things we cannot,
> —thrones and lordships and rulers and powers—
> All were created both through him and for him.
> [17]And he is ahead, prior to all else,
> and in him all things hold together;
> [18]And he himself is supreme, the head
> over the body, the church.

He is the start of it all,
firstborn from realms of the dead;
so in all things he might be the chief.
[19]For in him all the Fullness was glad to dwell
[20]and through him to reconcile all to himself,
making peace through the blood of his cross,
through him—yes, things on the earth,
and also the things in the heavens.[11]

It is of course only through imagery, through metaphor and symbol, that we can imagine the new world that God intends to make. That is right and proper. All our language about the future, as I have said, is like a set of signposts pointing into a bright mist. The signpost doesn't provide a photograph of what we will find when we arrive but offers instead a true indication of the direction we should be traveling in. What I am proposing is that the New Testament image of the future hope of the whole cosmos, grounded in the resurrection of Jesus, gives as coherent a picture as we need or could have of the future that is promised to the whole world, a future in which, under the sovereign and wise rule of the creator God, decay and death will be done away with and a new creation born, to which the present one will stand as mother to child. This picture, as some recent writers like John Polkinghorne have shown, gives a shape to the Christian hope that can address and enter into dialogue with cutting-edge physics in a way that the synthesis offered by Teilhard de Chardin and others simply cannot do. What creation needs is neither abandonment nor evolution but rather redemption and renewal; and this is both promised and guaranteed by the resurrection of Jesus from the dead. This is what the whole world's waiting for.

This in turn clears the way for the other topics concerning the Christian future hope: God's putting all things to rights through the coming of Jesus, and the bodily resurrection itself.

As I reflect on God's future plans for the world, I am reminded of the great teacher and pastor Bishop Lesslie Newbigin. Someone once asked him whether, as he looked to the future, he was optimistic or pessimistic. His reply was simple and characteristic. "I am," he said, "neither an optimist nor a pessimist. Jesus Christ is risen from the dead!" This chapter, building on the previous one, is a way of saying amen to that. The whole world is waiting, on tiptoe with expectation, for the moment when that resurrection life and power sweeps through it, filling it with the glory of God as the waters cover the sea.

Before we get to the topic of resurrection itself, however, we must turn to the other vital element of the New Testament picture of God's ultimate future. Central to the unveiling of God's new world will be the personal presence of Jesus himself.

7. JESUS, HEAVEN, AND NEW CREATION

THE ASCENSION

Belief that Jesus of Nazareth has been raised from the dead is closely linked in the New Testament with the belief that he has been taken into heaven, where, in the words of the psalm, he has been seated at the right hand of God.[1] Only Luke tells an explicit story about this event (though he, as if making up for his colleagues' omissions, tells it twice, once at the end of his gospel and once at the beginning of Acts). But we are safe in saying both that it is presupposed more or less throughout early Christianity.

What is more, despite the efforts of many, it is impossible to collapse the ascension into the resurrection or vice versa. You can't get away with the suggesting that "Jesus is raised from the dead" and "Jesus is ascended into heaven" are two ways of saying the same thing. Paul, our earliest writer, clearly distinguishes the two.[2] John, despite popular impressions to the contrary, sees them as two separate events; John 20:17 ("Don't touch me, since I haven't yet ascended to the Father") is puzzling in other respects but not in this one. Resurrection and ascension play quite different (though of course closely related) roles within the thought of the early church.

In fact, some kind of belief in Jesus's ascension has recently been shown to be not just a strange added extra to Christian belief, as has sometimes been thought, but a central and vital feature without which all sorts of other things start to go demonstrably wrong. In his magisterial work, *Ascension and Ecclesia*, Professor Douglas Farrow of McGill University goes through the entire range of Christian thought on the subject, showing that where the ascension has been ignored or misunderstood, one can trace a slide into muddled and even dangerous ideas and practices.[3] In our own day the problem is not unlike the problems about the second coming to which we shall presently turn: flat literalism, on the one hand, facing modernist skepticism, on the other, with each feeding off the other. Some people insist that Jesus must have done a kind of vertical take-off (despite the fact that the same people know that he isn't now living somewhere in outer space and despite the fact that a vertical take-off in one part of the world would be a downward movement seen from the other side of the globe, and so on). Many people insist—and I dare say that this is the theology many of my readers have been taught—that the language of Jesus's "disappearance" is just a way of saying that after his death he became, as it were, spiritually present everywhere, especially with his own followers. This is then often correlated with a nonliteral reading of the resurrection, that is, a denial of its bodily nature: Jesus simply "went to heaven when he died" in a rather special sense that makes him now close to each of us wherever we are. According to this view, Jesus has, as it were, disappeared without remainder. His "spiritual presence" with us is his only identity. In that case, of course, to speak of his second coming is then only a metaphor for his presence, in the same sense, eventually permeating all things.

What happens when people think like this? To answer this, we might ask a further question: why has the ascension been such a difficult and unpopular doctrine in the modern Western church? The answer is not just that rationalist skepticism mocks it (a possibility that the church has sometimes invited with those stained-glass windows that show Jesus's feet sticking downward out of a cloud). It is that the ascension demands that we think differently about how the whole cosmos is, so to speak, put together and that we also think differently about the church and about salvation. Both literalism and skepticism regularly operate with what is called a receptacle view of space; theologians who take the ascension seriously insist that it demands what some have called a relational view.[4] Basically, heaven and earth in biblical cosmology are not two different locations within the same continuum of space or matter. They are two different dimensions of God's good creation. And the point about heaven is twofold. First, heaven relates to earth tangentially so that the one who is in heaven can be present simultaneously anywhere and everywhere on earth: the ascension therefore means that Jesus is available, accessible, without people having to travel to a particular spot on the earth to find him. Second, heaven is, as it were, the control room for earth; it is the CEO's office, the place from which instructions are given. "All authority is given to me," said Jesus at the end of Matthew's gospel, "in heaven and on earth."[5]

The idea of the human Jesus now being in heaven, in his thoroughly embodied risen state, comes as a shock to many people, including many Christians. Sometimes this is because many people think that Jesus, having been divine, stopped being divine and became human, and then, having been human for a while, stopped being human and went back to being divine (at least, that's what many people think Christians are supposed to believe). More often it's because our culture is so used to the Platonic idea that heaven is, by definition, a place of "spiritual," nonmaterial reality so that the idea of a solid body being not only present but also thoroughly at home there seems like a category mistake. The ascension invites us to rethink all this; and, after all, why did we suppose we knew what heaven was? Only because our culture has suggested things to us. Part of Christian belief is to find out what's true about Jesus and let that challenge our culture.

This applies in particular to the idea of Jesus being in charge not only in heaven but also on earth, not only in some ultimate future but also in the present. Many will snort the obvious objection: it certainly doesn't look as though he's in charge, or if he is, he's making a proper mess of it. But that misses the point. The early Christians knew the world was still a mess. But they announced, like messengers going off on behalf of a global company, that a new CEO had taken charge. They discovered through their own various callings how his new way of running things was to be worked out. It wasn't a matter (as some people anxiously suppose to this day) of Christians simply taking over and giving orders in a kind of theocracy where the church could simply tell everyone what to do. That has sometimes been tried, of course, and it's always led to disaster. But neither is it a matter of the church backing off, letting the world go on its sweet way, and worshipping Jesus in a kind of private sphere.

Somehow there is a third option, which we shall explore in the third part of the present book. We can glimpse it in the book of Acts: the *method* of the kingdom will match the *message* of the kingdom. The kingdom will come as the church, energized by the Spirit, goes out into the world vulnerable, suffering, praising, praying, misunderstood, misjudged, vindicated, celebrating: always—as Paul puts it in one of his letters—bearing in the body the dying of Jesus so that the life of Jesus may also be displayed.

What happens when you downplay or ignore the ascension? The answer is that *the church expands to fill the vacuum.* If Jesus is more or less identical with the church—if, that is, talk about Jesus can be reduced to talk about his presence within his people rather than his standing over against them and addressing them from elsewhere as their Lord, then we have created a high road to the worst kind of triumphalism. This indeed is what twentieth-century English liberalism always tended toward: by compromising with rationalism and trying to maintain that talk of the ascension is really talk about Jesus being with us everywhere, the church effectively presented *itself* (with its structures and hierarchy, its customs and quirks) instead of presenting Jesus as its Lord and itself as the world's servant, as Paul puts it.[6] And the other side of triumphalism is of course despair. If you put all your eggs into the church-equals-Jesus basket, what are you left with when, as Paul says in the same passage, we ourselves are found to be cracked earthenware vessels?

If the church identifies its structures, its leadership, its liturgy, its buildings, or anything else with its Lord—and that's what happens if you ignore the ascension or turn it into another way of talking about the Spirit—what do you get? You get, on the one hand, what Shakespeare called "the insolence of office" and, on the other hand, the despair of late middle age, as people realize it doesn't work. (I see this all too frequently among those who bought heavily into the soggy rationalism of the 1950s and 1960s.) Only when we grasp firmly that the church is *not* Jesus and Jesus is *not* the church—when we grasp, in other words, the truth of the ascension, that the one who is indeed present with us by the Spirit is *also* the Lord who is strangely absent, strangely other, strangely different from us and over against us, the one who tells Mary Magdalene not to cling to him—only then are we rescued from both hollow triumphalism and shallow despair.

Conversely, only when we grasp and celebrate the fact that Jesus has gone on ahead of us into God's space, God's new world, and is both already ruling the rebellious present world as its rightful Lord and also interceding for us at the Father's right hand—when we grasp and celebrate, in other words, what the ascension tells us about Jesus's continuing *human* work in the present—are we rescued from a wrong view of world history and equipped for the task of justice in the present (we'll come back to both of those later).[7] We are also, significantly, rescued from the attempts that have been made to create alternative mediators, and in particular an alternative mediatrix, in his place.[8] Get the ascension right, and your view of the church, of the sacraments, and of the mother of Jesus can get back into focus.[9]

You could sum all this up by saying that the doctrine of the Trinity, which is making quite a comeback in current theology, is essential if we are to tell the truth not only about God, and more particularly about Jesus, but also about ourselves. The Trinity is precisely a way of recognizing and celebrating the fact of the human being Jesus of Nazareth as distinct from while still identified with

God the Father, on the one hand (he didn't just "go back to being God again" after his earthly life), and the Spirit, on the other hand (the Jesus who is near us and with us by the Spirit remains the Jesus who is other than us).[10] This places a full stop on all human arrogance, including Christian arrogance. And now we see at last why the Enlightenment world was determined to make the ascension appear ridiculous, using the weapons of rationalism and skepticism to do so: if the ascension is true, then the whole project of human self-aggrandizement represented by eighteenth-century European and American thought is rebuked and brought to heel. To embrace the ascension is to heave a sigh of relief, to give up the struggle to be God (and with it the inevitable despair at our constant failure), and to enjoy our status as *creatures:* image-bearing creatures, but creatures nonetheless.

The ascension thus speaks of the Jesus who remains truly human and hence in an important sense absent from us while in another equally important sense present to us in a new way. At this point the Holy Spirit and the sacraments become enormously important since they are precisely the means by which Jesus is present. Often in the church we have been so keen to stress the presence of Jesus by these means that we have failed to indicate his simultaneous absence and have left people wondering whether this is, so to speak, "all there is to it." The answer is: no, it isn't. The lordship of Jesus; the fact that there is already a human being at the helm of the world; his present intercession for us—all this is over and above his presence with us. It is even over and above our *sense of* that presence, which of course comes and goes with our own moods and circumstances.

Now it is of course one thing to say all this, to show how it fits together and sets us free from some of the nonsenses we would otherwise get into. It's quite another to be able to envisage or imagine it, to know what it is we're really talking about when we speak of Jesus being still human, still in fact an *embodied* human—actually, a *more solidly embodied* human than we are—but absent from this present world. We need, in fact, a new and better cosmology, a new and better way of thinking about the world than the one our culture, not least post-Enlightenment culture, has bequeathed us. The early Christians, and their fellow first-century Jews, were not, as many moderns suppose, locked into thinking of a three-decker universe with heaven up in the sky and hell down beneath their feet. When they spoke of up and down like that they, like the Greeks in their different ways, were using metaphors that were so obvious they didn't need spelling out. As some recent writers have pointed out, when a pupil at school moves "up" a grade, from (say) the tenth grade to the eleventh, it is unlikely that this means relocating to a classroom on the floor above. And though the move "up" from vice-chairman of the board to chairman of the board may indeed mean that at last you get an office in the penthouse suite, it would be quite wrong to think that "moving up" in this context meant merely being a few feet farther away from terra firma.

The mystery of the ascension is of course just that, a mystery. It demands that we think what is, to many today, almost unthinkable: that when the Bible speaks of heaven and earth it is not talking about two localities related to each other within the same space-time continuum or about a nonphysical world contrasted with a physical one but about two different *kinds* of what we call space, two different kinds of what we call matter, and also quite possibly (though this does not necessarily follow from the other two) two different kinds of what we call time. We post-Enlightenment Westerners are such wretched flatlanders. Although New Age thinkers, and indeed quite a lot of contemporary novelists, are quite capable of taking us into other parallel worlds, spaces, and times, we retreat into our rationalistic closed-system universe as soon as we think about Jesus. C. S. Lewis of course did a great job in the Narnia stories and elsewhere of imagining how two worlds could relate and interlock. But the generation that grew up knowing its way around Narnia does not usually know how to make the transition from a children's story to the real world of grown-up Christian devotion and theology.

Some church buildings do their best to indicate the interrelation of heaven and earth. The Eastern Orthodox churches do it by envisaging heaven as the inner sanctuary, the space around the altar, and earth as the part of the building outside that space. The two are separated by the iconostasis, upon which are portrayed the saints, whose presence in heaven is not far from the worshippers on earth. Western cathedrals and abbeys often did a similar thing through soaring Gothic architecture, giving us at floor level a sense of belonging within (but unable at the moment to inhabit more than a little of) great spaces of light and beauty, into which, significantly, only our music can penetrate.

All such aids to the Christian imagination are to be welcomed as long, of course, as they are not mistaken for the real thing. What we are encouraged to grasp precisely through the ascension itself is that God's space and ours—heaven and earth, in other words—are, though very different, not far away from one another. Nor is talk about heaven simply a metaphorical way of talking about our own spiritual lives. God's space and ours interlock and intersect in a whole variety of ways even while they retain, for the moment at least, their separate and distinct identities and roles. One day, as we saw in the last chapter, they will be joined in a quite new way, open and visible to one another, married together forever.

One day, in other words, the Jesus who is right now the central figure of God's space—the human Jesus, still wearing (as Wesley put it) "those dear tokens of his passion" on his "dazzling body"—will be present to us, and we to him, in a radically different way than what we currently know. The other half of the truth of the ascension is that Jesus will return, as the angels said in Acts 1:11.

At this point some of the regular prayers, in my tradition, let us down with a bump—which is actually the wrong metaphor because what they do is to say, in effect, "Jesus has been raised to heaven, and we pray that we may be raised there too." There is indeed a sense in which this is true, as in Ephesians 2:6 and Colossians 3:1–4. But when people hear those prayers today (speaking of Jesus being

SURPRISED BY HOPE

exalted to heaven and of us going in heart and mind to be with him forever; or speaking of the Holy Spirit as the one who will exalt us to the place where he has gone before), they are almost bound, within today's muddled worldview, to be reinforced in their view that the whole point of the Christian faith is to follow Jesus away from earth to heaven and stay there forever. And the New Testament insists, on the contrary, that the one who has gone into heaven will come back. At no point in the gospels or Acts does anyone say anything remotely like, "Jesus has gone into heaven, so let's be sure we can follow him." They say, rather, "Jesus is in heaven, ruling the whole world, and he will one day return to make that rule complete."

But what is this second coming all about? Isn't that too a strange, outlandish idea that we should abandon in our own day?

WHAT ABOUT THE SECOND COMING?

"Christ has died," we say in the Anglican Eucharist, "Christ is risen; *Christ will come again.*" And of course in the creed too: "He will come again in glory to judge the living and the dead." If we sing it once during the season of Advent, we sing it a dozen times. "Alleluia! Come, Lord, come!"

And if we are ordinary mainstream Christians in Britain today—and in many other places too, including parts of North America—we may well add under our breath, "even though I haven't a clue what it means." The so-called second coming of Jesus is not a hot topic in the preaching of the mainstream churches, even in Advent. (Some churches, of course, speak of little else; I shall come to them presently.) The more recent lectionaries we use in my church rather steer us away from it. What's more, the revival of a lively Eucharistic life in the Church of England in the postwar years carried with it, in some circles at least, a theology that seemed to leave no room for a final coming. "Why do we say, 'Christ will come again'?" asked one puzzled worshipper in the 1970s when the threefold phrase was first used in Anglican liturgy. "Surely we've been taught that he comes—that he is here with us—in the Eucharist itself?"

What then can we say about the second coming of Jesus?

We have reached the point in this book where we can address this question within the larger framework where it makes sense. We have looked in earlier chapters at the beliefs about life after death and the future of the world that are held in our own time and that were held in Jesus's day. We have seen that there are good historical arguments pointing to belief in Jesus's bodily resurrection. In particular, I sketched in the last chapter the large-scale future hope of Christians, the hope for the renewal of the whole world. Now, before we turn to examine more particularly the hope, or the fate, of the individual within this scheme of thought, we come to one central and vital aspect of the large-scale hope. When God renews the whole cosmos, the New Testament insists, Jesus himself will be personally present as the center and focus of the new world that will result. What does the Christian faith teach at this point? What is its sharp edge for us today? How can we make it our own?

Answering these questions has become more difficult in the past century. There are two reasons for this, more or less equal and opposite.

One reason is that the second coming of Jesus Christ has become the favorite topic of a large swath of North American Christianity, particularly but not exclusively in the fundamentalist and dispensationalist segment. Growing out of some millenarian movements of the nineteenth century, particularly those associated with J. N. Darby and the Plymouth Brethren, a belief has arisen, and taken hold of millions of minds and hearts, that we are now living in the end times, in which all the great prophecies are to be fulfilled at last. Central to these prophecies, it is believed, is the promise that Jesus will return in person, snatching the true believers away from this wicked world to be with him and then, after an interval of ungodliness, returning to reign over the world forever. The attempt to correlate these prophecies with the geopolitical events of the 1960s and 1970s, which reached a height in Hal Lindsey's best-selling book, *The Late Great Planet Earth*,[11] has somewhat palled, but its place has been taken by the fictional scenarios offered by a series of books by Tim LaHaye and Jerry Jenkins. The first volume of the series, called *Left Behind*, gave its name to a sequence of twelve books in all, most of which have done astonishingly well in the current American best-seller lists. In their fictitious scenario, the rapture has happened; all true Christians have been snatched away from the earth; and those left behind are now struggling to survive in a godless world. This is an exciting and entertaining scenario; I leave it to others to probe the social and political psychology that is going on when pseudotheological fiction takes off like this. Nor is it purely an American phenomenon. The books sell quite well in the United Kingdom too, though who is buying them in my own country I do not know.[12]

The American obsession—I don't think that's too strong a word—with the second coming of Jesus, or rather with one particular and, as we shall see, highly distorted interpretation of it, continues unabated. I first met it in person when I was giving some lectures in Thunder Bay, Ontario, in the early 1980s. I was talking about Jesus in his historical context, and to my surprise almost all the questions afterward were about ecology—about trees and water and crops, which is after all what there mostly is at Thunder Bay. It turned out (as I indicated in the previous chapter) that many conservative Christians in the area, and more importantly just to the south in the United States, had been urging that since we were living in the end times, with the world about to come to an end, there was no point worrying about trying to stop polluting the planet with acid rain and the like. Indeed, wasn't it unspiritual, and even a sign of a lack of faith, to think about such things? If God was intending to bring the whole world to a shuddering halt, what was the problem? If Armageddon was just around the corner, it didn't matter—and here, I suspect, is part of the real agenda—if General Motors went on pumping poisonous gases into the Canadian atmosphere.

We face similar questions today. So-called end-time speculation, which is the daily bread of many in the American religious right, is not unconnected to the agenda of some of America's leading politicians. More of that anon. For many millions of believing Christians in today's world, the second coming is part of a scenario in which the present world is doomed to destruction while the chosen few are snatched up to heaven.

Partly in reaction against such an idea, but partly powered by the energy of good old Enlightenment liberalism, many in the mainstream churches of the West have for some time been doing their best to divest themselves of the doctrine that Jesus Christ "will come again in glory to judge the living and the dead," at least in any recognizable form.

Both parts are disliked: the coming and the judging. The idea that Jesus will come to this world, invading it like a spaceman, smacks to many of an older supernatural or interventionist theology, which they have spent a lifetime rejecting or, at best, reinterpreting. They don't imagine that Jesus is still, so to speak, around the place somewhere in that way. The language of his coming must therefore be reinterpreted in terms of a general hope for world renewal. After all, they say, the early church expected Jesus to come very soon, and he didn't; we should obviously reinterpret their hope in a way that makes sense two thousand years later. In addition, the idea of judgment makes many people think of a vengeful, wrathful deity, determined to throw as many people as possible into hell. We have learned to distrust people who love accusing and punishing others. In the same way, we have learned to dislike and distrust theologies in which accusing and punishing take center stage. The Hebrew for "the accuser" is after all *hasatan,* "the satan."

We are therefore faced, as we look at today's large-scale picture, with two polar opposites. At one end, some have made the second coming so central that they can see little else. At the other, some have so marginalized or weakened it that it ceases to mean anything at all.

Both positions need to be challenged. I shall shortly show that the focus on the so-called rapture is based on a misunderstanding of two verses in Paul and that when we get that misunderstanding out of the way, we can find a doctrine of Jesus's coming that remains central and vital if the whole Christian faith is not to unravel before our eyes. At the same time, the older Enlightenment liberalism, with its dislike of all judgment, has itself been under attack. We have become a very moralistic, very judgmental, generation. We have judged apartheid and found it wanting. We judge child abusers and find them guilty. We judge genocide and find it outrageous. We have rediscovered what the Psalmists knew: that for God to judge the world meant that he would, in the end, put it all to rights, straighten it out, producing not just a sigh of relief all around but shouting for joy from the trees and the fields, the seas and the floods.[13]

At the same time, we may not as a culture be fond of old-fashioned supernaturalism, but we certainly like spirituality in whatever form we can get it.[14] I suspect that if anyone other than Jesus (Krishna, say, or Buddha) were suddenly put forward as being due for a second coming, millions in our postsecular society would embrace such a thing uncritically, leaving Enlightenment rationalism huffing and puffing in the rear. We are a puzzled and confused generation, embracing any and every kind of nonrationalism that may offer us a spiritual shot in the arm while lapsing back into rationalism (in particular, the old modernist critiques) whenever we want to keep traditional or orthodox Christianity at bay.

And yet it is Christian orthodoxy, properly understood, that can help us find the way through this morass and muddle and out the other side. But before we get any further I need to say a word about a word—a much misunderstood word, a word that may get in the way unless we demystify it. I refer to the blessed term *eschatology*.[15]

The word *eschatology* has often been used, in relation to early Christianity, to mean the expectation of the return of Jesus within a generation—and the redefinitions that took place when this did not happen. This expectation, it used to be thought, was based on and gave new focus to the expectation of first-century Jews that the world was about to come to an end.

When I wrote *The New Testament and the People of God* in 1992 I argued that though the early Christians did indeed expect Jesus's return, they were not bothered by its not happening within a generation and indeed that the Jewish expectation they had inherited was not about the end of the world but about a dramatic change within the present world order. An Oxford colleague who read the book said to me, "Now that you've abandoned eschatology," meaning, apparently, "Now that you've abandoned the idea that first-century Jews and Christians expected the world to end at once." I insisted then, and I insist now, that I have done no such thing. The word *eschatology*, which literally means "the study of the last things," doesn't just refer to death, judgment, heaven, and hell, as used to be thought (and as many dictionaries still define the word). It also refers to the strongly held belief of most first-century Jews, and virtually all early Christians, that history was going somewhere under the guidance of God and that where it was going was toward God's new world of justice, healing, and hope. The transition from the present world to the new one would be a matter not of the destruction of the present space-time universe but of its radical healing. As we saw in the last chapter, the New Testament writers, particularly Paul, looked forward to this time and saw Jesus's resurrection as the beginning, the firstfruits, of it. So when I (and many others) use the word *eschatology*, we don't simply mean the second coming, still less a particular theory about it; we mean, rather, the entire sense of God's future for the world and the belief that that future has already begun to come forward to meet us in the present. This is what we find in Jesus himself and in the teaching of the early church. They modified, but did not abandon, the Jewish eschatological beliefs they already shared.

So how can we understand the second coming? How, for that matter, do the biblical writers themselves understand it? This will take a further chapter to set out.

8. WHEN HE APPEARS

INTRODUCTION

Two chapters ago I sketched the big picture of cosmic redemption that the New Testament invites us to make our own. God will redeem the whole universe; Jesus's resurrection is the beginning of that new life, the fresh grass growing through the concrete of corruption and decay in the old world. That final redemption will be the moment when heaven and earth are joined together at last, in a burst of God's creative energy for which Easter is the prototype and source. When we put together that big picture with what we've said in the previous chapter about the ascension of Jesus, what do we get? Why, of course, the personal *presence* of Jesus, as opposed to his current *absence*.

The presence we know at the moment—the presence of Jesus with his people in word and sacrament, by the Spirit, through prayer, in the faces of the poor—is of course related to that future presence, but the distinction between them is important and striking. Jesus's appearing will be, for those of us who have known and loved him here, like meeting face-to-face someone we have only known by letter, telephone, or perhaps e-mail. Communication theorists insist that for full human communication you need not only words on a page but also a tone of voice. That's why a telephone call can say more than a letter, not in quantity but in quality. But for full communication between human beings you need not only a tone of voice but also body language, facial language, and the thousand small ways in which, without realizing it, we relate to one another. At the moment, by the Spirit, the word, the sacraments and prayer, and in those in need whom we are called to serve for his sake, the absent Jesus is present to us; but one day he will be there with us, face-to-face. Cecil Frances Alexander got it partly right in her classic nineteenth-century compromise:

And our eyes at last shall see him,
Through his own redeeming love,
For that child so dear and gentle
Is our Lord in heaven above.

Unless we feel the pull and yearning of those lines, we may not yet have learned to know him as we may know him in the present or to feel the tension between our present knowing and that which is promised in the future. But the hymn is quite wrong to suggest that for this knowledge *we* need to go and find *him:*

And he leads his children on
To the place where he is gone.

This is indeed true, as we shall see, of what happens to his people after death, in the interim state. But it isn't the main truth that the New Testament teaches, the main emphasis that the early Christians insisted on over and over again. The main truth is that *he* will come back to *us.*[1] That is the thing of which we must now speak, in two main movements. He will come again; and he will come again as judge.

COMING, APPEARING, REVEALING, ROYAL PRESENCE

We still speak in our culture about the sun rising and setting even though we know that in fact it is we, on our planet, who are moving in relation to the sun rather than the other way around. In the same way, the early Christians often spoke of Jesus coming, or returning; indeed, at least in John's gospel, Jesus himself speaks in that way. But the larger picture they use suggests that if we are to understand them properly, that language, common and even creedal though it is, may not be the most helpful way today of getting at the truth it affirms.

In fact, the New Testament uses quite a variety of language and imagery to express the truth that Jesus and his people will one day be personally present to each other as full and renewed human beings. It is perhaps an accident of history that the phrase "the second coming," which is very rare in the New Testament, has come to dominate discussion. When that phrase is identified, as it has often been in the United States, with a particular view of that coming as a literal downward descent, meeting halfway with the redeemed who are making a simultaneous upward journey, all sorts of problems arise that are avoided if we take the New Testament's multiple witness as a whole.

The first thing to get clear is that, despite widespread opinion to the contrary, during his earthly ministry Jesus said nothing about his return. I have argued this position at length and in detail in my various books about Jesus and don't have space to substantiate it here. Let me just say two things, quite baldly.[2]

First, when Jesus speaks of "the son of man coming on the clouds," he is talking not about the second coming but, in line with the Daniel 7 text he is quoting, about his vindication after suffering. The "coming" is an upward, not a downward, movement. In context, the key texts mean that though Jesus is going to his death, he will be vindicated by events that will take place afterward.[3] What those events are remains cryptic from the point of view of the passages in question, which is one good reason for thinking them authentic, but they certainly include both Jesus's resurrection and the destruction of the Temple, the system that opposed him and his mission. And the language, significantly, is precisely the language that the early church used as the least inadequate way of talking about the strange thing that happened after Jesus's resurrection: his "ascension," his glorification, his "coming," not to earth, but to heaven, to the Father.

Second, the stories Jesus tells about a king or master who goes away for a while and leaves his subjects or servants to trade with his money in his absence were not originally meant to refer to Jesus going away and leaving the church with tasks to get on with until his eventual second coming, even though they were read in that way from fairly early on.[4] They belong in the Jewish world of the first century, where everyone would hear the story to be about God himself, having left Israel and the Temple at the time of the exile, coming back again at last, as the postexilic prophets had said he would,[5] back to Israel, back to Zion, back to the Temple. In their original setting, the point of these stories is that Israel's God, YHWH, is indeed coming at last to Jerusalem, to the Temple—in and as the human person Jesus of Nazareth. The stories are, in that sense, not about the *second* coming of Jesus but about the first one. They are explaining, albeit cryptically, Jesus's own belief, that what he was doing in coming to Jerusalem to enact both judgment and salvation was what YHWH had said in scripture that he would do in person.

These two historical moves, about the "son of man" sayings and about the parables of the returning master or king, have left me open to the attack, particularly from American readers, that I have thereby given up believing or teaching the second coming. This is absurd, as the present chapter will make clear. The fact that Jesus didn't teach it doesn't mean it isn't true. (Similarly, the fact that I have written books about Jesus without mentioning it doesn't mean I don't believe in it; when a football commentator goes through a whole game without mentioning baseball, that doesn't mean he doesn't believe it exists or that he doesn't rate it highly as a sport.) Jesus was having a hard enough time explaining to his disciples that he had to die; they never really grasped that at all, and they certainly didn't take his language about his own resurrection as anything more than the general hope of all Jewish martyrs. How could they possibly have understood him saying something about further events in what would have been, for them, a still more unthinkable future?

Of course, when Jesus came to Zion as Israel's rightful Lord in the first century, that event did indeed point forward to his eventual return as the rightful Lord of the whole world. This means that, if we are careful what we are doing, we can read the parables I've mentioned in this new way if we so desire. The reason we need to be careful, though, is because they don't quite fit. Nowhere in the New Testament does any writer say that at Jesus's final coming some of his servants, some actual believing Christians, will be judged in the way that the wicked servant was judged for hiding his master's money in a napkin.

Nor will it do to say, as do some who grasp part of the point but have not worked it through, that the events of A.D. 70 were themselves the second coming of Jesus so that ever since then we have been living in God's new age and there is no further coming to await. This may seem to many readers, as indeed it seems to me, a bizarre position to hold, but there are some who not only hold it but also eagerly propagate it and use some of my arguments to support it. This results from a confusion: if the texts that speak of "the son of man coming on the clouds" refer to A.D. 70, as I have argued that (in part) they do, this doesn't mean that A.D. 70 was the "second coming" because the "son of man" texts aren't "second coming" texts at all, despite their frequent misreading that way. They are about Jesus's vindication. And Jesus's vindication—in his resurrection, ascension, and judgment on Jerusalem—requires a still further event for everything to be complete. Let me say it emphatically for the sake of those who are confused on the point (and to the amusement, no doubt, of those who are not): the second coming has not yet occurred.

So if the gospel accounts of Jesus's teaching do not refer to the second coming, where does the idea come from? Quite simply, from the rest of the New Testament. As soon as Jesus had been vindicated, raised and exalted, the church firmly believed and taught that he would return. "This same Jesus who has gone from you into heaven," said the angel to the disciples, "will return in the same way that you saw him go into heaven."[6] And, though Acts doesn't often refer again to this belief, clearly the whole book takes place under this rubric. This is what the disciples are doing to make Jesus's lordship known in all the world against the day when he will come once more to renew all things.[7]

But of course the primary witness is Paul. Paul's letters are full of the future coming or appearing of Jesus.[8] His worldview, his theology, his missionary practice, his devotion are all inconceivable without it. Yet what he has to say about this great event has often been misunderstood, not least by the proponents of rapture theology. It's almost time to address this directly, but first a word about another major and often misunderstood technical term.

Scholars and simple folk alike can get led astray by the use of a single word to refer to something when that word in its original setting means both more and less than the use to which it is subsequently put. In this case the word in question is the Greek word *parousia*. This is usually translated "coming," but literally it means "presence"—that is, presence as opposed to absence.

The word *parousia* occurs in two of the key passages in Paul (1 Thessalonians 4:15 and 1 Corinthians 15:23), and it is found frequently elsewhere in Paul and the New Testament. It seems clear that the early Christians knew the word well, and knew what was meant by it. People often assume that the early church used *parousia* simply to mean "the second coming of Jesus" and that by this event they all envisaged, in a quite literal fashion, the scenario of 1 Thessalonians 4:16–17 (Jesus coming down on a cloud and people flying upward to meet him). Neither of these assumptions is in fact correct.

The word *parousia* had two lively meanings in non-Christian discourse at the time. Both of these seem to have influenced it in its Christian meaning.

The first meaning was the mysterious presence of a god or divinity, particularly when the power of this god was revealed in healing. People would suddenly be aware of a supernatural and powerful presence, and the obvious word for this was *parousia.* Josephus sometimes uses this word when he is talking about YHWH coming to the rescue of Israel.[9] God's powerful, saving presence is revealed in action, for instance when Israel under King Hezekiah was miraculously defended against the Assyrians.

The second meaning emerges when a person of high rank makes a visit to a subject state, particularly when a king or emperor visits a colony or province. The word for such a visit is *royal presence:* in Greek, *parousia.* In neither setting, we note, obviously but importantly, is there the slightest suggestion of anybody flying around on a cloud. Nor is there any hint of the imminent collapse or destruction of the space-time universe.

Now suppose that Paul, and for that matter the rest of the early church, wanted to say two things. Suppose they wanted to say, first, that the Jesus they worshipped was near in spirit but absent in body but that one day he would be present in body and that then the whole world, themselves included, would know the sudden transforming power of that presence. A natural word to use for this would be *parousia.*

At the same time, suppose they wanted to say that the Jesus who had been raised from the dead and exalted to God's right hand was the rightful Lord of the world, the true Emperor before whom all other emperors would shake in their shoes and bow their knees in fear and wonder. And suppose they wanted to say that, just as Caesar might one day visit a colony like Philippi or Thessalonica or Corinth (the normally absent but ruling emperor appearing and ruling in person), so the absent but ruling Lord of the world would one day appear and rule in person within this world, with all the consequences that would result. Again, the natural word to use for this would be *parousia.* (This was particularly significant in that Paul and the others were keen to say that Jesus was the true Lord and that Caesar was a sham.)

Now these things are not just suppositions. This is exactly how it was. Paul and the others used the word *parousia* because they wanted to evoke these worlds. But they evoke them within a different context. For neither the first nor the last time, the Jewish story line and the Greco-Roman allusions and confrontations meet like two tectonic plates, throwing up the craggy mountain range we call New Testament theology. The Jewish story line in question was, of course, the story of the Day of the Lord, the Day of YHWH, the day when YHWH would defeat all Israel's enemies and rescue his people once and for all. Paul and the other writers regularly refer to "the Day of the Lord," and now of course they mean it in a Christian sense: "the Lord" here is Jesus himself.[10] In this sense, and in this sense only, there is a solid Jewish background for the Christian doctrine of the second coming of Jesus.[11] Of course, there could be nothing stronger because pre-Christian Judaism, including the disciples during Jesus's lifetime, never envisaged the death of the Messiah. That is why they never thought of his resurrection, let alone an interim period between such events and the final consummation, during which he would be installed as the world's true Lord while still waiting for that sovereign rule to take full effect.

What happened, it seems, was this. The early Christians had lived within and breathed and prayed that old Jewish story line. In the resurrection and ascension of Jesus, shocking and unexpected though they were, they grasped the fact that in this way Israel's God had indeed done what he'd always intended, though it hadn't looked like they thought it would. Through this they came to see that Jesus, as Israel's Messiah, was already the world's true Lord and that his secret presence by his Spirit in the present time was only a hint of what was still to come, when he would finally be revealed as the one whose power would trump all other powers both earthly and heavenly. The Jesus story thus created a radical intensification and transformation from within the Jewish story, and the language that results in describing the Jesus event that is yet to come is the language that says, in relation to the future: Jesus is Lord and Caesar isn't.

Parousia is itself, in fact, one of those terms in which Paul is able to say that Jesus is the reality of which Caesar is the parody. His theology of the second coming is part of his political theology of Jesus as Lord.[12] In other words, we have the language of *parousia,* of royal presence, sitting in a typically Pauline juxtaposition with the language of Jewish apocalyptic. This would not, I think, have presented many problems for Paul's first hearers. It has certainly created problems for subsequent readers, not least in the last century or so.

This is so especially when we read 1 Thessalonians 4:16–17:

> The Lord himself will come down from heaven with a shouted order, with the voice of an archangel and the sound of God's trumpet. The Messiah's dead will rise first; then we who are alive, who are left, will be snatched up with them among the clouds, to meet the Lord in the air. And in this way we shall always be with the Lord.

The point to notice above all about these tricky verses is that they are *not* to be taken as a literal description of what Paul thinks will happen. They are simply a different way of saying what he is saying in 1 Corinthians 15:23–27 and 51–54, and in Philippians 3:20–21.

We had better get those other passages straight in our minds to start with. In 1 Corinthians 15:23–27 Paul speaks of the *parousia* of the Messiah as the time of the resurrection of the dead, the time when his present though secret rule will become manifest in the conquest of the last enemies, especially death. Then in verses 51–54 he speaks of what will happen to those who, at Jesus's coming, are not yet dead. They will be *changed,* transformed. This is clearly the same event as he is speaking of in 1 Thessalonians 4; we have the trumpet in both, and the resurrection of the dead in both; but whereas in 1 Thessalonians he speaks of those presently alive being "snatched up in the air," in 1 Corinthians he speaks of them being "transformed." So too in Philippians 3:21, where the context is quite explicitly ranging Jesus over against Caesar, Paul speaks of the *transformation* of the present lowly body to be like Jesus's glorious body, as a result of his all-conquering power.

So why does Paul speak in this peculiar way in 1 Thessalonians about the Lord descending and the living saints being snatched up in the air? I suggest that he is finding richly metaphorical ways of alluding to three other stories that he is deliberately bringing together. (Paul was good at richly mixed metaphors: in the next chapter, 1 Thessalonians 5, he says that the thief will come in the night, so the woman will go into labor, so you mustn't get drunk but must stay awake and put on your armor. As the television programs say, don't try that one at home.)

We must remind ourselves yet once more that all Christian language about the future is a set of signposts pointing into a mist. Signposts don't normally provide you with advance photographs of what you'll find at the end of the road, but that doesn't mean they aren't pointing in the right direction. They are telling you the truth, the particular sort of truth that can be told about the future.

The three stories Paul is here bringing together start with the story of Moses coming down the mountain. The trumpet sounds, a loud voice is heard, and after a long wait Moses appears and descends from the mountain to see what's been going on in his absence.

Then there is the story of Daniel 7, in which the persecuted people of God are vindicated over their pagan enemy by being raised up on the clouds to sit with God in glory. This "raising up on the clouds," which Jesus applies to himself in the gospels, is now applied by Paul to the Christians who are presently suffering persecution.[13]

Putting these two stories together, in a typically outrageous mix of metaphors, enables Paul to bring in the third story, to which we have already alluded. When the emperor visited a colony or province, the citizens of the country would go to meet him at some distance from the city. It would be disrespectful to have him actually arrive at the gates as though his subjects couldn't be bothered to greet him properly. When they met him, they wouldn't then stay out in the open country; they would escort him royally into the city itself. When Paul speaks of "meeting" the Lord "in the air," the point is precisely not—as in the popular rapture theology—that the saved believers would then stay up in the air somewhere, away from earth. The point is that, having gone out to meet their returning Lord, they will escort him royally into his domain, that is, back to the place they have come from. Even when we realize that this is highly charged metaphor, not literal description, the meaning is the same as in the parallel in Philippians 3:20. Being citizens of heaven, as the Philippians would know, doesn't mean that one is expecting to go back to the mother city but rather means that one is expecting the emperor to come *from* the mother city to give the colony its full dignity, to rescue it if need be, to subdue local enemies and put everything to rights.

These two verses in 1 Thessalonians 4, then, have been grievously abused by those who have constructed out of them a big picture of a supposed rapture. This has had its effect not only on popular fundamentalism but also on a fair amount of New Testament scholarship, which has assumed that Paul really meant what the fundamentalists think he meant. Only when we put together the several different things he says on the same topic does the truth emerge. This is a typical piece of highly charged and multiply allusive rhetoric. The reality to which it refers is this: Jesus will be personally present, the dead will be raised, and the living Christians will be transformed. That, as we shall now see, is pretty much what the rest of the New Testament says as well.

Note, though, something else of great significance about the whole Christian theology of resurrection, ascension, second coming, and hope. This theology was born out of confrontation with the political authorities, out of the conviction that Jesus was already the true Lord of the world who would one day be manifested as such. The rapture theology avoids this confrontation because it suggests that Christians will miraculously be removed from this wicked world. Perhaps that is why such theology is often Gnostic in its tendency toward a private dualistic spirituality and toward a political laissez-faire quietism. And perhaps that is partly why such theology, with its dreams of Armageddon, has quietly supported the political status quo in a way that Paul would never have done.

Before turning away from Paul, notice a significant pair of passages. First, at the end of 1 Corinthians, Paul suddenly writes a phrase in Aramaic: *Marana tha.*[14] It means, "Our Lord, come!" and goes back (like the word *Abba,* "father") to the very early Aramaic-speaking church. There is no reason why the Greek-speaking church would have invented a prayer in Aramaic; we must be in touch at this point with extremely early and pre-Pauline tradition. The early church was from the beginning praying to Jesus that he would return.

Second, a very different passage in Colossians 3. Here we have in a nutshell Paul's theology of resurrection and ascension as applied to present Christian living and future Christian hope:

> If you've been raised with the Messiah, seek the things that are above, because that's where the Messiah is, sitting at God's right hand. Think about the things above, not about the things below; for you died, and your life is hidden with the Messiah in God. When the Messiah appears [*hotan ho Christos phanerōthē*], the one who is your life, then you too will appear with him in glory.[15]

This is clearly in the same ballpark as the other texts we've been looking at. But notice the key thing: that instead of "coming," or the blessed word *parousia,* Paul can here use the word *appear.* It's the same thing from a different angle, and this helps us to demystify the idea that the "coming" of Jesus means that he will descend like a spaceman from the sky. Jesus is at present in heaven. But, as we saw earlier, heaven, being God's space, is not somewhere within the space of our world but is rather a different though closely related space. The promise is not that Jesus will simply reappear within the present world order, but that when heaven and earth are joined together in the new way God has promised, then he will appear to us—and we will appear to him, and to one another, in our own true identity.

This is, in fact, remarkably close to a key passage in the first letter of John (1 John 2:28 and 3:2):

Now, children, abide in him; so that, when he appears [*ean phanerō thē*], we may have confidence and not be shrink from him in shame at his presence [*parousia*]. . . . Beloved, we are now God's children; and it has not yet appeared [*oupō ephanerōthē*] what we shall be; but we know that when he appears [*ean phanerōthē*], we shall be like him, because we shall see him just as he is.

Here we have more or less exactly the same picture as in Colossians, though this time with *appearing* and *parousia* happily side by side. Of course, when he "appears" he will be "present." But the point of stressing "appearing" here is that, though in one sense it will seem to us that he is "coming," he will in fact be "appearing" right where he presently is—not a long way away within our own space-time world but in his own world, God's world, the world we call heaven. This world is different from ours (earth) but intersects with it in countless ways, not least in the inner lives of Christians themselves. One day the two worlds will be integrated completely and be fully visible to one another, producing that transformation of which both Paul and John speak.

Of course, Paul and John are not the only writers to mention all of this. The Revelation of St. John the Divine also speaks of the coming of Jesus; and here we find the word *come* itself. The Spirit and the Bride say, "Come," and the closing prayer of the book, as with 1 Corinthians, is that the Lord Jesus will come, and come soon. The same theme is scattered elsewhere in the book.[16] There is no space here to look at these passages in detail or indeed at the relevant passages in the other, smaller, New Testament books.[17] The one place in the New Testament where the issue of delay is addressed head-on is, famously, 2 Peter 3; and it's worth noting that those who reckon this a problem are precisely, in context, those who are arguing for a rather different, nonhistorical, form of Christianity.[18]

What we have here, with minor variations, is a remarkably unanimous view spread throughout the early Christianity known to us. There will come a time, which might indeed come at any time, when, in the great renewal of the world that Easter itself foreshadowed, Jesus himself will be personally present and will be the agent and model of the transformation that will happen both to the whole world and also to believers. This expectation and hope, expressed so clearly in the New Testament, continues undiminished in the second and subsequent centuries. Mainstream Christians throughout the early period were not worried by the fact that the event had not happened within a generation. The idea that the problem of "delay" set out in 2 Peter 3 was widespread in second-generation Christianity is a modern scholars' myth rather than a historical reality.[19] Nor was the idea of Jesus's "appearing" or "coming" simply part of a tradition that was passed on uncritically without later generations really tuning in to what it was saying. As with the ascension, so with Jesus's appearing: it was seen as a vital part of a full presentation of the Jesus who was and is and is to come. Without it the church's proclamation makes no sense. Take it away, and all sorts of things start to unravel. The early Christians saw this as clearly as anyone since, and we would do well to learn from them.

But it is now high time to look at the second aspect of the appearing or coming of Jesus. When he comes, according to the same biblically grounded tradition, he will have a specific role to play: that of judge.

9. JESUS, THE COMING JUDGE

INTRODUCTION

From the very beginning of Christianity—it's already there in some of the earliest traditions—we discover the belief that the Jesus who will appear at the end will take the role of judge. This is not an isolated belief. Indeed, within its Jewish context, it is more readily explicable than the *parousia* itself. However, it's important that we explore its meaning within early Christianity and its significance for today and tomorrow.

The picture of Jesus as the coming judge is the central feature of another absolutely vital and nonnegotiable Christian belief: that there will indeed *be* a judgment in which the creator God will set the world right once and for all. The word *judgment* carries negative overtones for a good many people in our liberal and postliberal world. We need to remind ourselves that throughout the Bible, not least in the Psalms, God's coming judgment is a good thing, something to be celebrated, longed for, yearned over. It causes people to shout for joy and the trees of the field to clap their hands.[1] In a world of systematic injustice, bullying, violence, arrogance, and oppression, the thought that there might come a day when the wicked are firmly put in their place and the poor and weak are given their due is the best news there can be. Faced with a world in rebellion, a world full of exploitation and wickedness, a good God *must* be a God of judgment. The liberal optimism of the nineteenth century

137

had a long run for its money, outlasting some of the more obvious counterarguments provided by the huge systemic evil of the twentieth century. But more recent theology has returned to the theme of judgment, recognizing that the biblical analysis of evil corresponds more closely to reality.[2]

The Old Testament hope for the creator God to bring judgment and justice to the world, to set the world right, became focused in the later biblical period on Israel's longing to see God overturn the oppressive regimes of the pagan world. It would be like a great, cosmic court scene. Israel (or at least the righteous within Israel) would play the part of the helpless defendant. The Gentiles (or at least the particularly wicked ones) would play the part of the arrogant bullies who would at last meet their match and get the justice (the "judgment") they deserved.

The most famous scenario expressing all this is Daniel 7. There the Gentile nations are depicted as huge, powerful monsters while Israel, or the righteous within Israel, is depicted as an apparently defenseless human being, "one like a son of man." The scene is a great court setting whose climax comes when the judge, the Ancient of Days, takes his seat and rules in favor of the son of man against the monsters, in favor of Israel against the pagan empires. The son of man is then given authority and dominion over all the nations, in a deliberate echo of Adam being given authority over the animals in Genesis 1 and 2.

What happens when this is transposed to the New Testament? Answer: we find Jesus himself taking on the role of the son of man, suffering then vindicated. Then, as in Daniel, he receives from the Supreme Judge the task of bringing this judgment to bear on the world. This accords with many biblical and postbiblical passages in which Israel's Messiah, the one who represents Israel in person, is given the task of judgment. In Isaiah 11 the Messiah's judgment creates a world where the wolf and the lamb lie down side by side. In Psalm 2 the Gentiles tremble when the Messiah is enthroned. Again and again the Messiah is stated to be God's agent to bring the whole world, not just Israel, back into the state of justice and truth for which God longs as much as we do. So the early Christians, who had concluded from Easter that Jesus was indeed the Messiah, naturally identified him as the one through whom God would put the world to rights. They didn't simply deduce this from their belief in his future coming or appearing. Actually, it may have been the other way around: their belief in Jesus's messiahship may have been a decisive factor in the emergence of the belief in his final coming as judge.

Certainly by the time of Paul this belief is well established. Paul's speech on the Areopagus in Athens concludes with the statement that God has fixed a day on which he will judge the world by a man whom he has appointed, giving assurance of the fact by raising him from the dead.[3] Paul can refer almost casually (in Romans 2:16) to the fact that according to the gospel he preaches, God will judge the secrets of all hearts through Jesus the Messiah. Although people often suppose that because Paul taught justification by faith, not works, there can be no room for a future judgment "according to works," this only goes to show how much some have radically misunderstood him. The future judgment according to deeds, a judgment exercised by Jesus at his "judgment seat," is clearly taught in, for instance, Romans 14:9–10, 2 Corinthians 5:10, and elsewhere. Equally important, these are not isolated places where Paul is quoting a tradition that doesn't fully fit with his developed theology. They are fully and tightly integrated into his thinking and preaching. For him, as much as for anyone else in the early church, the final judgment exercised by Jesus the Messiah was a vital element, without which all sorts of other things simply wouldn't stand up.

In particular (though there isn't space to develop this here) this picture of future judgment according to works is actually the *basis* of Paul's theology of justification by faith.[4] The point of justification by faith isn't that God suddenly ceases to care about good behavior or morality. Justification by faith cannot be collapsed, as so many in the last two centuries tried to do, either into a generalized liberal view of a laissez-faire morality or into the romantic view that what we do outwardly doesn't matter at all since the only thing that matters is what we're like inwardly. (Those who overanxiously defend a doctrine from which all mention of works has been rigorously excluded should consider with whom they are colluding at this point!) No: justification by faith is what happens in the *present time,* anticipating the verdict of the *future day* when God judges the world. It is God's advance declaration that when someone believes the gospel, that person is already a member of his family no matter who their parents were, that their sins are forgiven because of Jesus's death, and that on the future day, as Paul says, "there is now no condemnation" (Romans 8:1). Clearly further questions can be asked about how the verdict issued in the present can so confidently be supposed to anticipate correctly the verdict issued in the future on the basis of the entire life led. Paul addresses those questions in several ways at several points, particularly in his expositions of the work of the Holy Spirit. But for Paul (and this is the only point I am making in the present context), there was no clash between present justification by faith and future judgment according to works. The two actually need, and depend upon, one another. To go any further would demand a fairly thorough exposition of Romans and Galatians, for which there is obviously no space here.[5]

Once again, the Pauline picture is filled out by other references in the New Testament. This is no flash in the pan or Pauline idiosyncrasy; it is common early Christian belief.[6] It is the central point in that long paragraph in John 5 (verses 22–30), which caused so many headaches to those earlier scholars who tried to make John's gospel teach simply a present eternal life rather than also the future one:

The father doesn't judge anyone; he has handed over all judgment to the son, so that everyone should honour the son just as they honour the father. Anyone who doesn't honour the son doesn't honour the father who sent him. I'm telling you the solemn truth: anyone who hears my word, and believes in the one who sent me, has eternal life. Such a person won't come into judgment; they will have passed out of death into life. I'm telling you the solemn truth: the time is coming—in fact, it's here already!—when the dead will hear the voice of God's son, and those who hear it will live. You see, just as the father has life in himself, in the same way he has given the son the privilege of having life in himself. He has even given him authority to pass judgment, because he is the son of man. Don't be surprised at this. The time is coming, you see, when everyone in the tombs will hear his voice. They will come out—those who have done good, to the resurrection of life, and those who have done evil, to the resurrection of judgment. I can't do anything on my own authority. I judge on the basis of what I hear. And my judgment is just, because I'm not trying to carry out my own wishes, but the wishes of the one who sent me.[7]

The main point to notice, once more, is that all the future judgment is highlighted basically as good news, not bad. Why so? It is good news, first, because the one through whom God's justice will finally sweep the world is not a hard-hearted, arrogant, or vengeful tyrant but rather the Man of Sorrows, who was acquainted with grief; the Jesus who loved sinners and died for them; the Messiah who took the world's judgment upon himself on the cross. Of course, this also means that he is uniquely placed to judge the systems and rulers that have carved up the world between them, and the New Testament points this out here and there.[8] In particular, as we have already seen and as some medieval theologians and artists highlighted, Jesus comes as judge much as Moses descended the mountain into the camp where idolatry and revelry were in full swing. The Sistine Chapel itself reminds us of the day when careless and casual living, as well as downright wickedness, will be brought to book.[9]

Within the New Testament, and within subsequent Christian theology, this judgment is *anticipated* under certain circumstances.

I have already spoken of justification by faith. The same is true, in 1 Corinthians, for the Eucharist: eating and drinking the body and blood of Jesus means confronting here and now the one who is the judge as well as the savior of all.[10] And the same is true, of course, of the work of the Spirit, as we see once more in John 16. When the Spirit comes, declares Jesus, he will convict the world of sin, of righteousness and judgment.[11] The final judgment, in other words, will be anticipated in the present world through the Spirit-led work and witness of Jesus's followers.

SECOND COMING AND JUDGMENT

The so-called second coming of Jesus, then, when properly understood in the New Testament and subsequent Christian teaching, is no afterthought to the basic Christian message. It hasn't been, as it were, bolted on to the outside of a gospel message that could stand complete without it. We cannot relegate it to the margins of our thinking, our living, and our praying; if we do, we shall pull everything else out of shape. I now want, briefly, to draw out a few final points of relevance for us today.

First, the appearing or coming of Jesus offers the complete answer to both the literalist fundamentalists and to the proponents of that cosmic Christ idea I outlined in chapter 5. Jesus remains other than the church, other than the world, even while being present to both by the Spirit. He confronts the world in the present, and will do so personally and visibly in the future. He is the one to whom every knee shall bow (Philippians 2:10–11) as well as the one who took the form of a servant and was obedient to the death of the cross (Philippians 2:6–8). Indeed, as Paul stresses, he is the first *because* he did the second. In his appearing we find neither a dualist rejection of the present world nor simply his arrival like a spaceman into the present world but rather the *transformation* of the present world, and ourselves within it, so that it will at last be put to rights and we with it. Death and decay will be overcome, and God will be all in all.

This means, second, that a proper shape and balance are given to the Christian worldview. Like the Jewish worldview, but radically opposed to the Stoic, the Platonic, the Hindu, and the Buddhist worldviews, the Christian worldview is a story with a beginning, a middle, and an end. Not to have closure at the end of the story—to be left with a potentially endless cycle, round and round with either the same things happening again and again or simply perhaps the long outworking of karma—would be the very antithesis of the story told by the apostles and by the long line of their Jewish predecessors. And precisely because Jesus is not collapsed into the church, or indeed the world, we can renounce both the triumphalism that conveniently makes his sovereign lordship an excuse for its own and the despair that comes when we see such hopes dashed, as they always will be, in the follies and failings of even the best and greatest Christian organizations, structures, leaders, and followers. Because we live between ascension and appearing, joined to Jesus Christ by the Spirit but still awaiting his final coming and presence, we can be *both* properly humble *and* properly confident. "We proclaim not ourselves, but Jesus Christ as Lord, and ourselves as your servants through Jesus."[12]

Third, following directly from this, the task of the church between ascension and *parousia* is therefore set free both from the self-driven energy that imagines it has to build God's kingdom all by itself and from the despair that supposes it can't do anything until Jesus comes again. We do not "build the kingdom" all by ourselves, but we do build *for* the kingdom. All that we do in faith, hope, and love in the present, in obedience to our ascended Lord and in the power of his Spirit, will be enhanced and transformed at his appearing.[13] This too brings a note of judgment, of course, as Paul makes clear in 1 Corinthians 3:10–17. The "day" will disclose what sort of work each builder has done.

In particular, the present rule of the ascended Jesus Christ and the assurance of his final appearing in judgment should give us—which goodness knows we need today—some clarity and realism in our political discourse. Far too often Christians slide into a vaguely spiritualized version of one or other major political system or party. What would happen if we were to take seriously our stated belief that Jesus Christ is already the Lord of the world and that at his name, one day, every knee would bow?

You might suppose that this would merely inject a note of pietism and make us then avoid the real issues—or, indeed, to attempt a theocratic takeover bid. But to think in either of those ways would only show how deeply we have been conditioned by the Enlightenment split between religion and politics. What happens if we reintegrate them? As with specifically Christian work, so with political work done in Jesus's name: confessing Jesus as the ascended and coming Lord frees us up from needing to pretend that this or that program or leader has the key to utopia (if only we would elect him or her). Equally, it frees up our corporate life from the despair that comes when we realize that once again our political systems let us down. The ascension and appearing of Jesus constitute a radical challenge to the entire thought structure of the Enlightenment (and of course several other movements). And since our present Western politics is very much the creation of the Enlightenment, we should think seriously about the ways in which, as thinking Christians, we can and should bring that challenge to bear. I know this is giving a huge hostage to fortune, raising questions to which I certainly don't know the answers, but I do know that unless I point all this out one might easily get the impression that these ancient doctrines are of theoretical or abstract interest only. They aren't. People who believe that Jesus is already Lord and that he will appear again as judge of the world are called and equipped (to put it mildly) to think and act quite differently in the world from those who don't. I shall pursue these questions a bit further in the final part of the book.

In particular, of course, the hope of Jesus's coming as judge to put right all that is wrong in the world and to give new life to the dead is the context for one of our central themes, to which we can at last turn. If all this is so, what can we say about the future that awaits every one of us, every baptized believer in Jesus Christ? What precisely do we mean, for ourselves, when we speak of the future resurrection?

10. THE REDEMPTION OF OUR BODIES

As we saw in the first two chapters, there is no agreement in the church today about what happens to people when they die. Not surprisingly, therefore, there is also confusion in the wider, non-Christian world not only about the fate of the dead but also about *what Christians are supposed to believe* on the subject.

This is all the more curious in that the New Testament itself, which most churches officially regard as their primary doctrinal source, is crystal clear on the matter. In a classic passage, Paul speaks of "the redemption of our bodies" (Romans 8:23). There is no room for doubt as to what he means: God's people are promised a new type of bodily existence, the fulfillment and redemption of our present bodily life. The rest of the early Christian writings, where they address the subject, are completely in tune with this.

This expression of hope—hope for the resurrection of the body—was, however, so out of tune with several of the prevailing moods of Christian thought down the years that it became muzzled and distorted and then not even known. In this chapter I shall lay out the basic picture of final bodily resurrection offered by the New Testament and the early church fathers and explain how I think it can be reemphasized today. This can be done briefly because I am merely drawing together what I have set out in much more detail elsewhere.[1]

My proposition is that the traditional picture of people going to either heaven or hell as a one-stage postmortem journey (with or without the option of some kind of purgatory or continuing journey as an intermediate stage) represents a serious distortion and diminution of the Christian hope. Bodily resurrection is not just one odd bit of that hope. It is the element that gives shape and meaning to the rest of the story we tell about God's ultimate purposes. If we squeeze it to the margins, as many have done by implication, or indeed if we leave it out altogether, as some have done quite explicitly, we don't just lose an extra feature, like buying a car that happens not to have electrically operated mirrors. We lose the central engine, which drives it and gives every other component its reason for working. Instead of talking vaguely about heaven and then trying to fit the language of resurrection into that, we should talk with biblical precision about the resurrection and reorganize our language about heaven around *that*. What is more, as I shall show in the final part of this book, when we do this we discover an excellent foundation, not, as some suppose, for an escapist or quietist piety (that belongs more with the traditional and misleading language about heaven), but for lively and creative Christian work within the present world.

RESURRECTION: LIFE *AFTER* LIFE AFTER DEATH

We saw in the second chapter that whereas Greco-Roman paganism and second-temple Judaism both held a wide variety of beliefs about life beyond death, the early Christians were remarkably unanimous on the topic. There is space here only for a brief survey of the massive evidence.

We begin once more with Paul. I stressed in the previous chapter that when Paul speaks in Philippians 3 of being "citizens of heaven," he doesn't mean that we shall retire there when we have finished our work here. He says in the next line that Jesus will come *from* heaven in order to transform the present humble body into a glorious body like his own and that he will do this by the power through which he makes all things subject to himself. This little statement contains in a nutshell more or less all Paul's thought on the subject. The risen Jesus is both the *model* for the Christian's future body and the *means* by which it comes about.

Similarly in Colossians 3:1–4: when the Messiah appears, the one who is your life, then you too will appear with him in glory. Paul does not say "one day you will go to be with him." No, you already possess life in him. This new life, which the Christian possesses secretly, invisible to the world, will burst forth into full bodily reality and visibility.

The clearest and strongest passage, often ignored, is Romans 8:9–11. If the Spirit of God, the Spirit of Jesus the Messiah, dwells in you, says Paul, then the one who raised the Messiah from the dead will give life to your mortal bodies as well, through his Spirit who dwells in you. God will give life, not to a disembodied spirit, not to what many people have thought of as a spiritual body in the sense of a nonphysical one, but "to your mortal bodies also."

Paul is not the only New Testament writer to hold this view. The first letter of John declares that when Jesus appears, we shall be like him, for we shall see him as he is.[2] The resurrection body of Jesus, which at the moment is almost unimaginable to us in its glory and power, will be the model for our own. And of course within John's gospel, despite the puzzlement of those who want to read the book in a very different way, we have some of the clearest statements of future bodily resurrection. Jesus reaffirms the widespread Jewish expectation of resurrection and announces that the hour for this has already arrived. In the passage we glanced at in the previous chapter, it is quite explicit: "The hour is coming," he says, "indeed, it is already here, when the dead will hear the voice of the son of God, and those who hear will live; when all in the graves will come out, those who have done good, to the resurrection of life, and those who have done evil, to the resurrection of judgment."[3]

This clearly depends on Daniel 12 and other passages such as Isaiah 26 and Ezekiel 37. It exhibits a surface tension with the position of Paul, who mostly seems to regard resurrection as God's future gift by the Spirit for those who are in Christ, not for everyone (though, as we shall see presently, 2 Corinthians 5:10 may indicate otherwise). Some of the early church fathers enthusiastically follow John at this point, emphasizing that resurrection is necessary for the wicked as well so that they may be judged in the body. To this we shall return.

Here we need to revisit a point we made earlier. What does Jesus mean when he declares that there are "many dwelling places" in his father's house?[4] This has regularly been taken, not least when used in the context of bereavement, to mean that the dead (or at least dead Christians) will simply go to heaven permanently rather than being raised again subsequently to new bodily life. But the word for "dwelling places" here, *monai,* is regularly used in ancient Greek not for a final resting place but for a temporary halt on a journey that will take you somewhere else in the long run.

This fits closely with Jesus's words to the dying brigand in Luke: "Today you will be with me in Paradise."[5] Despite a long tradition of misreading, paradise is here, as in some other Jewish writing, not a final destination but the blissful garden, the parkland of rest and tranquillity, where the dead are refreshed as they await the dawn of the new day.[6] The main point of the sentence lies in the apparent contrast between the brigand's request and Jesus's reply: "Remember me," he says, "*when you come in your kingdom,*" implying (whether ironically or not does not concern us here) that this will be at some far distant future. Jesus's answer brings this future hope into the present, implying of course that with his death the kingdom is indeed coming even though it doesn't look like what anyone had imagined: "*Today* you will be with me in Paradise." There will still, of course, be a future completion involving ultimate resurrection; Luke's overall theological understanding leaves no doubt on that score. Jesus, after all, didn't rise again "today," that is, on Good Friday. Luke must have understood him to be referring to a state of being-in-paradise, which would be true, for him and for the man dying beside him, at once, that very day—in other words, *prior to the resurrection*. With Jesus, the future hope has come forward into the present. For those who die in faith, before that final reawakening, the central promise is of being "with Jesus" at once. "My desire is to depart," wrote Paul, "and be with Christ, which is far better."[7]

Resurrection itself then appears as what the word always meant, whether (like the ancient pagans) people disbelieved it or whether (like many ancient Jews) they affirmed it. It wasn't a way of talking about life after death. It was a way of talking about a new bodily life *after* whatever state of existence one might enter immediately upon death. It was, in other words, life *after* life after death.

What then about such passages as 1 Peter 1, which speak of a salvation that is "kept in heaven for you" so that in your present believing you are receiving "the salvation of your souls"? Here, I suggest, the automatic assumption of Western Christianity leads us badly astray. Most Christians today, reading a passage like this, assume that it means that heaven is where you go to receive this salvation—or even that salvation *consists in* "going to heaven when you die." This then provides a dangerously distorted framework within which some of the key gospel sayings are interpreted, such as those in Matthew where Jesus talks of "entering the kingdom of heaven" or "having a reward in heaven" or "storing up riches in heaven." Quite simply, the way we now understand that language in the Western world is totally different from what Jesus and his hearers meant and understood.

For a start, *heaven* is actually a reverent way of speaking about God so that "riches in heaven" simply means "riches in God's presence" (as we see when, elsewhere, Jesus talks about someone being or not being "rich toward God").[8] But then, by derivation from this primary meaning, heaven is the place where *God's purposes for the future are stored up*. It isn't where they are meant to stay so that one would need to go to heaven to enjoy them; it is where they are kept safe against the day when they will become a reality on earth. If I say to a friend, "I've kept some beer in the fridge for you," that doesn't mean that he has to climb into the fridge in order to drink the beer. God's future inheritance, the incorruptible new world and the new bodies that are to inhabit that world, are already kept safe, waiting for us, not so that we can go to heaven and put them on there but so that they can be brought to birth in this world or rather in the new heavens and new earth, the renewed world of which I spoke earlier.

We should note as well, in relation to the passage in 1 Peter and some others, that the word *soul* is rare in this sense in the early Christian writings. The word *psyche* was very common in the ancient world and carried a variety of meanings. Despite its frequency both in later Christianity and (for instance) in Buddhism, the New Testament doesn't use it to describe, so to speak, the bit of you that will ultimately be saved. The word *psyche* seems here to refer, like the Hebrew *nephesh,* not to a disembodied inner part of the human being but to what we might call the person or even the personality. And the point in 1 Peter 1 is that this person, the "real you," is *already* being saved and will one day receive that salvation in full bodily form. That is why Peter quite rightly plants the hope for salvation firmly in the resurrection of Jesus. God has, he says, "given us new birth to a living hope by the resurrection of Jesus the Messiah from the dead."[9]

RESURRECTION IN CORINTH

All discussions of the future resurrection must sooner or later do business with Paul and particularly with his two letters to Corinth. These are tricky and controversial, and I've spent a long time elsewhere going through them in detail. Let me simply sum up the main argument, working back from 2 Corinthians to 1 Corinthians.[10]

The passage about resurrection in 2 Corinthians 4 and 5 comes within Paul's long and passionate description of his own apostleship. He speaks of his ministry in terms of "having treasure in jars of clay, to show that what matters is God's power" and not his own. To give substance to this, he spells out the future hope, within which the present life of ambiguity and suffering makes sense. If all we had were the final verses of chapter 4, it might be possible to say—and some do try to argue this—that Paul was referring to a future hope in which the body would be left behind and a pure spirit would remain: "The outer nature," he says, "is wasting away, but the inner nature is being renewed day by day." Is this not three-quarters of the way down the road to Plato, eager to be done with the perishable mortal body and to be left with the glorious, immortal, and disembodied soul?

Certainly not. In chapter 5 Paul speaks of the new tent or tabernacle that is waiting for us. There is a new house, a new dwelling, a new body, waiting within God's sphere (again, "heaven"), ready for us to put it on over the present one so that what is mortal may be swallowed up with life. As always, so here, Paul insists that God will accomplish this by the Spirit.

This is the point at which we modern Westerners are called to make a huge leap of the imagination. We have been buying our mental furniture for so long in Plato's factory that we have come to take for granted a basic ontological contrast between "spirit" in the sense of something immaterial and "matter" in the sense of something material, solid, physical. We think we know that solid objects are one sort of thing and ideas or values or spirits or ghosts are a different sort of thing (often not noticing that they are themselves all rather different sorts of things). We know that bodies decay and die; that houses, temples, cities, and civilizations fall to dust; and so we assume that to be bodily, to be physical, is to be impermanent, changeable, transitory, and that the only way to be permanent, unchanging, and immortal is to become nonphysical.

Paul's point here is that this is not so. Actually, it wasn't so even in the dominant cosmology of his day, which was Stoic rather than

Platonic. Still less was it so within the Jewish creation theology, which formed the seedbed out of which, because of the resurrection of Jesus himself, Paul grew his theology of new creation.[11] Paul is making his Corinthian readers think in new patterns, and he has the same effect on us.

What Paul is asking us to imagine is that there will be a new mode of physicality, which stands in relation to our present body as our present body does to a ghost. It will be as much more real, more firmed up, more *bodily*, than our present body as our present body is more substantial, more touchable, than a disembodied spirit. We sometimes speak of someone who's been very ill as being a shadow of their former self. If Paul is right, a Christian in the present life is a mere shadow of his or her *future* self, the self that person will be when the body that God has waiting in his heavenly storeroom is brought out, already made to measure, and put on over the present one—or over the self that will still exist after bodily death. This is where one of the great Easter hymns gets it exactly right:

> O how glorious and resplendent
> Fragile body, shalt thou be,
> When endued with so much beauty,
> Full of health, and strong, and free!
> Full of vigour, full of pleasure,
> That shall last eternally.[12]

Paul is anxious not to pretend he has already attained this state. Indeed, he is anxious to stress that the present work of an apostle involves him precisely in sharing the weakness and suffering of the present state of the world. But his point is that we must all appear before the judgment seat of the Messiah (2 Corinthians 5:10), and for that we shall need bodies. Here Paul, like John, is on track with Daniel 12 and other similar Jewish texts. Indeed, it may be at this point that Paul hints after all at a resurrection of the wicked (in order to be judged in the body) as well as of the righteous.

This brings us to the heart of the New Testament view of the resurrection, 1 Corinthians 15.

The hope of resurrection underlies the whole of 1 Corinthians, not just chapter 15. But here Paul addresses it head-on as of central importance. Some in Corinth are denying the future resurrection, almost certainly on the normal pagan grounds that everyone knows dead people don't rise again. In reply, Paul speaks, as we saw in the previous chapter, of Jesus as the firstfruits and of the great harvest still to come when all Jesus's people are raised as he has been.

The whole chapter echoes and alludes to Genesis 1–3. It is a theology of new creation, not of the abandonment of creation. The heart of the chapter is an exposition of the two different types of bodies, the present one and the future one. This is where all sorts of problems have arisen.

Several popular translations, notably the Revised Standard Version and its offshoots, translate Paul's key phrases as "a physical body" and "a spiritual body."[13] Simply in terms of the Greek words Paul uses, this cannot be correct. The technical arguments are overwhelming and conclusive. The contrast is between the present body, corruptible, decaying, and doomed to die, and the future body, incorruptible, undecaying, never to die again. The key adjectives, which are quoted endlessly in discussions of this topic, do not refer to a physical body and a nonphysical one, which is how people in our culture are bound to hear the words *physical* and *spiritual.*

The first word, *psychikos,* does not in any case mean anything like "physical" in our sense. For Greek speakers of Paul's day, the *psychē,* from which the word derives, means the soul, not the body.

But the deeper, underlying point is that adjectives of this type, Greek adjectives ending in *-ikos,* describe not *the material out of which things are made* but *the power or energy that animates them.* It is the difference between asking, on the one hand, "Is this a wooden ship or an iron ship?" (the material from which it is made) and asking, on the other, "Is this a steamship or a sailing ship?" (the energy that powers it). Paul is talking about the present body, which is animated by the normal human *psychē* (the life force we all possess here and now, which gets us through the present life but is ultimately powerless against illness, injury, decay, and death), and the future body, which is animated by God's *pneuma,* God's breath of new life, the energizing power of God's new creation.

This is why, in a further phrase that became controversial as early as the mid-second century, Paul declares that "flesh and blood cannot inherit God's kingdom."[14] He doesn't mean that physicality will be abolished. "Flesh and blood" is a technical term for that which is corruptible, transient, heading for death. The contrast, again, is not between what we call physical and what we call nonphysical but between *corruptible physicality,* on the one hand, and *incorruptible physicality,* on the other.

This underlies the remarkable concluding verse of 1 Corinthians 15, to which we shall return. For Paul, the bodily resurrection does not leave us saying, "So that's all right; we shall go, at the last, to join Jesus in a nonbodily, Platonic heaven," but, "So, then, since the person you are and the world God has made will be gloriously reaffirmed in God's eventual future, you must be steadfast, immovable, always abounding in the Lord's work, because you know that in the Lord your labour is not in vain." Belief in the bodily resurrection includes the belief that what is done in the present in the body, by the power of the Spirit, will be reaffirmed in the eventual future, in ways at which we can presently only guess.

RESURRECTION: LATER DEBATES

There were of course all kinds of debates and further discussions about the bodily resurrection in the second century and beyond.[15] What is remarkable is that apart from the small corpus of Gnostic and semi-Gnostic writings, the early church fathers at least as far as Origen insisted on this doctrine, though the pressures on them to abandon it must have been very great. Ignatius of Antioch, Justin Martyr, Athenagoras, Irenaeus, Tertullian—all of them stress bodily resurrection.

What is more, they all link this doctrine very closely to two others, which enable them to stand out against all kinds of other teachings, not least Docetism and Gnosticism: first, the doctrine of creation and, second, the doctrine of God's justice and final judgment. As in Judaism, resurrection is the point where creation and judgment meet. Where one is abandoned, for whatever reason, the others soon follow.

With Tertullian in particular, we start to find questions about what precisely bodily resurrection will involve. (Some of these questions are also raised in the rabbinic sources, which were wrestling with similar problems around the same time.) Suppose a cannibal eats a Christian, and suppose the cannibal is then himself converted. The Christian's body has become part of the cannibal's body; who will have which bits at the resurrection?

Tertullian gives a brusque answer. It's God's business, he says; he's the creator, so he can and will sort it out. Origen, faced with similar questions, replies more subtly. Our bodies, he points out, are in any case in a state of flux. It isn't just that hair and fingernails grow and are cut off; our entire physical substance is slowly changing. What we today call atoms and molecules pass through us, leaving us with continuity of form but transience of matter. (C. S. Lewis, summarizing this argument, offers an illustration: I am in that respect, he says, like a curve in a waterfall.)[16] This argument is repeated by Thomas Aquinas a millennium after Origen and nearly a millennium before Lewis. It's a good argument: as we now know, we change our entire physical kit, every atom and molecule, over a period of seven years or so. I am physically a totally different person now from the person I was ten years ago. And yet I am still me. Thus it really doesn't matter whether we get the identical molecules back or not, though some continuity is perfectly possible. The ones we use for a while have been used by other organisms before us and will be used by others when we are done with them. Dust we are, and to dust we shall return. But God can do new things with dust.

Many of the leading theologians in the patristic and medieval periods were quite clear about the two-stage postmortem future. Gregory the Great (540–604), for instance, taught that the soul of the dead Christian enjoys the beatific vision while still awaiting the resurrection of the body. Anselm (1033–1109) stressed that our resurrection bodies will transcend our present bodies in a new kind of being. The Victorine theologians, following Hugh of St. Victor (d. 1142), taught that the resurrection body will be identical with our earthly body but transfigured:

> It will be immune from death and sorrow; it will be at the height of its powers, free from disease and deformity, and around thirty years old, the age at which Christ began his ministry. It will surpass anything we can imagine, even from the accounts of Christ's appearances on earth after his own resurrection.[17]

Mainstream medieval theologians like Thomas and Bernard insisted on the bodily resurrection. They, like the New Testament and the early church fathers, held a strong view of God's good creation. They knew that it must be reaffirmed, not abandoned. But a good deal of Western medieval piety then took a very different turn, in which the twin destinations of heaven and hell and the possible intermediate destination of purgatory became far more important and in which the language of resurrection, insofar as it was retained at all, seemed simply to be a rather special way of talking about heaven, which was the primary category. This has had all kinds of unfortunate results, to which we shall come in a moment. But first we must draw out and underline the key elements of the early Christian view of the resurrection and consider how we can reappropriate it for today.

RETHINKING RESURRECTION TODAY:
WHO, WHERE, WHAT, WHY, WHEN, AND HOW

Who will be raised from the dead? All people, according to John and perhaps Paul, but for Paul at least there is a special sense of resurrection that clearly applies to those who are in Christ and indwelt by the Spirit. This raises other questions that we shall have to address in the next chapter.

Where will the resurrection take place? On the new earth, joined as it will then be to the new heaven. That has been the burden of my song in the shape and argument of this whole part of the book. In this new world there will be no problem of overcrowding (as some, at the risk of bathos, have ventured to suggest). Apart from the question of whether every human will be raised or only some, we need to remind ourselves that roughly half the humans who have ever lived are alive at the moment. World population has grown at an enormous rate in the last century; we easily forget that for much of history huge tracts of land were hardly inhabited at all. Even the civilized and somewhat crowded cities of biblical times were mostly, by today's standards, like small market towns. In any case, if we take seriously the promise of new heavens and new earth, none of this is a problem. God is the creator, and his new world will be exactly what we need and want, with the love and beauty of this present world taken up and transformed.

More fully, then, what precisely will the resurrection body be? Here I pay homage again to one of the few modern writers who has tried to help us with the task of *imagining* what the risen body might be like: C. S. Lewis. In a variety of places, but particularly in his remarkable book *The Great Divorce,* he manages to get us to envisage bodies that are more solid, more real, more substantial than our present ones.[18] That is the task that 2 Corinthians in particular invites us to. These will be bodies of which the phrase "the weight of glory," taken from that letter (4:17), will be seen, felt, and known to be appropriate.

Further questions were asked in the ancient world at this point and often reemerge in contemporary discussion. Which of our present characteristics, and indeed present blemishes, will be retained in the transformed physicality? When I taught a course on resurrection at Harvard in 1999, one of my students complained in her term paper that since she had never liked the shape of her nose she hoped she wouldn't have to put up with it in a future life as well. There is no way we can answer such questions. All we can surmise from the picture of Jesus's resurrection is that just as his wounds were still visible, not now as sources of pain and death but as signs of his victory, so the Christian's risen body will bear such marks of his or her loyalty to God's particular calling as are appropriate, not least where that has involved suffering.

In particular, this new body will be immortal. That is, it will have passed *beyond* death not just in the *temporal* sense (that it happens to have gone through a particular moment and event) but also in the *ontological* sense of no longer being subject to sickness, injury, decay, and death itself. None of these destructive forces will have any power over the new body. That indeed may be one of the ways of understanding the *strangeness* of the risen body of Jesus. The disciples were looking at the first, and so far the only, piece of incorruptible physicality.

At this point we must notice that once again our language gets us into trouble. The word *immortality* is often used to mean "*disembodied* immortality," and it is sometimes then used in a sharp contrast with resurrection. As a result, we easily forget Paul's point about the resurrection body. It will be a body, but it will not be subject to mortality. An "immortal body" is something most people find so strange that they don't even pause to wonder if that's what Paul and the other early Christians were talking about. But it is.

There is a world of difference between this belief and a belief in an "immortal soul." Platonists believe that all humans have an immortal element within them, normally referred to as "soul." (Having praised C. S. Lewis, I should say that he seems to fall into this trap.)

In the New Testament, however, immortality is something that only God possesses by nature and that he then shares, as a gift of grace rather than an innate possession, with his people.[19]

Why will we be given new bodies? According to the early Christians, the purpose of this new body will be to rule wisely over God's new world. Forget those images about lounging around playing harps. There will be work to do and we shall relish doing it. All the skills and talents we have put to God's service in this present life—and perhaps too the interests and likings we gave up because they conflicted with our vocation—will be enhanced and ennobled and given back to us to be exercised to his glory. This is perhaps the most mysterious, and least explored, aspect of the resurrection life. But there are several promises in the New Testament about God's people "reigning," and these cannot just be empty words.[20] If, as we have already seen, the biblical view of God's future is of the renewal of the entire cosmos, there will be plenty to be done, entire new projects to undertake. In terms of the vision of original creation in Genesis 1 and 2, the garden will need to be tended once more and the animals renamed. These are only images, of course, but like all other future-oriented language they serve as true signposts to a larger reality—a reality to which most Christians give little or no thought.

The new body will be a gift of God's grace and love. However, there are several passages in the New Testament, not least in the words of Jesus himself, that speak of God's future blessings in terms of *reward* (a further answer, in other words, to the question why). Many Christians find this uncomfortable. We have been taught that we are justified by faith, not works, and, somehow, the very idea of being a Christian for what we will get out of it is distasteful.

But the image of reward in the New Testament doesn't work like that. It isn't a matter of calculation, of doing a difficult job in order to be paid a wage. It is much more like working at a friendship or a marriage in order to enjoy the other person's company more fully. It is more like practicing golf in order that we can go out on the course and hit the ball in the right direction. It is more like learning German or Greek so that we can read some of the great poets and philosophers who wrote in those languages. The "reward" is *organically connected to the activity,* not some kind of arbitrary pat on the back, otherwise unrelated to the work that was done. And it is always far in abundance beyond any sense of direct or equivalent payment. The reward of being able to read and enjoy Homer for the rest of your life is way beyond any kind of one-for-one payment for the slog of learning Greek. As we have already seen and shall pick up again later, all this relates directly to what Paul says in 1 Corinthians 15:58: the resurrection means that what you do in the present, in working hard for the gospel, is not wasted. It is not in vain. It will be completed, will have its fulfillment, in God's future.

When will the resurrection happen? Some have supposed that we go immediately upon death into the resurrection state.[21] I find that very difficult. Paul says that if Christ is the firstfruits, those who belong to him will be raised "at his coming," which clearly hasn't happened yet. The book of Revelation speaks, as do many Jewish writings of the period, of the dead waiting patiently, and sometimes not so patiently, for the time when they will finally be raised to new life.[22] This intermediate state, in fact, is more or less a constant feature of resurrection belief both Jewish and Christian.

In particular, if it is true (as I argued earlier) that the new creation will be in important senses continuous with the present one, we cannot think that it has already arrived, any more than it would have made sense for Jesus's resurrection body to be already alive and active before his crucifixion. The new is the *transformation,* not merely the replacement, of the old. And since the old is quite obviously not yet transformed, the resurrection, its central feature, cannot yet have happened. Time matters; it was part of the original good creation. Though it may well itself be transformed in ways we cannot at present even begin to imagine, we should not allow ourselves to be seduced by the language of eternity (as in the phrase "eternal life," which in the New Testament regularly refers not to a nontemporal future existence but to "the life of the coming age") into imagining, as one old song puts it, that "time shall be no more."[23] No: "the old field of space, time, matter and the senses is to be weeded, dug, and sown for a new crop. We may be tired of that old field: God is not."[24]

How will it happen? As John Polkinghorne and others have urged, what we are talking about is a great act of new creation. Polkinghorne, in fact, offers a contemporary metaphor that I find appealing (but that, I have discovered, some people find appalling). He, of course, puts it in a much more nuanced way, but I don't think it's too much of a caricature to express it like this: God will download our software onto his hardware until the time when he gives us new hardware to run the software again.[25] Paul says that God will give us new bodies; there may well be some bodily continuity, as with Jesus himself, but God is well capable of recreating people even if (as with the martyrs of Lyons) their ashes are scattered into a fast-flowing river.

Whenever the question of "how" is raised in the early Christian writings, the answer comes back: by the Spirit. The Spirit who brooded over the waters of chaos, the Spirit who indwelt Jesus so richly that it became known as the Spirit *of* Jesus: this Spirit, already present within Jesus's followers as the firstfruits, the down payment, the guarantee of what is to come, is not only the beginning of the future life, even in the present time, but also the energizing power through which the final transformation will take place. The early creed spoke of "the Holy Spirit, the Lord *and giver of life*." That is exactly true to the New Testament.

All this raises in an acute form the question: so where are the dead right now? How should we think of them?

11. PURGATORY, PARADISE, HELL

INTRODUCTION

Before the sixteenth century most Western Christians thought of the church as divided into three parts. First there was the church triumphant, consisting of the saints, the holy souls, who had already arrived at the beatific vision of God. Officially they were still awaiting the final resurrection, but increasingly that wasn't emphasized, and in many medieval portrayals it has dropped out altogether. Think of Dante and the medieval mystery plays. There was such a place as heaven; some souls had already made it there, and they were therefore to be thought of as saints; they were in the presence of God; what more could they want?

Within this picture, some saints had got there by the direct route, immediately upon death, while others had arrived in heaven after a period elsewhere, to which we shall come presently. But, once there, such saints could act as friends at court for those already on the way. And these triumphant saints had their own celebration: All Saints Day.

At the other end was the church militant. (Militant means "fighting," in the sense of "fighting the good fight of faith," as in 1 Timothy.)[1] This is, of course, the company of God's people in the present life, about whom we are not presently concerned.

In between was the church expectant, that is, "waiting," and the place where they were waiting was purgatory. This is a complex topic and needs further examination.

PURGATORY

Purgatory is basically a Roman Catholic doctrine. It is not held as such in the Eastern Orthodox church, and it was decisively rejected, on biblical and theological grounds and not merely because of antipathy to particular abuses, at the Reformation. The main statements on purgatory come from Aquinas in the thirteenth century and Dante in the early fourteenth, but the notion became woven deeply into the entire psyche of the whole period.[2] Huge energy was expended in the late medieval period in developing the picture of purgatory and rearranging present Christian life around it. Most Christians, it was taught, remain sinful in some measure right up to death; they therefore need both punishment and purging, though they can be helped through this time by the prayers, and especially the masses, of the church militant. It was as an outcrop from this that the sale of indulgences was invented in the early sixteenth century, to the horror not only of Martin Luther but also of several other Roman Catholic theologians of the day.

The poetic and dramatic power of the idea of purgatory is evident both from Dante seven hundred years ago and, closer to our time, from works like Cardinal Newman's famous *Dream of Gerontius,* set to music even more famously by Elgar. This vision, and the teaching that goes with it, still forms the staple diet of a large part of the Roman church and of some others that look to it for a lead. But in the last generation two major and central Roman teachers have expounded very different views.

Karl Rahner, who died in 1984, tried to combine Roman and Eastern teaching on the place of the soul between death and resurrection. Instead of concentrating on what he saw as the overindividualized concern with the fate of a particular soul, he supposed that after death souls became more closely united with the cosmos as a whole, through which process, while still awaiting the resurrection, the soul is more aware of the effects of its own sin on the world in general. This, he thought, is purgatory enough.[3]

More remarkable still is the view of Cardinal Ratzinger, now Pope Benedict XVI. Building on 1 Corinthians 3, he argued that the Lord himself is the fire of judgment, which transforms us as he conforms us to his glorious, resurrected body. This happens not during a long, drawn-out process but in the moment of final judgment itself. By thus linking purgatory to Jesus Christ himself as the eschatological fire, Ratzinger detached the doctrine of purgatory from the concept of an intermediate state and broke the link that in the Middle Ages gave rise to the idea of indulgences and so provided a soft target for Protestant polemic. Whatever we think of that, it is clear that two of the most central, important, and conservative Roman theologians of the last generation offered a quite radical climb-down from Aquinas, Dante, Newman, and all that went in between.[4]

At the same time, however—and this is where many Anglicans come in—there was a tendency in much twentieth-century theology to soft-pedal the "sure and certain hope" spoken of so enthusiastically by the Reformers. It seems (we are often told) very arrogant. If we know our own hearts, and those of the people to whom we minister, we know that we are not ready for final bliss. In addition, the tendency toward universalism so evident in the last hundred years of Protestant thinking has produced a new situation, where not only professed Christians but also the mass of professed non-Christians are going to have to be got ready for salvation in the time after death. Like a badly sprung double bed, this has propelled the people who used to be positioned at either side, in either heaven or hell, into an uneasy huddle in the middle. Non-Christians, in this view, will continue after death to pursue whatever "journey" they have been on up till then, until they eventually come round to accepting God's salvation. Christians, likewise, will continue the "journey" they have been on, proceeding by unhurried steps through uncharted spiritual country until they too arrive at the goal. Sometimes, as in the American Prayer Book, this process is spoken of as growth—though why that metaphor is preferred over others is not clear. We thus have a sort of purgatory-for-all. It isn't very unpleasant, and it's certainly not punitive—since the liberalism that gives rise to these ideas doesn't make much fuss of sin and certainly doesn't want to think it needed or needs to be punished.[5]

Purgatory, in either its classic or its modern form, provides the rationale for All Souls Day (November 2), a tenth-century Benedictine innovation. This commemoration assumes a sharp distinction between the "saints," who are already in heaven, and the "souls," who aren't and who are therefore still less than completely happy and need our help (as we say today) to "move on." The double commemoration of All Saints and All Souls stands on the foundation of this radical distinction. It is this that I now want to challenge.

There are four points to be made.

First, as I said earlier, the resurrection is still in the future. This is the official view of all mainstream orthodox theologians, Catholic and Protestant, East and West, except for those who think that after death we pass into an eternity in which all moments are present. We should recall in particular that the use of the word *heaven* to denote the *ultimate* goal of the redeemed, though of course hugely popularized by medieval and subsequent piety, is severely misleading and does not begin to do justice to the Christian hope. I am repeatedly frustrated by how hard it is to get this point through the thick wall of traditional thought and language that most Christians put up. The ultimate destination is (once more) *not* "going to heaven when you die" but being bodily raised into the transformed, glorious likeness of Jesus Christ. (The point of all this is not, of course, merely our own happy future, important though that is, but the glory of God as we come fully to reflect his image.) Thus, if we want to speak of "going to heaven when we die," we should be clear that this represents the first, and far less important, stage of a two-stage process. Resurrection isn't life after death; it is life *after* life after death.

Second, there is no reason in the New Testament to suppose that there are any category distinctions between different Christians in heaven as they await the resurrection. In the early Christian writings all Christians are "saints," including the muddled and sinful Corinthians. When Paul speaks of his desire "to depart and be with Christ, for that is far better," he isn't suggesting that he is going to be "with Christ" while less proficient Christians will have an interim waiting period.[6] He will not, in that sense, be with the "saints" *while the "souls" are somewhere else.* This is recognized in Eastern orthodoxy, which celebrates the saints in all sorts of ways but doesn't imagine that they have already obtained final bliss. They won't until we all do. That's why the Orthodox pray *for* the saints as well as with them.

The only passage in the New Testament that makes any kind of distinction at this point is 1 Corinthians 3, which speaks of Christian workers who build with gold, silver, and precious stones and others who build with wood, hay, and stubble. But Paul doesn't say that the one group will go straight to heaven while the others go to purgatory. Both will be saved; the same destination awaits both; but the first group will arrive gloriously, the second by the skin of their teeth. This is a solemn passage, to be taken very seriously by Christian workers and teachers, but, as the pope now appears to acknowledge, it doesn't indicate that there is a difference of status or of celestial geography or of temporal progression between one category of Christians after death and another.

In fact, there are so many things said in the New Testament about the greatest becoming least and the least becoming greatest that we shouldn't be surprised at this lack of distinction between the postmortem state of different Christians. I appreciate that it may be hard for some to come to terms with this, but in the light of the basic and central Christian gospel, the message and achievement of Jesus, and the preaching of Paul and the others, there is no reason whatever to say, for instance, that Peter or Paul, Aidan and Cuthbert, or even, dare I say, the mother of Jesus herself is more advanced, closer to God, has achieved more spiritual growth, or whatever, than those Christians who have been martyred in our own day or indeed those who have died quietly in their beds. If we are to be true to our foundation charter, we must say that all Christians, living and departed, are to be thought of as saints and that all Christians who have died are to be thought of, and treated, as such.

Third, therefore, I do not believe in purgatory as a place, a time, or a state. It was in any case a late Western innovation, without biblical support, and its supposed theological foundations are now questioned, as we saw, by leading Roman Catholic theologians themselves. As the reformers insisted, bodily death itself is the destruction of the sinful person. Someone once accused me of suggesting that God was a magician if he could wonderfully make a still-sinful person into a no-longer-sinful person just like that. But that's not the point. Death itself gets rid of all that is still sinful; this isn't magic but good theology. There is nothing then left to purge. Some older teachers suggested that purgatory would still be necessary because one would still need to bear some punishment for one's sins, but any such suggestion is of course abhorrent to anyone with even a faint understanding of Paul, who teaches that "there is no condemnation for those who are in Christ."[7]

The last great paragraph of Romans 8, so often and so appropriately read at funerals, leaves no room for purgatory in any form. "Who shall lay any charge against us . . . ? Who shall condemn us . . . ? Who shall separate us from the love of Christ? Neither death nor life nor anything in all creation shall be able to separate us from the love of God in Christ Jesus our Lord."[8] And if you still want to say that Paul really meant "though of course you'll probably have to go through purgatory first," I think with great respect that you ought to see not a theologian but a therapist.

In fact, Paul makes it clear here and elsewhere that it's the *present* life that is meant to function as a purgatory. The sufferings of the present time, not of some postmortem state, are the valley through which we have to pass in order to reach the glorious future. I think I know why purgatory became so popular, why Dante's middle volume is the one people most easily relate to. *The myth of purgatory is an allegory, a projection from the present onto the future.* This is why purgatory appeals to the imagination. It is our story, here and now. If we are Christians, if we believe in the risen Jesus as Lord, if we are baptized members of his body, then we are passing right now through the sufferings that form the gateway to life. Of course, this means that for millions of our theological and spiritual ancestors death brought a pleasant surprise. They had been gearing themselves up for a long struggle ahead, only to find it was already over.

The revival of a quasi purgatory in our own day, therefore, is beside the point. It is a strange return to mythology just when we should be having our feet on the ground. It is ironic that in some circles the aim seems to be to sidle up to Rome in a friendly way, at the very moment when two of the leading conservative theologians in Rome, Rahner and Ratzinger, have been transforming the doctrine into something else. It's time for a deep breath, some clear thinking, and a sigh of relief.

PARADISE

I therefore arrive, fourth, at this view: that all the Christian departed are in substantially the same state, that of restful happiness. Though this is sometimes described as sleep, we shouldn't take this to mean that it is a state of unconsciousness. Had Paul thought that, I very much doubt that he would have described life immediately after death as "being with Christ, which is far better." Rather, *sleep* here means that the *body* is "asleep" in the sense of "dead," while the real person—however we want to describe him or her—continues.

This state is not, clearly, the final destiny for which the Christian dead are bound, which is, as we have seen, the bodily resurrection.

But it is a state in which the dead are held firmly within the conscious love of God and the conscious presence of Jesus Christ while they await that day. There is no reason why this state should not be called heaven, though we must note once more how interesting it is that the New Testament routinely doesn't call it that and uses the word *heaven* in other ways.

An important point follows from all this. Since both the departed saints and we ourselves are in Christ, we share with them in the "communion of saints." They are still our brothers and sisters in Christ. When we celebrate the Eucharist they are there with us, along with the angels and archangels. Why then should we not pray for and with them? The reason the Reformers and their successors did their best to outlaw praying for the dead was because that had been so bound up with the notion of purgatory and the need to get people out of it as soon as possible. Once we rule out purgatory, I see no reason why we should not pray for and with the dead and every reason why we should—not that they will get out of purgatory but that they will be refreshed and filled with God's joy and peace. Love passes into prayer; we still love them; why not hold them, in that love, before God?

I do not, however, find in the New Testament or in the earliest Christian fathers any suggestion that those at present in heaven or (if you prefer) paradise are actively engaged in praying *for* those of us in the present life. Nor do I find any suggestion that Christians who are still alive should pray to the saints to intercede to the Father on their behalf. I know that I touch here on a sensitive nerve within the devotional habits of many Christians, but I think this point of view deserves to be heard. It is true that if the Christian dead are conscious, and if they are "with Christ" in a sense that, as Paul implies, is closer than we ourselves are at the moment, there is every reason to suppose that they are at least, like the souls under the altar in Revelation, urging the Father to complete the work of justice and salvation in the world. If that is so, there is no reason in principle why they should not urge the Father similarly on our behalf. Or if, from another point of view, they are indeed "with Christ," and if part of the work of the ascended Christ is indeed to be ruling the world as the agent of his Father, we might indeed suppose that the dead are somehow involved in that, not merely as spectators of that ongoing work. But—and this is very important for those who, like me, believe that it's vital to ground one's beliefs in scripture itself—I see no evidence in the early Christian writings to suggest that the Christian dead are in fact engaged in work of that sort, still less any suggestion that presently alive Christians should, so to speak, encourage them to do it by invoking them specifically.

In particular, we should be very suspicious of the medieval idea that the saints can function as friends at court so that while we might be shy of approaching the King ourselves, we know someone who is, as it were, one of us, to whom we can talk freely and who will maybe put in a good word for us. The practice seems to me to call into question, and even actually to deny by implication, the immediacy of access to God through Jesus Christ and in the Spirit, which is promised again and again in the New Testament. In the New Testament it is clear: because of Christ and the Spirit, every single Christian is welcome at any time to come before the Father himself. If you have a royal welcome awaiting you in the throne room itself, for whatever may be on your heart and mind, whether great or small, why would you bother hanging around the outer lobby trying to persuade someone there, however distinguished, to go in and ask for you? To question this, even by implication, is to challenge one of the central blessings and privileges of the gospel.

Explicit invocation of saints may be, in fact—I do not say it always is, but it may be—a step toward that semipaganism of which the Reformers were rightly afraid. The world of late Roman antiquity found it difficult to rid its collective imagination of the many-layered panoply of gods and lords, of demigods and heroes, that had been collecting in the culture for well over a thousand years. The second-century church began, quite understandably, to venerate the martyrs as special witnesses to the victory of Christ over death. Once Christianity had become established and persecution ceased, it was not a large transition to nominate for veneration others who, though not martyred, had nevertheless been notable Christians in whatever way. But the whole process of developing not only hierarchies among such people but also elaborate systems for designating them (canonization and the like) seems to me a huge exercise in missing the point.

So then: instead of the three divisions of the medieval church—triumphant, expectant, and militant—I believe that there are only two. The church in heaven or paradise is both triumphant and expectant. I do not expect all my readers to agree with this conclusion, but I would urge them at least to search the scriptures and see whether these things be so. And in particular I urge those whose churches, like my own, have revived the practice of All Souls commemorations, not least those who find them pastorally helpful, to think seriously about the theology they are implicitly embracing and teaching. The two appropriate times for remembering the Christian dead, and for doing so in a way that expresses genuine Christian hope, are Easter and All Saints. To add other commemorations detracts from the meaning of those great festivals. Here, as in some other points of theology and liturgy, more is less.

These are of course matters of detail, applying to some churches but not all. But all churches are rightly concerned, at least from time to time, with addressing the questions of what happens immediately after death as well as the ultimate future. Without some reflection on these matters, which have been so central and contentious within the tradition, our discussions will be impoverished and run the risk of repeating old mistakes. The important thing is that we grasp the central hope of the ultimate resurrection, set within the new creation itself, and that we reorder all our thinking and speaking about every other after-death question in that light.

Whenever I have spoken about these issues over the last decade or so, someone always asks, "What about hell?" This question really demands a book in itself, and I am torn between my lack of desire to write such a book and my recognition that one must at least say something.

Part of the difficulty of the topic, as with the others we have been studying, is that the word *hell* conjures up an image gained more from medieval imagery than from the earliest Christian writings. Just as many who were brought up to think of God as a bearded old gentleman sitting on a cloud decided that when they stopped believing in such a being they had therefore stopped believing in God, so many who were taught to think of hell as a literal underground location full of worms and fire, or for that matter as a kind of torture chamber at the center of God's castle of heavenly delights, decided that when they stopped believing in that, so they stopped believing in hell. The first group decided that because they couldn't believe in childish images of God, they must be atheists. The second decided that because they couldn't believe in childish images of hell, they must be universalists.

There are of course better reasons for becoming an atheist and better reasons for becoming a universalist. Many who occupy one of those positions have gone by a much more sophisticated route than the ones I just described. But, at least at a popular level, it is not the serious early Christian doctrine of final judgment that has been rejected but rather one or other gross caricature.

The most common New Testament word sometimes translated by *hell* is *Gehenna*. Gehenna was a place, not just an idea: it was the rubbish heap outside the southwest corner of the old city of Jerusalem. There is to this day a valley at that point that bears the name Ge Hinnom. When I was in Jerusalem a few years ago, I was taken to a classy restaurant on the western slope of this famous valley, and we witnessed a spectacular fireworks display, organized no doubt without deliberate irony, on the site to which Jesus was referring to when he spoke about the smoldering fires of Gehenna. But, as with his language about heaven, so with his talk of Gehenna: once Christian readers had been sufficiently distanced from the original meaning of the words, alternative images would come to mind, generated not by Jesus or the New Testament but by the stock of images, some of them extremely lurid, supplied by ancient and medieval folklore and imagination.

The point is that when Jesus was warning his hearers about Gehenna, he was not, as a general rule, telling them that unless they repented in this life they would burn in the next one. As with God's kingdom, so with its opposite: it is *on earth* that things matter, not somewhere else. His message to his contemporaries was stark and (as we would say today) political. Unless they turned back from their hopeless and rebellious dreams of establishing God's kingdom in their own terms, not least through armed revolt against Rome, then the Roman juggernaut would do what large, greedy, and ruthless empires have always done to smaller countries (not least in the Middle East) whose resources they covet or whose strategic location they are anxious to guard. Rome would turn Jerusalem into a hideous, stinking extension of its own smoldering rubbish heap. When Jesus said, "Unless you repent, you will all likewise perish," that is the primary meaning he had in mind.[9]

It is therefore only by extension, and with difficulty, that we can extrapolate from the many gospel sayings that articulate this urgent, immediate warning to the deeper question of a warning about what may happen after death itself. The two parables that appear to address this question directly are, we should remember, *parables,* not actual descriptions of the afterlife. They use stock imagery from ancient Judaism, such as "Abraham's bosom," not to teach about what happens after death but to insist on justice and mercy within the present life.[10] This is not to say that Jesus would have dissented from their implied picture of postmortem realities. It is, rather, to point out that to take the scene of Abraham, the Rich Man, and Lazarus literally is about as sensible as trying to find out the name of the Prodigal Son. Jesus simply didn't say very much about the future life; he was, after all, primarily concerned to announce that God's kingdom was coming "on earth as in heaven." He gave (as we have seen) no fresh teaching on the question of the resurrection apart from dark hints that it was going to happen, and happen soon, to one person ahead of everyone else; for the rest, he was content to reinforce the normal Jewish picture. In the same way, he was not concerned to give any fresh instruction on postmortem judgment apart from the strange hints that it was going to be dramatically and horribly anticipated in one particular way, in space-time history, within a generation.

We cannot therefore look to Jesus's teaching for any fresh detail on whether there really are some who finally reject God and, as it were, have that rejection ratified. All the signs, of course, are that he went along with the normal first-century Jewish perception: there would indeed be such people, with the only surprise being the surprise experienced, by sheep and goats alike, at their fate and at the evidence on which it was based.[11] And the early Christian writers go along with this. Hell, and final judgment, is not a major topic in the letters (though when it comes it is very important, as for instance in Romans 2:1–16); it is not mentioned at all in Acts; and the vivid pictures toward the end of the book of Revelation, while being extremely important, have always proved among the hardest parts of scripture to interpret with any certainty. All this should warn us against the cheerful double dogmatism that has bedeviled discussion of these topics—the dogmatism, that is, both of the person who knows exactly who is and who isn't "going to hell" and of the universalist who is absolutely certain that there is no such place or that if there is it will, at the last, be empty.

That latter kind of universalism was the normal working assumption of many theologians and clergy in the liberal heyday of the 1960s and 1970s and has remained a fixed point, almost in some cases *the* fixed point, for many whose thinking was shaped in that period. I well remember, in one of my first tutorials at Oxford, being told by my tutor that he and many others believed that "though hell may exist, it will at the last be untenanted"—in other words, that hell would turn out to be purgatory after all, an unpleasant preparation for eventual bliss. The merest mention of final judgment has been squeezed out of Christian consciousness in several denominations, including my own, by the cavalier omission of verses from public biblical reading. Whenever you see, in an official lectionary, the command to omit two or three verses, you can normally be sure that they contain words of judgment. Unless, of course, they are about sex.

But the worm has turned, theologically speaking, in the last twenty years. The failure of liberal optimism in Western society has been matched by the obvious failure of the equivalent liberal optimism in theology, driven as it was by the spirit of the age. It is a shame to have to rerun the story of nearly a hundred years ago, with Karl Barth furiously rejecting the liberal theology that had created the climate for the First World War, but it does sometimes feel as though that is what has happened. Faced with the Balkans, Rwanda, the Middle East, Darfur, and all kinds of other horrors that enlightened Western thought can neither explain nor alleviate, opinion in many quarters has, rightly in my view, come to see that there must be such a thing as judgment. Judgment—the sovereign declaration that *this* is good and to be upheld and vindicated, and *that* is evil and to be condemned—is the only alternative to chaos. There are some things, quite a lot of them in fact, that one must not tolerate lest one merely collude with wickedness. We all know this perfectly well, yet we conveniently forget it whenever squeamishness or the demands of current opinion make it easier to go with the flow of social convention. The problem is that much theology, having lived for so long on the convenience food of an easygoing tolerance of everything, an "inclusivity" with as few boundaries as McWorld, has become depressingly flabby, unable to climb even the lower slopes of social and cultural judgment let alone the steep upper reaches of that judgment of which the early Christians spoke and wrote.

But judgment is necessary—unless we were to conclude, absurdly, that nothing much is wrong or, blasphemously, that God doesn't mind very much. In the justly famous phrase of Miroslav Volf, there must be "exclusion" before there can be "embrace": evil must be identified, named, and dealt with before there can be reconciliation. That is the basis on which Desmond Tutu has built his mind-blowing work on the South African Commission for Truth and Reconciliation.[12] And—this is of course the crunch—where those who have acted wickedly refuse to see the point, there can be no reconciliation, no embrace.

God is utterly committed to set the world right in the end. This doctrine, like that of resurrection itself, is held firmly in place by the belief in God as creator, on the one side, and the belief in his goodness, on the other. And that setting right must necessarily involve the elimination of all that distorts God's good and lovely creation and in particular of all that defaces his image-bearing human creatures. Not to put too fine a point upon it, there will be no barbed wire in the kingdom of God. And those whose whole being has become dependent upon barbed wire will have no place there either.

For "barbed wire," of course, read whichever catalog of awfulnesses you prefer: genocide, nuclear bombs, child prostitution, the arrogance of empire, the commodification of souls, the idolization of race. The New Testament has several such categories, functioning as red flashing lights to warn against going down a road that leads straight to a fenceless cliff. And in the analysis offered by early Christians from Paul onward, such patterns of behavior have three things to be said about them.

First, they all stem from the primal fault, which is idolatry, worshipping that which is not God as if it were. Second, they all show the telltale marks of the consequent fault, which is subhuman behavior, that is, the failure fully to reflect the image of God, that missing the mark as regards full, free, and genuine humanness for which the New Testament's regular word is *hamartia,* "sin." (Sin, we note, is not the breaking of arbitrary rules; rather, the rules are the thumbnail sketches of different types of dehumanizing behavior.) Third, it is perfectly possible, and it really does seem to happen in practice, that this idolatry and dehumanization become so endemic in the life and chosen behavior of an individual, and indeed of groups, that unless there is a specific turning away from such a way of life, those who persist are conniving at their own ultimate dehumanization.

This is at the heart of the way in which I believe we can today restate the doctrine of final judgment. I find it quite impossible, reading the New Testament on the one hand and the newspaper on the other, to suppose that there will be no ultimate condemnation, no final loss, no human beings to whom, as C. S. Lewis put it, God will eventually say, "*Thy* will be done." I wish it were otherwise, but one cannot forever whistle "There's a wideness in God's mercy" in the darkness of Hiroshima, of Auschwitz, of the murder of children and the careless greed that enslaves millions with debts not their own. Humankind cannot, alas, bear very much reality, and the massive denial of reality by the cheap and cheerful universalism of Western liberalism has a lot to answer for.

But if there is indeed final condemnation for those who, by their idolatry, dehumanize themselves and drag others down with them, the account I have suggested of how this works in practice provides a somewhat different picture from those normally imagined.

The traditional view is that those who spurn God's salvation, who refuse to turn from idolatry and wickedness, are held forever in conscious torment. Sometimes this is sharpened up by overenthusiastic preachers and teachers who claim to know precisely which sorts of behavior are bound to lead to hell and which, though reprehensible, are still forgivable. But the traditional picture is clear: such human beings will continue to be, in some sense, human beings, and they will be punished in an endless time.

This account is then opposed by the universalists. Sometimes they suggest (rather after the manner of Shakespeare in *Measure for Measure*) that God will be merciful even to the utterly abhorrent, to mass murderers and child rapists. Sometimes they modify this: God will continue, after death, to offer all people the chance of repentance until they finally give in to the offer of his love.

A middle way is offered by the so-called conditionalists. They propose "conditional immortality": those who persistently refuse God's love and his way of life in the present world will simply cease to exist. Immortality, such theories point out, is not (despite the popularity of Platonism!) an innate human characteristic; it is something that, as Paul says, only God possesses by right and hence is a gift that God can choose to bestow or withhold.[13] According to this theory, then, God will simply not confer immortality on those who in this life continue impenitently to worship idols and thereby to destroy their own humanness. This view is therefore sometimes known as annihilationism; such people will cease to exist. That word, however, is perhaps too strong, suggesting that such people are actively destroyed rather than merely failing to receive a gift that had been held out to them and that they consistently rejected.

Over against these three options, I propose a view that combines what seem to me the strong points of the first and third. The greatest objection to the traditional view in recent times—and the last two hundred years have seen a massive swing toward universalism in the Western churches, at least the so-called mainstream ones—has come from the deep revulsion many feel at the idea of the torture chamber in the middle of the castle of delights, the concentration camp in the middle of the beautiful countryside, the idea that among the delights of the blessed we should include the contemplation of the torments of the wicked. However much we tell ourselves that God must condemn evil if he is a good God and that those who love God must endorse that condemnation, as soon as these pictures present themselves to our minds, we turn away in disgust. The conditionalist avoids this at the apparent cost of belittling those scriptural passages that appear to speak unambiguously of a *continuing* state for those who reject the worship of the true God and the way of humanness, which follows from it.

Using that analysis, though, presents us with the following possibility, which I believe does justice both to the key texts and to the realities of human life of which, after a century of horror mostly dreamed up by human beings, we are now all too well aware. When human beings give their heartfelt allegiance to and worship that which is not God, they progressively cease to reflect the image of God. One of the primary laws of human life is that you become like what you worship; what's more, you *reflect* what you worship not only back to the object itself but also outward to the world around. Those who worship money increasingly define themselves in terms of it and increasingly treat other people as creditors, debtors, partners, or customers rather than as human beings. Those who worship sex define themselves in terms of it (their preferences, their practices, their past histories) and increasingly treat other people as actual or potential sexual objects. Those who worship power define themselves in terms of it and treat other people as either collaborators, competitors, or pawns. These and many other forms of idolatry combine in a thousand ways, all of them damaging to the image-bearing quality of the people concerned and of those whose lives they touch. My suggestion is that it is possible for human beings so to continue down this road, so to refuse all whisperings of good news, all glimmers of the true light, all promptings to turn and go the other way, all signposts to the love of God, that after death they become at last, by their own effective choice, *beings that once were human but now are not,* creatures that have ceased to bear the divine image at all. With the death of that body in which they inhabited God's good world, in which the flickering flame of goodness had not been completely snuffed out, they pass simultaneously not only beyond hope but also beyond pity. There is no concentration camp in the beautiful countryside, no torture chamber in the palace of delight. Those creatures that still exist in an ex-human state, no longer reflecting their maker in any meaningful sense, can no longer excite in themselves or others the natural sympathy some feel even for the hardened criminal.

I am well aware that I have now wandered into territory that no one can claim to have mapped. Jesus, Christians believe, has been to hell and back, but to say that is to stand gaping into the darkness, not to write a travel brochure for future visitors. The last thing I want is for anyone to suppose that I (or anyone else) know very much about all this. Nor do I want anyone to suppose I enjoy speculating in this manner. But I find myself driven, by the New Testament and the sober realities of this world, to this kind of a resolution to one of the darkest theological mysteries. I should be glad to be proved wrong but not at the cost of the foundational claims that this world is the good creation of the one true God and that he will at the end bring about that judgment at which the whole creation will rejoice.

CONCLUSION: HUMAN GOALS AND NEW CREATION

But I cannot end this chapter on that note—for the very good reason that the New Testament, again and again, refuses to end on it either. Paul in Romans is quite clear that there will indeed be final condemnation for "those who are factious and disobey the truth, but obey wickedness"; but, as the letter goes on, his great emphasis falls on the fact that God has shut up all people in the prison house of disobedience in order that he may have mercy upon all.[14] True, it is clear from that passage and others like it that he does not mean "all people individually" but rather "people of all sorts." But when Paul says "all" he regularly reaches out beyond what his hearers might have expected to show that God's powerful love embraces the unexpected as well as the obvious. Since Paul knew that his own hard and bitter heart had been changed by God's grace, he also knew that there was nobody this side of the grave who could not in principle be similarly reached and changed.

Likewise, the majestic but mysterious ending of the Revelation of John leaves us with fascinating and perhaps frustrating hints of future purposes, further work of which the eventual new creation is just the beginning. The description of the New Jerusalem in chapters 21 and 22 is quite clear that some categories of people are "outside": the dogs, the fornicators, those who speak and make lies. But then, just when we have in our minds a picture of two nice, tidy categories, the insiders and the outsiders, we find that the river of the water of life flows *out of* the city; that growing on either bank is the tree of life, not a single tree but a great many; and that "the leaves of the tree are for the healing of the nations." There is a great mystery here, and all our speaking about God's eventual future must make room for it. This is not at all to cast doubt on the reality of final judgment for those who have resolutely worshipped and served the idols that dehumanize us and deface God's world. It is to say that God is always the God of surprises.

But the most important thing to say at the end of this discussion, and of this section of the book, is that heaven and hell are not, so to speak, what the whole game is about. This is one of the central surprises in the Christian hope. The whole point of my argument so far is that the question of what happens to me after death is *not* the major, central, framing question that centuries of theological tradition have supposed. The New Testament, true to its Old Testament roots, regularly insists that the major, central, framing question is that of God's purpose of rescue and re-creation for the whole world, the entire cosmos. The destiny of individual human beings must be understood within that context—not simply in the sense that we are only part of a much larger picture but also in the sense that part of the whole point of being saved in the present is so that we can play a vital role (Paul speaks of this role in the shocking terms of being "fellow workers with God") within that larger picture and purpose. And that in turn makes us realize that the question of our own destiny, in terms of the alternatives of joy or woe, is probably the wrong way of looking at the whole question. The question ought to be, *How will God's new creation come?* and then, *How will we humans contribute to that renewal of creation and to the fresh projects that the creator God will launch in his new world?* The choice before humans would then be framed differently: are you going to worship the creator God and discover thereby what it means to become fully and gloriously human, reflecting his powerful, healing, transformative love into the world? Or are you going to worship the world as it is, boosting your corruptible humanness by gaining power or pleasure from forces within the world but merely contributing thereby to your own dehumanization and the further corruption of the world itself?

This reflection leads to a further, and sobering, thought. If what I have suggested is anywhere near the mark, then to insist on heaven and hell as the ultimate question—to insist, in other words, that what happens eventually to individual humans is the most important thing in the world—may be to make a mistake similar to the one made by the Jewish people in the first century, the mistake that both Jesus and Paul addressed. Israel believed (so Paul tells us, and he should know) that the purposes of the creator God all came down to this question: how is God going to rescue Israel? What the gospel of Jesus revealed, however, was that the purposes of God were reaching out to a different question: how is God going to rescue the world *through Israel* and thereby rescue Israel itself as part of the process but not as the point of it all? Maybe what we are faced with in our own day is a similar challenge: to focus not on the question of which human beings God is going to take to heaven and how he is going to do it but on the question of how God is going to redeem and renew his creation *through human beings* and how he is going to rescue those humans themselves as part of the process but not as the point of it all. If we could reread Romans and Revelation—and the rest of the New Testament, of course—in the light of this reframing of the question, I think we would find much food for thought.

And if—to revisit for a moment the discussions we had in chapter 2—we could rework the church's liturgies so that they expressed the surprising hope held out in the New Testament, we would find ourselves sustained and strengthened by that larger vision.

We would find, in particular, that the question of the church's mission was suddenly catapulted into center stage and reshaped in the process. But for that we must move to the final part of the book.

PART III

HOPE IN PRACTICE: RESURRECTION
AND THE MISSION OF THE CHURCH

12. RETHINKING SALVATION: HEAVEN, EARTH, AND THE KINGDOM OF GOD

INTRODUCTION

We have now reached the point where we must ask: So what? Is all this talk about God's ultimate future, about "life after life after death," simply a matter of tidying up our beliefs about what will happen in the very end, or does it have any practical consequences here and now? Is it simply a matter of getting our teaching and preaching right and of ordering our funerals and other liturgies so that they reflect biblical teaching about death and what lies beyond instead of nonbiblical and even antibiblical ideas that have crept into the church here and there?

Let me approach this question obliquely. Among the objections that are regularly raised to believing in the bodily resurrection of Jesus, I recently came across a remarkable one that shows, it seems to me, a total misunderstanding of what Christianity is all about. One of the leading American writers on early Christianity, Dominic Crossan, has asked on a number of occasions: Even if Jesus did rise from the dead, so what? Very nice for him, but what's it got to do with anything else? Why should he be so specially favored? If God can pull off a stunt like that, why can't he intervene and do a lot more useful things like stopping genocide or earthquakes?[1] And this objection chimes in with things that have been said, for instance, by my distinguished predecessor Bishop David Jenkins, constituting what you might call the moral objection (as opposed to the historical or scientific one) to believing in Jesus's bodily resurrection.

I don't want to comment here on the objection itself—though we may note that when historians start to make arguments about what happened on the grounds of what ought (or ought not) to have happened, they put themselves on very thin ice indeed. What I want to do, rather, is to show what the New Testament says by way of answer to the question, What's the resurrection of Jesus got to do with anything else? and to point to some conclusions from this for the life of the church and of Christians today.[2]

Part of the energy for this undertaking comes from two further observations, this time about the way we keep Easter in the contemporary church. (The church I know best is the Church of England, but conversations with friends in other churches indicate that similar phenomena can be found in plenty of other churches too.)

A good many Easter hymns start by assuming that the point of Easter is that it proves the existence of life after death and encourages us to hope for it. This is then regularly, but ironically, combined with a view of that life after death in which the specific element of resurrection has been quietly removed. "May we go where he is gone," we sing at the end of one well-known hymn, "rest and reign with him in heaven!" But that is precisely *not* the point that the New Testament draws from Jesus's resurrection. Yes, there is a promised rest after the labors of this life, and the word *heaven* may be an appropriate, though vague, way of denoting where this rest takes place. But this time of rest is the prelude to something very different, which will emphatically involve earth as well. Earth—the renewed earth—is where the reign will take place, which is why the New Testament regularly speaks not of our going to be where Jesus is but of his coming to where we are, as we saw in the previous part of the book.

But even when we become more precise and focused about what the New Testament says about our own future hope—the final resurrection itself and whatever intermediate state may precede it, which we discussed in chapters 10 and 11—this is still, maybe to our surprise, not what the New Testament sees as the main result of the resurrection of Jesus of Nazareth. Yes, that resurrection does indeed give us a sure and certain hope. If that's not the case, we are of all people, as Paul says, most to be pitied.[3] But when the New Testament strikes the great Easter bell, the main resonances it sets up are not simply about ourselves and about whatever future world God is ultimately going to make, when heaven and earth are joined together and renewed at last from top to bottom. Precisely because the resurrection has happened as an event *within our own world,* its implications and effects are to be felt within our own world, here and now.

This is one of the points at which it simply won't do to say (as, according to various opinion polls, a lot of clergy and even some bishops are inclined to say) that believing in the bodily resurrection of Jesus is a take-it-or-leave-it option. Jesus's bodily resurrection marks a watershed. It may look like only a few steps this way or that to move from one side to the other, but if you accept the bodily resurrection of Jesus all the streams flow in one direction, and if you don't they all flow in the other direction. And, to put it kindly but bluntly, if you go in the other direction, away from the bodily resurrection, you may be left with something that looks a bit like Christianity, but it won't be what the New Testament writers were talking about. Please note, this is not at all a matter of putting a check beside some dogmas and not others, with the resurrection simply being a rather more difficult box to check off than some others. It is a matter of a belief that is a symptom of an entire worldview, an accurate index to a way of looking at everything else.

The point of this final section of the book is that a proper grasp of the (surprising) *future* hope held out to us in Jesus Christ leads directly and, to many people, equally surprisingly, to a vision of the *present* hope that is the basis of all Christian mission. To hope for a better future in this world—for the poor, the sick, the lonely and depressed, for the slaves, the refugees, the hungry and homeless, for the abused, the paranoid, the downtrodden and despairing, and in fact for the whole wide, wonderful, and wounded world—is not something *else,* something extra, something tacked on to the gospel as an afterthought. And to work for that intermediate hope, the surprising hope that comes forward from God's ultimate future into God's urgent present, is not a *distraction from* the task of mission and evangelism in the present. It is a central, essential, vital, and life-giving part of it. Mostly, Jesus himself got a hearing from his contemporaries because of what he was *doing.* They saw him saving people from sickness and death, and they heard him talking about a salvation, the message for which they had longed, that would go beyond the immediate into the ultimate future. But the two were not unrelated, the present one a mere visual aid of the future one or a trick to gain people's attention. The whole point of what Jesus was up to was that he was doing, close up, in the present, what he was promising long-term, in the future. And what he was promising for that future, and doing in that present, was not saving souls for a disembodied eternity but rescuing people from the corruption and decay of the way the world presently is so they could enjoy, already in the present, that renewal of creation which is God's ultimate purpose—and so they could thus become colleagues and partners in that larger project.

When we turn to Paul, the verse that has always struck me in this connection is 1 Corinthians 15:58. Paul, we remind ourselves, has just written the longest and densest chapter in any of his letters, discussing the future resurrection of the body in great and complex detail. How might we expect him to finish such a chapter? By saying, "Therefore, since you have such a great hope, sit back and relax because you know God's got a great future in store for you"? No. Instead, he says, "Therefore, my beloved ones, be steadfast, immovable, always abounding in the work of the Lord, because you know that in the Lord your labour is not in vain."

What does he mean? How does believing in the future resurrection lead to getting on with the work in the present? Quite straightforwardly. The point of the resurrection, as Paul has been arguing throughout the letter, is that *the present bodily life is not valueless just because it will die.* God will raise it to new life. What you do with your body in the present matters because God has a great future in store for it. And if this applies to ethics, as in 1 Corinthians 6, it certainly also applies to the various vocations to which God's people are called. What you *do* in the present—by painting, preaching, singing, sewing, praying, teaching, building hospitals, digging wells, campaigning for justice, writing poems, caring for the needy, loving your neighbor as yourself—*will last into God's future.* These activities are not simply ways of making the present life a little less beastly, a little more bearable, until the day when we leave it behind altogether (as the hymn so mistakenly puts it, "Until that day when all the blest to endless rest are called away"). They are part of what we may call *building for God's kingdom.*

I shall come back to the meaning of "God's kingdom" presently. But let us note, at the outset of this final section of the book, that the promise of new creation—the promise we have been studying throughout this book—is not and cannot be simply about straightening out ideas about life after death. It is about the mission of the church. There has been a lot of talk where I work about a "mission-shaped church," following a report with that title, urging today's church to regard mission not as an extra, something to fit in if there's any time left over from other concerns, but as the central and shaping dynamic of its life.[4] But if this is to mean what it ought to mean, we must also reshape our ideas of mission itself. It's no good falling back into the tired old split-level world where some people believe in evangelism in terms of saving souls for a timeless eternity and other people believe in mission in terms of working for justice, peace, and hope in the present world. That great divide has nothing to do with Jesus and the New Testament and everything to do with the silent enslavement of many Christians (both conservative and radical) to the Platonic ideology of the Enlightenment. Once we get the resurrection straight, we can and must get mission straight. If we want a mission-shaped church, what we need is a hope-shaped mission. And if that is surprising, we ought to be getting used to it by now.

We begin with one of the largest topics of all, which most Christians take for granted but which is in urgent need of a radical rethink: salvation.

THE MEANING OF SALVATION

The truly exciting, surprising, and perhaps frightening thing about where we have now got to in this book is that we are now forced to rethink the very meaning of salvation itself.

Mention salvation, and almost all Western Christians assume that you mean going to heaven when you die. But a moment's thought, in the light of all we have said so far, reveals that this simply cannot be right. Salvation means, of course, rescue. But what are we ultimately to be rescued from? The obvious answer is death. But if, when we die, all that happens is that our bodies decompose while our souls (or whatever other word we want to use for our continuing existence) go on elsewhere, this doesn't mean we've been *rescued from* death. It simply means that we've died.

And if God's good creation—of the world, of life as we know it, of our glorious and remarkable bodies, brains, and bloodstreams—really *is* good, and if God wants to reaffirm that goodness in a wonderful act of new creation at the last, then to see the death of the body and the escape of the soul as salvation is not simply slightly off course, in need of a few subtle alterations and modifications. It is totally and utterly wrong. It is colluding with death. It is conniving at death's destruction of God's good, image-bearing human creatures while consoling ourselves with the (essentially non-Christian and non-Jewish) thought that the really important bit of ourselves is saved from this wicked, nasty body and this sad, dark world of space, time, and matter! As we have seen, the whole of the Bible, from Genesis to Revelation, speaks out against such nonsense. *It is, however, what most Western Christians, including most Bible Christians of whatever sort, actually believe.* This is a serious state of affairs, reinforced not only in popular teaching but also in liturgies, public prayers, hymns, and homilies of every kind.

All this was borne in on me recently when I read a popular-level book by the well-known Christian writer Adrian Plass. Plass doesn't claim to be a profound theologian, though actually his great contribution, through humor, irony, and the occasional deeply poignant story, is often to make us think afresh about things we take for granted. So when someone gave me his new book, *Bacon Sandwiches and Salvation,* I looked forward to more of the same. And I wasn't disappointed: the book is funny, shrewd, deliberately silly, and deliberately serious.[5]

When it came to the most serious bit, on salvation itself, I was looking forward to some fresh thinking. Plass himself raises the questions that puzzle many people today:

> But what is it all about? What does it mean to be saved? Saved from what? Saved *for* what? Should the whole business of salvation have a significant impact on my present as well as on my future? Speaking of the future, what can we expect from an eternity spent in heaven? How can we possibly make sense of heaven when our feet remain so solidly on Earth? Where is the interface, the meeting point between the flesh and the Spirit? And when all the strange religious terms and voices and patterns and mantras and man-made conventions have faded away, what will be left?[6]

Well, quite. That is indeed the puzzle we found in the early chapters of the present book. I turned the page, eager to see what Plass would come up with as a fresh statement of salvation. But I was disappointed:

> [God's] plan was for us to live in perfect harmony with him. . . . Then something went horribly, dreadfully wrong. . . . This truly

ghastly thing that happened somehow separated human beings from God, who nevertheless continued to love them/us with a passion that is impossible to comprehend. Desperate to heal the rift, he devised a rescue plan. . . . Because Jesus was executed on the cross it is now possible for any or all of us, through repentance, baptism and obedience, *to recover the magnificent relationship with God* that was destroyed in days gone by. . . . If you and I accept the death and resurrection of Jesus as a living, divine, working mechanism in our own lives *we shall one day go home to God and find peace.* . . . The Holy Spirit, sent by Jesus himself after his death, offers support and strength for those who call on him.[7]

Now I know it is hardly fair to take on Adrian Plass in a book like this. He does not claim to be writing a work of theology, and as I said, his book has many wonderful insights (as well as many corny jokes). I cite him simply as a classic example—all the more powerful because at this point he is so clearly articulating what so many take for granted—of the normal Western Christian view: that salvation is about "my relationship with God" in the present and about "going home to God and finding peace" in the future. The fact that, though asking so many probing questions and clearly being dissatisfied with the stock answers he has received, he has not thought to question these answers themselves shows how deeply rooted they are in an entire tradition. Those of us who have known this tradition all our lives—not just an evangelical tradition, by the way, but at this point the entire tradition of the Western church—will recognize his summary as being what most Christians believe and, indeed, what most non-Christians assume Christians believe. And, to make the point once more as forcibly as I can, this belief is simply not what the New Testament teaches.

The day after writing this paragraph I had another, and sharply personal, example of the same problem. An anguished e-mail appeared from the man who is translating my book *Judas and the Gospel of Jesus* into one of the Balkan languages. He had just got to the point where I was warning that some Western Christians have embraced something worryingly similar to second-century Gnosticism when they think of the present world as evil and the only solution being to escape it and to go to heaven instead. This produced a tirade of accusations from the translator, for whom that seemed to be precisely what he thought the gospel was all about. Hadn't I read the Bible? Didn't I believe in heaven? Or in Jesus? Was I trying to invent a new religion?

Thus far, I am simply rubbing in the point I have been making throughout the book. But in this closing section we have to look head-on at the problem that directly results from this widespread misperception of the Christian view of salvation. As long as we see salvation in terms of going to heaven when we die, the main work of the church is bound to be seen in terms of saving souls for that future. But when we see salvation, as the New Testament sees it, in terms of God's promised new heavens and new earth and of our promised resurrection to share in that new and gloriously embodied reality—what I have called life after life after death—then the main work of the church here and now demands to be rethought in consequence.

At this point the well-known slogan of Christian Aid, "We Believe in Life Before Death," comes into its own. Life *before* death is what is threatened, called into question, by the idea that salvation is merely life *after* death. If we're heading for a timeless, bodiless eternity, then what's the fuss about putting things right in the present world? But if what matters is the newly embodied life *after* life after death, then the presently embodied life *before* death can at last be seen not as an interesting but ultimately irrelevant present preoccupation, not simply as a "vale of tears and soul-making" through which we have to pass to a blessed and disembodied final state, but as the essential, vital time, place, and matter into which God's future purposes have already broken in the resurrection of Jesus and in which those future purposes are now to be further anticipated through the mission of the church. Life after death, it seems, can be a serious distraction not only from the ultimate life *after* life after death, but also from life *before* death. To ignore this is in fact to collude not only with death but also with all sorts of other powers that gain their force from their own alliance with that ultimate enemy.

Salvation, then, is not "going to heaven" but "being raised to life in God's new heaven and new earth." But as soon as we put it like this we realize that the New Testament is full of hints, indications, and downright assertions that this salvation isn't just something we have to wait for in the long-distance future. We can enjoy it here and now (always partially, of course, since we all still have to die), genuinely anticipating in the present what is to come in the future. "We were saved," says Paul in Romans 8:24, "in hope." The verb "we were saved" indicates a past action, something that has already taken place, referring obviously to the complex of faith and baptism of which Paul has been speaking in the letter so far. But this remains "in hope" because we still look forward to the ultimate future salvation of which he speaks in (for instance) Romans 5:9, 10.

This explains at a stroke the otherwise puzzling fact that the New Testament often refers to salvation and being saved in terms of bodily events within the present world. "Come and save my daughter," begs Jairus; as Jesus is on his way to do so, the woman with the issue of blood thinks to herself, "If I can only touch his clothes I will be saved"; "Daughter," says Jesus to her after her healing, "your faith has saved you."[8] Matthew, telling the same story, abbreviates it drastically, but at this point he adds an extra note: "And the woman was saved from that moment on."[9] It is fascinating to see how passages like this—and there are many of them—are often juxtaposed with others that speak of salvation in larger terms, seeming to go beyond present physical healing or rescue. This juxtaposition makes some Christians nervous (surely, they think, salvation ought to be a *spiritual* matter!), but it doesn't seem to have troubled the early church at all.[10] For the first Christians, the ultimate salvation was all about God's new world, and the point of what Jesus and the apostles were doing when they were healing people or being rescued from shipwreck or whatever was that this was a proper anticipation of that ultimate salvation, that healing transformation of space, time, and matter. The future rescue that God had planned and promised was starting to come true in the present. We are saved not as souls but as wholes.

(All sorts of things follow from this. We might notice, for instance, that theories of atonement, of the meaning of the cross, are not simply a set of alternative answers to the same question. They give the answers they give because of the question they ask. If the question is, How can I get to heaven despite the sin because of which I deserve to be punished? the answer may well be, Because Jesus has been punished in your place. But if the question is, How can God's plan to rescue and renew the entire world go ahead despite the corruption and decay that have come about because of human rebellion? the answer may well be, Because on the cross Jesus defeated the powers of evil, which have enslaved rebel humans and so ensured continuing corruption. Please note, *these and other possible questions and answers are not mutually exclusive.* My point is that reframing the question will mean rethinking the various answers we might give and the relationship between them. This is a large topic for another occasion.)[11]

But as soon as we grasp this—and I appreciate it takes quite a bit of latching onto for people who have spent their whole lives thinking the other way—we see that if salvation is that sort of thing, it can't be confined to human beings. When human beings are saved, in the past as a single coming-to-faith event, in the present through acts of healing and rescue, including answers to the prayer "lead us not into temptation, but deliver us from evil," and in the future when they are finally raised from the dead, this is always so that they can be genuine human beings in a fuller sense than they otherwise would have been. And genuine human beings, from Genesis 1 onward, are given the mandate of looking after creation, of bringing order to God's world, of establishing and maintaining communities. To suppose that we are saved, as it were, for our own private benefit, for the restoration of our own relationship with God (vital though that is!), and for our eventual homecoming and peace in heaven (misleading though that is!) is like a boy being given a baseball bat as a present and insisting that since it belongs to him, he must always and only play with it in private. But of course you can only do what you're meant to do with a baseball bat when you're playing with other people. And salvation only does what it's meant to do when those who have been saved, are being saved, and will one day fully be saved realize that they are saved not as souls but as wholes and not for themselves alone but for what God now longs to do through them.

The point is this. When God saves people in this life, by working through his Spirit to bring them to faith and by leading them to follow Jesus in discipleship, prayer, holiness, hope, and love, such people are designed—it isn't too strong a word—to be a sign and foretaste of what God wants to do for the entire cosmos. What's more, such people are not just to be a sign and foretaste of that ultimate salvation; they are to be *part of the means by which* God makes this happen in both the present and the future. That is what Paul insists on when he says that the whole creation is waiting with eager longing not just for its own redemption, its liberation from corruption and decay, but *for God's children to be revealed:* in other words, for the unveiling of those redeemed humans through whose stewardship creation will at last be brought back into that wise order for which it was made.[12] And since Paul makes it quite clear that those who believe in Jesus Christ, who are incorporated into him through baptism, are already God's children, are already themselves saved, this stewardship cannot be something to be postponed for the ultimate future. It must begin here and now.

In other words—to sum up where we've got so far—the work of salvation, in its full sense, is (1) about whole human beings, not merely souls; (2) about the present, not simply the future; and (3) about what God does *through* us, not merely what God does *in and for* us. If we can get this straight, we will rediscover the historic basis for the full-orbed mission of the church. To pursue this further, we need to look at the larger picture within which all this makes sense: the kingdom of God.

THE KINGDOM OF GOD

We have seen at several points in this book that the normal Christian understanding of kingdom, especially of kingdom of heaven, is simply mistaken. "God's kingdom" and "kingdom of heaven" mean the same thing: the sovereign rule of God (that is, the rule of heaven, of the one who lives in heaven), which according to Jesus was and is breaking in to the present world, to earth. That is what Jesus taught us to pray for. We have no right to omit that clause from the Lord's Prayer or to suppose that it doesn't really mean what it says.

This, as we have seen, is what the resurrection and ascension of Jesus and the gift of the Spirit are all about. They are designed not to take us away from this earth but rather to make us agents of the transformation of this earth, anticipating the day when, as we are promised, "the earth shall be full of the knowledge of the Lord, as the waters cover the sea." When the risen Jesus appears to his followers at the end of Matthew's gospel, he declares that all authority in heaven *and on earth* has been given to him. When John the Seer hears the thundering voices in heaven, they are singing, "The kingdom of the world has become the kingdom of our Lord and of his Messiah, and he shall reign for ever and ever."[13] And the point of the gospels—of Matthew, Mark, Luke, and John together with Acts—is that *this has already begun.*

The question of *how* it has begun—in what sense it is inaugurated, anticipated, or whatever—has been the stuff of debate for a long time. But part of the problem with that debate is that those taking part in it do not usually clarify the question of *what precisely it is* that is begun, launched, or initiated. At one level it is clearly the hope of Israel, as expressed in classic kingdom passages such as

Isaiah 52:7–12. There, "God becoming king at last" means the end of exile, the defeat of evil, and the return of Israel's God to Zion. We can see all of that becoming the major theme not only of Jesus's life and public career but also of his own interpretation of his death.[14]

But underneath that again, when we stand back, is the meaning of God's kingdom, to which the hope of Israel was designed to contribute—or, to put it another way, the meaning because of which God called Israel in the first place. Faced with his beautiful and powerful creation in rebellion, God longed to set it right, to rescue it from continuing corruption and impending chaos and to bring it back into order and fruitfulness. God longed, in other words, to reestablish his wise sovereignty over the whole creation, which would mean a great act of healing and rescue. He did not want to rescue humans *from* creation any more than he wanted to rescue Israel *from* the Gentiles. He wanted to rescue Israel *in order that Israel might be a light to the Gentiles,* and he wanted thereby to rescue humans *in order that humans might be his rescuing stewards over creation.* That is the inner dynamic of the kingdom of God.

That, in other words, is how the God who made humans to be his stewards over creation and who called Israel to be the light of the world is to become king, in accordance with his original intention in creation, on the one hand, and his original intention in the covenant, on the other. To snatch saved souls away to a disembodied heaven would destroy the whole point. God is to become king of the whole world at last. And he will do this not by declaring that the inner dynamic of creation (that it be ruled by humans) was a mistake, nor by declaring that the inner dynamic of his covenant (that Israel would be the means of saving the nations) was a failure, but rather by fulfilling them both. That is more or less what Paul's letter to the Romans is all about.[15]

This is the purpose that has been realized in Jesus Christ. One of the greatest problems of the Western church, ever since the Reformation at least, is that it hasn't really known what the gospels were there for. Imagining that the point of Christianity was to enable people to go to heaven, most Western Christians supposed that the mechanism by which this happened was the one they found in the writings of Paul (I stress, the one *they found;* I have argued elsewhere that this involved misunderstanding Paul as well) and that the four gospels were simply there to give backup information about Jesus, his teaching, his moral example, and his atoning death. This long tradition screened out the possibility that when Jesus spoke of God's kingdom, he was talking not about a heaven for which he was preparing his followers but about something that was happening in and on this earth, through his work, then through his death and resurrection, and then through the Spirit-led work to which they would be called.

Part of the difficulty people still have in coming to terms with the gospels, read in this way, is that *kingdom of God* has been a flag of convenience under which all sorts of ships have sailed. Some used the phrase as a cover for pursuing business of their own—programs of moral, social, or political improvement or upheaval, agendas of the left and the right, of the well-meaning but muddled and of the less well-meaning but all too clear. Many who went this route treated the gospels as though they were simply stories about Jesus going around helping people as best he could, with the unfortunate sequel of his untimely death. And many other Christians, seeing this shallow and confused exegesis and application, reacted angrily against what is called kingdom theology as though it were simply an outdated and shallow corporate version of faddish self-help moralism. (This is a serious problem in some parts of America, where *kingdom* has become a slogan of this kind and has then been used to rule out or marginalize many aspects of orthodox Christian faith—precipitating among some would-be orthodox Christians a reaction against any social or political dimension to the gospel and against kingdom language altogether. By such means do we project our own confusions onto the text.)

But the fact that some people, and some movements, have misappropriated the kingdom theology of the gospels doesn't mean there isn't a reality of which such ideas are a caricature. What we find in the gospels is much, much more profound. Here we meet again a familiar problem, the problem of how Jesus's initial ministry joins up with his self-giving to death. I have argued at length elsewhere that Jesus never imagined that the kingdom he was launching through his healings, feastings, and teachings would be fulfilled without his death. Or, to put it the other way around, I and others have stressed that Jesus's death was not (and he did not think it was) about something other than the kingdom work to which he had devoted his short public career. The problem of evil, which looms up as the backdrop to the gospels, is not going to be dealt with even by Jesus's healings, feastings, and teachings. It certainly won't be dealt with by his then providing his followers with a fast-track route to a distant and disembodied heaven. It can only be dealt with—the kingdom can only come on earth as in heaven—through Jesus's own death and resurrection. That is a whole other story, though of course a central and vital one.[16]

But when we reintegrate what should never have been separated—the kingdom-inaugurating public work of Jesus and his redemptive death and resurrection—we find that the gospels tell a different story. It isn't just a story of some splendid and exciting social work with an unhappy conclusion. Nor is it just a story of an atoning death with an extended introduction. It is something much bigger than the sum of those two diminished perspectives. It is the story of God's kingdom being launched on earth as in heaven, generating a new state of affairs in which the power of evil has been decisively defeated, the new creation has been decisively launched, and Jesus's followers have been commissioned and equipped to put that victory and that inaugurated new world into practice. Atonement, redemption, and salvation are what happen on the way because engaging in this work demands that people themselves be rescued from the powers that enslave the world in order that they can in turn be rescuers. To put it another way, if you want to help inaugurate God's kingdom, you must follow in the way of the cross, and if you want to benefit from Jesus's saving death, you must become part of his kingdom project. There is only one Jesus, only one gospel story, albeit told in four kaleidoscopic patterns.[17]

Heaven's rule, God's rule, is thus to be put into practice in the world, resulting in salvation in both the present and the future, a salvation that is both *for* humans and, *through* saved humans, for the wider world. This is the solid basis for the mission of the church. But to explore this further will need another chapter.

13. BUILDING FOR THE KINGDOM

Many people, faced with the challenge to work for God's kingdom in the present, will at once object. "Doesn't that sound," they will ask, "as though you're trying to build God's kingdom by your own efforts?" Well, if it does sound like that, I'm sorry. It wasn't meant like that. Perhaps some further clarification is needed.

Let's be quite clear on two points. First, God builds God's kingdom. But God ordered his world in such a way that his own work within that world takes place not least through one of his creatures in particular, namely, the human beings who reflect his image. That, I believe, is central to the notion of being made in God's image. God intends his wise, creative, loving presence and power to be *reflected*—imaged, if you like—into his world *through* his human creatures. He has enlisted us to act as his stewards in the project of creation. And, following the disaster of rebellion and corruption, he has built into the gospel message the fact that through the work of Jesus and the power of the Spirit, he equips humans to help in the work of getting the project back on track. So the objection about us trying to build God's kingdom by our own efforts, though it seems humble and pious, can actually be a way of hiding from responsibility, of keeping one's head well down when the boss is looking for volunteers. Not that one can go on eluding God's call forever . . . but still.

Second, we need to distinguish between the final kingdom and the present anticipations of it. The final coming together of heaven and earth is, of course, God's supreme act of new creation, for which the only real prototype—other than the first creation itself—was the resurrection of Jesus. God alone will sum up all things in Christ, things in heaven and things on earth. He alone will make the "new heavens and new earth." It would be the height of folly to think that we could assist in that great work.

But what we can and must do in the present, if we are obedient to the gospel, if we are following Jesus, and if we are indwelt, energized, and directed by the Spirit, is to build *for* the kingdom. This brings us back to 1 Corinthians 15:58 once more: what you do in the Lord *is not in vain.* You are not oiling the wheels of a machine that's about to roll over a cliff. You are not restoring a great painting that's shortly going to be thrown on the fire. You are not planting roses in a garden that's about to be dug up for a building site. You are— strange though it may seem, almost as hard to believe as the resurrection itself—accomplishing something that will become in due course part of God's new world. Every act of love, gratitude, and kindness; every work of art or music inspired by the love of God and delight in the beauty of his creation; every minute spent teaching a severely handicapped child to read or to walk; every act of care and nurture, of comfort and support, for one's fellow human beings and for that matter one's fellow nonhuman creatures; and of course every prayer, all Spirit-led teaching, every deed that spreads the gospel, builds up the church, embraces and embodies holiness rather than corruption, and makes the name of Jesus honored in the world—all of this will find its way, through the resurrecting power of God, into the new creation that God will one day make. That is the logic of the mission of God. God's recreation of his wonderful world, which began with the resurrection of Jesus and continues mysteriously as God's people live in the risen Christ and in the power of his Spirit, means that what we do in Christ and by the Spirit in the present is not wasted. It will last all the way into God's new world. In fact, it will be enhanced there.

I have no idea what precisely this will mean in practice. I am putting up a signpost, not offering a photograph of what we will find once we get to where the signpost is pointing. I don't know what musical instruments we shall have to play Bach in God's new world, though I'm sure Bach's music will be there. I don't know how my planting a tree today will relate to the wonderful trees that there will be in God's recreated world, though I do remember Martin Luther's words about the proper reaction to knowing the kingdom was coming the next day being to go out and plant a tree. I do not know how the painting an artist paints today in prayer and wisdom will find a place in God's new world. I don't know how our work for justice for the poor, for remission of global debts, will reappear in that new world. But I know that God's new world of justice and joy, of hope for the whole earth, was launched when Jesus came out of the tomb on Easter morning, and I know that he calls his followers to live in him and by the power of his Spirit and so to be new-creation people here and now, bringing signs and symbols of the kingdom to birth on earth as in heaven. The resurrection of Jesus and the gift of the Spirit mean that we are called to bring real and effective signs of God's renewed creation to birth even in the midst of the present age. Not to bring works and signs of renewal to birth within God's creation is ultimately to collude, as Gnosticism always does, with the forces of sin and death themselves. But don't focus on the negative. Think of the positive: of the calling, in the present, to share in the surprising hope of God's whole new creation.

The image I often use in trying to explain this strange but important idea is that of the stonemason working on part of a great cathedral. The architect already drew up the plans and passed on instructions to the team of masons as to which stones need carving in what way. The foreman distributes these tasks among the team. One shapes stones for a particular tower or turret; another carves the delicate pattern that breaks up the otherwise forbidding straight lines; another works on gargoyles or coats of arms; another is making statues of saints, martyrs, kings, or queens. They are vaguely aware that the others are getting on with their tasks, and they know, of course, that many other entire departments are busy about quite different tasks as well. When they're finished with their stones and their statues, they hand them over without necessarily knowing very much about where in the eventual building their work will find its home. They may not have seen the complete architect's drawing of the whole building with their bit identified in its proper place. They may not live, either, to see the completed building with their work at last where it belongs. But they trust the architect that the work they have done in following instructions will not be wasted. They are not, themselves, building the cathedral, but they are building *for* the cathedral, and when the cathedral is complete their work will be enhanced, ennobled, will mean much more than it could have meant as they were chiseling it and shaping it down in the stonemasons' yard.

That image, of course, is itself incomplete since actually the cathedral is eventually built by the combination of all the artisans and craftspeople working together, whereas God's eventual kingdom will, as I have said, be a fresh gift of transformation and renewal from the Architect himself. But it is enough to indicate the way in which there is continuity as well as discontinuity between the present life, and the work we do in it, and the ultimate future life in which God has gathered all things together and transformed them, "making all things new" in Christ. What we do in the Lord is "not in vain," and that is the mandate we need for every act of justice and mercy, every program of ecology, every effort to reflect God's wise stewardly image into his creation. In the new creation the ancient human mandate to look after the garden is dramatically reaffirmed, as John hints in his resurrection story, where Mary supposes Jesus is the gardener. The resurrection of Jesus is the reaffirmation of the goodness of creation, and the gift of the Spirit is there to make us the fully human beings we were supposed to be, precisely so that we can fulfill that mandate at last.

The work we do in the present, then, gains its full significance from the eventual design in which it is meant to belong. Applied to the mission of the church, this means that we must work in the present for the advance signs of that eventual state of affairs when God is "all in all," when his kingdom has come and his will is done "on earth as in heaven." This will of course be radically different from the kind of work we would engage in if our sole task was to save souls for a disembodied heaven or simply to help people enjoy a fulfilling relationship with God as though that were the end of the matter. It will also be significantly different from the kind of work we might undertake if our sole task was to forget any God dimension at all and to try simply to make life better within the continuation of the world as it is.

This throws us headlong into some contentious, but important and necessary, areas. Today's church (including "emerging church," "liquid church," "fresh expressions of church," "mission-shaped church," and many others) is grappling with the question of what its mission and life might look like in the days to come. But the present mood of frustration with existing patterns of church life coupled with postmodern free-for-all experimentation, on the one hand, and residual Protestant fears about the created order, on the other, have conspired together to produce cheerful and sometimes not-so-cheerful chaos. This is the context within which a proper vision of biblical eschatology can and should generate a fresh, and no doubt controversial, vision of the church's mission.

To put it bluntly, creation is to be redeemed; that is, space is to be redeemed, time is to be redeemed, and matter is to be redeemed. God said "very good" over his space-time-and-matter creation, and though the redeeming of this world from its present corruption and decay will mean transformations we cannot imagine, the one thing we can be sure of is that this redeeming of creation will not mean that God will say, of space, time and matter, "Oh, well, nice try, good while it lasted but obviously gone bad, so let's drop it and go for a nonspatiotemporal, nonmaterial world instead." But if God really does intend to *redeem* rather than reject his created world of space, time, and matter, we are faced with the question: what might it look like to celebrate that redemption, that healing and transformation, in the present, and thereby appropriately to anticipate God's final intention?

A note before we launch in, to anticipate the obvious objection. As long as the present world lasts, there will be an ever-present danger of idolatry, of worshipping the creature instead of the creator. Since space, time, and matter are the raw materials out of which idols have been formed, some devout folks have supposed that they must reject space, time, and matter themselves so that any object used in worship, any action performed, any holy place, becomes instantly suspect.

Fair enough: there is such a thing as idolatry, and we must guard against it. Indeed, we must put it to death without pity. *But idolatry is always the perversion of something good.* Greed—worshipping the appetites and what they feed on—is the perversion of the God-given instinct for the proper enjoyment of the good creation. The proper response to idolatry is therefore not dualism, the rejection of space, time, or matter as themselves evil or dangerous, but the renewed worship of the Creator God, which sets the context for the proper enjoyment and use of the created order without the danger of worshipping it. Our living within and enjoyment and use of space, time, and matter must constantly be measured against the story of Jesus, in his sharing of space, time, and matter as the Incarnate Son; in his death, which passes judgment on all idolatry and sin; and in his resurrection, in which space, time, and matter are renewed in his body, anticipating the final renewal of all things. The danger of idolatry and the proper response to it stand as a rubric over what is now to come. The church is called to a mission of implementing Jesus's resurrection and thereby anticipating the final new creation. What might that look like?

The first major category I want to explore is justice. I use this word as a shorthand for the intention of God, expressed from Genesis to Revelation, to set the whole world right—a plan gloriously fulfilled in Jesus Christ, supremely in his resurrection (following his victory over the powers of evil and death on the cross), and now to be implemented in the world. We cannot get off the hook of present responsibility, as many Christians try to do, not least within some parts of fundamentalism, by declaring that the world is currently in such a mess and there's nothing that can be done about it until the Lord returns. That is classic dualism. Many people embrace it enthusiastically. It leaves the church with nothing to do in the present except care for the wounded as best we can while we wait for a different kind of salvation altogether.

To say that there's more to it than that, though, is not to return to the old social gospel. It is rather to live consciously between the resurrection of Jesus in the past and the making of God's new world in the future. This is why the theology of liberal modernism, at its best, was always fighting its social agendas with one hand tied behind its back. Of course, some Christians have spoken of the resurrection as a way of reinforcing a dualism that leaves them with no social concern. But that always was a gross distortion. Precisely because Jesus Christ rose from the dead, God's new world has already broken in to the present and Christian work for justice in the present, for instance, in the ongoing campaigns for debt remission and ecological responsibility, take the shape they do. If Jesus left his body behind in the tomb and if we are going to do the same, as many theologians of the last generation thought, then we are robbed both of the ground and the energy for our work to bring real, bodily, concrete signs of hope to the present world.

Think back to the Sadducees. They were the powerful elite in Jesus's world. They were held in place by Rome, and they enjoyed wealth, status, and prestige within Judaean society. Their denial of the resurrection and of any future life was argued, it seems, on the basis of their belief that the doctrine was a newfangled thing, invented by late prophets like Daniel; you couldn't find it, they claimed, in the Five Books of Moses. The Pharisees argued against this, as did Jesus himself, with his quotation from Exodus, where God declares that he is the God of Abraham, Isaac, and Jacob. Now when Jesus quotes that verse he isn't simply pulling a rabbit out of an exegetical hat, finding a passage in the Books of Moses that speaks of the patriarchs as still alive and therefore by implication still awaiting their final resurrection. The point of God saying to Moses that he is the God of Abraham, Isaac, and Jacob is to underline what he's going to say in the next few verses: that he has heard the cry of his people in slavery and is coming down to rescue them and to bring them to their promised land.[1]

Within the first-century world of Jesus, the Pharisees, and the Sadducees, the doctrine of resurrection was a *revolutionary* doctrine. It spoke of God's determination to bring about the new Exodus, the real return from exile, the great liberation from oppression and slavery, the liberation for which Israel longed. And the real reason the Sadducees opposed it—behind the smokescreens of theological argument and silly stories about women with seven husbands—was that they knew that the resurrection doctrine was a threat to their own position. They knew it meant that God was turning the world upside down. And people who believe that God will turn the world upside down—people like Mary with her Magnificat, pulling down the mighty from their thrones and exalting the humble and meek—are not going to be backward in getting on with some world-changing activities in the present. It isn't that, like suicide bombers, people who believe in the resurrection are more cheerful about dying for the cause because they are happy to leave this present world and escape into a glorious future. It is, rather, that people who believe in the resurrection, in God making a whole new world in which everything will be set right at last, are unstoppably motivated to work for that new world in the present.

If that was true even of the Pharisees, even before anyone *had* in fact been raised from the dead, how much more ought it to be true of us, who celebrate and proclaim Jesus not only as risen from the dead but also as the one who has thereby been installed as Lord of the whole world? The world has *already* been turned upside down; that's what Easter is all about. It isn't a matter of waiting until God eventually does something different at the end of time. God has brought his future, his putting-the-world-to-rights future, into the present in Jesus of Nazareth, and he wants that future to be implicated more and more in the present. That's what we pray for every time we say the Lord's Prayer: "Thy kingdom come, thy will be done on earth as it is in heaven." And that's why that prayer goes on to pray for bread and forgiveness, which is, I suggest, where the issue of justice comes closest to our global village today.

Once again there are two extremes toward which Christian people tend to slide. To begin with, there are those who declare that if Jesus is the true revolutionary then the single main Christian task is to build the kingdom here on earth through social, political, and cultural revolution. Alas, this social gospel (as it used to be called) has singularly failed to deliver the goods in the century or so since it was advocated in this modern form. An enormous amount of good has been done: social conditions have been improved vastly, though how much that has been due to Christian work and how much to other influences it's hard to say. But we are still a fragmented, frightened, and battered world. Even in the affluent West there are many places where Dickensian conditions, or worse, still obtain, all the more appalling for being mostly out of sight and mind as far as the glossy media are concerned.

At the other end of the scale there are those who declare that nothing can be done until the Lord returns and everything is put to rights. The forces of evil are too entrenched, and nothing save a great apocalyptic moment of divine power can address them or change the deep structures of the way things are. This kind of dualism breeds very effectively within societies where, though injustice can be seen and named, it is politically inconvenient to do anything about it. We will get on, such a view says, with the real business of the gospel, which is that of saving souls for the future world. We will even do mopping-up operations, Band-Aid activities, to look after the people at the bottom of the pile. But we won't do anything about the structures that put them there and keep them there. This kind of dualism banishes the continuing healing activity of the Father from the world he made, of the Son from the world of which he is already the Lord, and of the Spirit from the world within which he (she?) groans in travail.

Neither of these views begins to do justice—in any sense—to Paul's injunction to be steadfast and immovable in doing the work of the Lord because in the Lord our labor is not in vain. The universal early Christian belief was that Jesus had already been demonstrated publicly to be Israel's Messiah and the world's true Lord through his resurrection. That, as we've seen, is part of the whole point of the Christian story. And if we believe it and pray, as he taught us, for God's kingdom to come on earth as in heaven, there is no way we can rest content with major injustice in the world. We must recognize, as the second view does, that the final putting to rights of everything does indeed wait for the last day. We must therefore avoid the arrogance or triumphalism of the first view, imagining that we can build the kingdom by our own efforts without the need for a further great divine act of new creation. But we must agree with the first view that doing justice in the world is part of the Christian task, and we must therefore reject the defeatism of the second view, which says there's no point in even trying.

As far as I can see, the major task that faces us in our generation, corresponding to the issue of slavery two centuries ago, is that of the massive economic imbalance of the world, whose major symptom is the ridiculous and unpayable Third World debt. I have spoken about this many times over the last few years, and I have a sense that some of us, like old Wilberforce on the subject of slavery, are actually called to bore the pants off people by going on and on about it until eventually the point is taken and the world is changed. There are many good books on the subject from different points of view, and I don't want to go into the arguments now. I simply want to record my conviction that this is the number one moral issue of our day. Sex matters enormously, but global justice matters far, far more. The present system of global debt is the real immoral scandal, the dirty little secret—or rather the dirty enormous secret—of glitzy, glossy Western capitalism. Whatever it takes, we must change this situation or stand condemned by subsequent history alongside those who supported slavery two centuries ago and those who supported the Nazis seventy years ago. It is that serious. I can't develop the arguments here; I just want to make four brief comments, in light of the subject matter we have explored in this book, about the nature of the debates that you run into when you raise the subject. (I know this only too well: every time I write on these issues some commentators, usually in the United States, write to tell me that I should stick to Jesus and Paul and not meddle in economics and politics. Fortunately, there are plenty of others, in that country and elsewhere, who encourage me to keep going.)

First, notice how the rhetoric regularly employed against the remission of global debts echoes the arguments used against the abolition of slavery. Read the writings of the eighteenth-century Quaker John Woolman (1720–1772). Read again the story of Wilberforce (1759–1833).[2] The patronizing, temporizing, and sometimes bullying they had to put up with; the tone of voice that says, "We know how the world works; don't bother us with moral arguments"; the powerful interests that lobbied the great and the good against them: all this is routine today as the Western global empire fights back against the cry for justice. But every time we put it off one more day, several hundred children die. And that's just the start.

We must learn, therefore, to recognize the complex arguments against debt remission as what they are. People tell you it's a tricky and many-sided subject. Yes, it is; so was slavery. So are all major moral problems. The fact remains that what is now going on amounts to theft by the strong from the weak, by the rich from the poor. I am choosing my words carefully; read the literature and see. If a police officer catches a thief red-handed, the officer doesn't need complicated arguments about the thief's motives, the complexities of the thief's and the victim's intertwined economic situations, or any other prevarication; the important thing is to stop the thieving and stop it right away. In the light of this, we should learn to recognize the complex stories told by those with vested interests as corresponding closely to the complex stories told by the Sadducees to show how impossible it was to believe in the resurrection. Jesus's answer was blunt and to the point: you're wrong because you don't know the Bible and you don't know God's power (Mark 12:24). Our response must be that because we believe in the resurrection of Jesus as an event within history, we believe that the living God has already begun the process of new creation, and what may seem impossible in human terms is possible to God.

Thus when people object, as they do, to me and others pointing out that the rich are getting richer and the poor are getting poorer—by commenting that wealth is not finite, that statist and globalist solutions and handouts will merely strip the poor of their human dignity and vocation to work, and that all this will encourage the poor toward a sinful envy of the rich, a slothful escapism, and a counterproductive reliance on Caesar rather than God—I want to take such commentators to refugee camps, to villages where children die every day, to towns where most adults have already died of AIDS, and show them people who haven't got the energy to be envious, who aren't slothful because they are using all the energy they've got to wait in line for water and to care for each other, who know perfectly well that they don't need handouts so much as justice. I know, and such people often know in their bones, that wealth isn't a zero-sum game, but reading the collected works of F. A. Hayek in a comfortable chair in North America simply doesn't address the moral questions of the twenty-first century.[3]

Second, return to what I said a few moments ago: the way in which the liberal theology of the last century, in denying the bodily resurrection, joined forces with the Sadducees in keeping God at arm's length and thus holding at bay any chance of theologically grounded work for God's new world, for the kingdom to come on earth as in heaven. There are multiple ironies here too, as social-gospel liberalism was also embracing modernist denials of God's action in history, when that action was just what they needed as their foundation. The heirs of that liberal theology are today keen to marginalize the Bible, declaring that it supports slavery and other wicked things, because they don't like what it says on other topics such as sexual ethics. But if you push the Bible off the table, you are merely colluding with pagan empire, denying yourself the sourcebook for your kingdom critique of oppression. The Sadducees didn't know the Bible or God's power; that's why they denied the resurrection and supported Rome.[4]

Third, however, look at the mirror-image point: that much conservative theology, not least in the United States, where it counts heavily at the moment, has also served to reinforce the dominance of the West. The Cold War years enabled the United States to build up its persona as God's answer to communism. Many conservative churches there still live by the belief that what's good for America is good for God—with the result, for instance, that if their country needs to produce more acid rain in order to keep up car production, then God must be happy with it and anyone who talks about pollution or is disappointed that the president didn't sign the Kyoto protocol is somehow anti-Christian or is simply producing a "baptized neosocialism," as one reviewer accused me of. Rampant belief in the rapture lends strong support to this, as we saw earlier: Armageddon is coming, so who cares what state the planet is in? The irony is that those American churches that protest most vocally against the teaching of Darwinism in their schools are often, in their public policies, supporting a kind of economic Darwinism, the survival of the fittest in world markets and military power.

In particular, fourth, the strong belief in Jesus's bodily resurrection among conservative Christians in many parts of the world, especially in the United States, has taken that belief out of its biblical context and put it instead in a different one, where it serves agendas diametrically opposed to the biblical ones. For many conservative Christians today, belief in Jesus's bodily resurrection is all about God's supernatural action in the world, legitimating an upstairs-downstairs view of reality—a dualism, in other words—in which the supernatural is the real world and the natural, the this-worldly, is secondary and largely irrelevant. The resurrection is thus affirmed as the orthodox belief over against liberal modernism, but what you get instead is *conservative* modernism, which leaves intact the modernist split between heaven and earth and indeed reinforces it. From this viewpoint, of course, what matters is the supernatural, world-denying salvation offered by the gospel. Any attempt to work for God's justice *on earth* as in heaven is condemned as the sort of thing those wicked antisupernatural liberals try to do. That is precisely not what the resurrection is about, and in defending the orthodox position on Easter, I have become aware in the last few years that many liberals are really attacking not Easter itself but the escapist and socially conservative politics of those they perceive to be defending it. This convoluted distortion of the gospel is not, alas, confined to North American fundamentalism.

Thus from both sides within would-be Christian culture—those who deny the resurrection and thereby cut off the branch from which true Christian work for justice must grow, and those who affirm it but use it to reinforce their anti-this-worldly theology—we find apparently powerful reasons for doing nothing about the plight of the world and for letting things take their own course, which means of course letting the strong go on winning. Implicit social Darwinism again. We should know where that got us a hundred years ago, as preachers in Britain and Germany solemnly declared that a few good wars might be God's way of enabling the human race to become fitter and stronger. As we learn the lessons of God's future, let us not forget the tragic lessons of our own past.

The paradigm I have set out in this book tells heavily against both sides. This is the point where a genuine biblical theology can come out of the forest and startle both those who thought that the Bible was irrelevant or dangerous for political ethics and those who thought that taking the Bible seriously meant being conservative politically as well as theologically. The truth is very different—as we should have guessed from Jesus's own preaching of the kingdom, not to mention his death as a would-be rebel king. His resurrection, and the promise of God's new world that comes with it, creates a program for change and offers to empower it. Those who believe the gospel have no choice but to follow.

And if people tell you that after all there isn't very much they can do, remember what the answer is. What would you say to someone who said, rightly, that God would make them completely holy in the resurrection and that they would never reach this state of complete holiness until then—and who then went on to say, wrongly, that therefore there was no point in even trying to live a holy life until that time? You would press for some form of inaugurated eschatology. You would insist that the new life of the Spirit, in obedience to the lordship of Jesus Christ, should produce radical transformation of behavior in the present life, *anticipating* the life to come even though we know we shall never be complete and whole until then. That is, actually, the lesson of Romans 6. Well, apply the same to Romans 8! How do you answer someone who says, rightly, that the world will not be completely just and right until the new creation and who deduces, wrongly, that there is no point trying to bring justice to the world (or for that matter ecological health, another topic for which there is no space here) until that time? Answer, from everything I have said so far: insist on inaugurated eschatology, on a radical transformation of the way we behave as a worldwide community, *anticipating* the eventual time when God will be all in all even though we all agree things won't be complete until then. There is the challenge. The resurrection of Jesus points us to it and gives us the energy for it. Let us overcome our surprise that such a hope should be set before us and go to the task with prayer and wisdom.

BEAUTY

An apparently quite different theme now emerges as part of the work of mission within a theology of new creation. I believe that taking creation and new creation seriously is the way to understand and revitalize aesthetic awareness and perhaps even creativity among Christians today. Beauty matters, dare I say, almost as much as spirituality and justice.[5] Of course, if you have to choose between beautiful slavery and an ugly Exodus, you must go for the Exodus, but, as William Temple said in a different (though related) context, fortunately we don't have to make that choice.

Romans 8, with its rich theology of new creation, offers us a way of appreciating natural beauty. Paul speaks of the creation groaning in travail, waiting to give birth to God's new world. The beauty of the present world, I suggested earlier in the book, has something about it of the beauty of a chalice, beautiful in itself but more hauntingly beautiful in what we know it's meant to be filled with; or that of the violin, beautiful in itself but particularly because we know the music it's capable of. Another example might be the engagement ring, which is meant as it is to delight the eye but which is meant even more to delight the heart because of what it promises. I want now to develop this further in terms of the new creativity to which I believe Christians are called as we find ourselves poised between creation and new creation.

We are moving away, I think, from the old split in which it was expected that good Christians couldn't be artists and good artists couldn't be Christians. We now have, thank God, some wonderful Christian painters, composers, sculptors, and even poets who are showing the way forward. We even have some splendid theoreticians, such as Jeremy Begbie and his project, Theology Through the Arts, which has done so much in this area. I want to offer a proposal about where the artistic endeavor belongs, where what we loosely call human culture belongs, within the discipline of Christian mission, within the map of creation and new creation.

It is, I believe, part of being made in God's image that we are ourselves creators or at least procreators. The extraordinary ability to bring forth new life, supremely of course through begetting children but in millions of other ways as well, is central to the mandate the human race receives in Genesis 1 and 2. To make sense of and celebrate a beautiful world through the production of artifacts that are themselves beautiful is part of the call to be stewards of creation, as was Adam's naming of the animals. Genuine art is thus itself a response to the beauty of creation, which itself is a pointer to the beauty of God.

But we don't live in the Garden of Eden, and art that attempts to do so quickly becomes flaccid and trivial. (The church doesn't have a monopoly on kitsch or sentimentalism, but if you want to find it, the church may well be the easiest place to start.) We live in a fallen world, and any attempt to plug in to some kind of pantheism, worshipping the creation as if it were itself divine, always runs up against the problem of evil. At that point art, like philosophy and politics, often swings the other way and determinedly responds to ugliness with more ugliness. (This reflects the supposed swing in Greek tragedy from Sophocles, describing the world as it ought to be, to Euripides, describing the world as it is.) We have a rash of this in the British arts world at the moment, a kind of brutalism that under the guise of realism simply expresses futility and boredom. We are back here on the fault line between those who refuse to recognize evil, on the one hand, and those who see nothing but evil, on the other.

This presents a wonderful opportunity for Christians with an integrated worldview, and with a theology of both creation and new creation, to find the way forward, perhaps to *lead* the way forward, beyond such a sterile impasse. When we read Romans 8, we find Paul affirming that the whole of creation is groaning in travail as it longs for its redemption. Creation is good, but it is not God. It is beautiful, but its beauty is at present transient. It is in pain, but that pain is taken into the very heart of God and becomes part of the pain of new birth. The beauty of creation, to which art responds and which it tries to express, imitate, and highlight, is not simply the beauty it possesses in itself but the beauty it possesses in view of what is promised to it: back to the chalice, the violin, the engagement ring. We are committed to describing the world not just as it should be, not just as it is, but as—by God's grace alone!—one day it will be. And we should never forget that when Jesus rose from the dead, as the paradigm, first example, and generating power of the whole new creation, the marks of the nails were not just visible on his hands and his feet. They were the way he was to be identified. When art comes to terms with *both* the wounds of the world *and* the promise of resurrection and learns how to express and respond to both at once, we will be on the way to a fresh vision, a fresh mission.

A parody of this is found in the passionate belief of many artists and writers of the last generation that the only true art is art that is politically committed. At least the Marxists who thought like that had grasped the point that neither sentimentality nor brutalism will do, but only eschatology in the process of being realized. If Christian artists can glimpse the truth of which that Marxist vision is a parody, they may find a way forward to celebrating beauty without lapsing into either pantheism or cynicism. This will take serious imagination, imagination fueled by reflection and prayer at the foot of the cross and before the empty tomb, imagination that will discern the mysteries of God's judgment on evil and God's reaffirmation, through resurrection, of his beautiful creation. Art at its best draws attention not only to the way things are but also to the way things will be, when the earth is filled with the knowledge of God as the waters cover the sea. That remains a surprising hope, and perhaps it will be the artists who are best at conveying both the hope and the surprise.

EVANGELISM

If we are engaging in the work of new creation, in seeking to bring advance signs of God's eventual new world into being in the present, in justice and beauty and a million other ways (there is no space for more in this book, and justice and beauty themselves cry out, of course, for fuller treatment), then at the center of the picture stands the personal call of the gospel of Jesus to every child, woman, and man.

The word *evangelism* still sends shivers down the spines of many people. There are various reasons for this. Some people have been scared off by frightening or bullying harangues or tactless and offensive behavior or embarrassing and naive presentations of the gospel. Others have never suffered such indignities but heard or read about them and are glad to have a good excuse to pour scorn on all evangelism—as though, because some people do it badly, nobody should ever do it at all. And, of course, many in the media still confuse *evangelist* (one who preaches the gospel) with *evangelical* (someone who holds certain doctrines in certain particular ways), and hence *evangelism* (the preaching of the gospel) with *evangelicalism* (the broad coalition of evangelicals, which cuts across the lines of official denominations). This is not the place to address the many issues of the nature of evangelism itself or what counts as preaching the gospel or the relation of evangelism to mission as abstract categories—though I hope the present chapter will give food for thought on all these topics. Rather, I simply want to show how the paradigm I have advanced in this book, of the surprising hope we find in the resurrection of Jesus and the New Testament's exploration of its significance, gives a new perspective on what evangelism might actually be and hence how one might go about it.

Much evangelism has, of course, consisted of taking the traditional framework of a heaven-and-hell expectation and persuading people that it's time they consider the heaven option and grab it while they have the chance. What's stopping them getting there is sin; the solution is provided in Jesus Christ; all they have to do is to accept it! Millions of Christians today are Christians because they heard that message and responded to it. Am I therefore saying—since plainly I think that way of putting things is at best lopsided—that they have been deceived or mistaken?

No. God gloriously honors all kinds of ways of announcing the good news. I do not suppose for a moment that my own way of preaching or talking to individuals about God is perfect and without flaws, and yet God (I believe) has graciously honored some at least of what I do. No doubt he would have been far more honored if I had done it better and more prayerfully. No doubt the flaws in my own preaching, and the different flaws in other presentations, will eventually show up in the Christian lives of those who come to faith as a result, and no doubt we all ought to polish up and improve what we do for the sake of our hearers and the honor of God. But, as every generation knows, it isn't the quality of the preaching that counts but the faithfulness of God.

And, of course, the praying that goes with the preaching. The first time I preached a proper sermon, my mentor gave me some good advice: your praying and your preaching should be of the same length. You don't want to find yourself limping, with one leg shorter than the other. God works as a result of prayer and faithfulness, not technique and cleverness.

But none of this is an excuse for not understanding what happens when we evangelize or not shaping the way we do it in accordance with the full biblical gospel. So let's start with the latter point and say clearly at once: the gospel, in the New Testament, is the good news that God (the world's creator) is at last becoming king and that Jesus, whom this God raised from the dead, is the world's true lord. There are a thousand different ways of saying this, depending on where the audience is starting from and what sort of occasion it is. (Compare the various speeches in Acts!) Some people will know who Jesus is, others will have only a hazy idea about him; some will hear the word *God* and think of an old man with a white beard while others will think of a sort of heavenly gas. Almost everyone will need help to understand what the message is about at some point or another.

The power of the gospel lies not in the offer of a new spirituality or religious experience, not in the threat of hellfire (certainly not in the threat of being "left behind"), which can be removed if only the hearer checks this box, says this prayer, raises a hand, or whatever, but in the powerful announcement that God is God, that Jesus is Lord, that the powers of evil have been defeated, that God's new world has begun. This announcement, stated as a fact about the way the world is rather than as an appeal about the way you might like your life, your emotions, or your bank balance to be, is the foundation of everything else. Of course, once the gospel announcement is made, in whatever way, it means instantly that all people everywhere are gladly invited to come in, to join the party, to discover forgiveness for the past, an astonishing destiny in God's future, and a vocation in the present. And in that welcome and invitation, all the emotions can be, and one hopes will eventually be, fully engaged.

But how can the church announce that God is God, that Jesus is Lord, that the powers of evil, corruption, and death itself have been defeated, and that God's new world has begun? Doesn't this seem laughable? Well, it would be if it wasn't happening. But if a church is working on the issues we've already looked at—if it's actively involved in seeking justice in the world, both globally and locally, and if it's cheerfully celebrating God's good creation and its rescue from corruption in art and music, and if, in addition, its own internal life gives every sign that new creation is indeed happening, generating a new type of community—then suddenly the announcement makes a lot of sense.

So what account can we give, within this theology of new creation, of what happens when the gospel takes root? It happens again and again, thank God: people discover, firing up within themselves, the sense that it does make sense, that they really believe it, that they find it transforming the way they are thinking and feeling about all sorts of other things, that the presence of Jesus is suddenly a reality for them, that reading the Bible becomes exciting, that they can't get enough of Christian worship and fellowship. We use various words for this moment or this process (with some people it happens in a flash; with others it takes a long time): conversion, which means turning around to travel in the opposite direction; regeneration, which means new birth; "entering into Christ," which means joining the family, which takes its name and its character from Jesus himself. The New Testament speaks of such a person "dying with Christ" and "being raised with him" (Romans 6, Colossians 2 and 3), of passing through the water of baptism as the sign and means of leaving behind the old life and beginning the new, of identifying with the death and resurrection of Jesus himself. And in terms of the big picture of new creation, which we have been drawing throughout, what we must say is this: such a person is a living, breathing little bit of "new creation"—that new creation that has already begun to happen in Jesus's resurrection and that will be complete when God finally makes his new heavens and new earth and raises us to share in that new world. Paul puts it like this: "If anyone is in Christ—new creation!"[6]

Stating the matter like this avoids three problems into which evangelism can run. First, it makes it clear that to become a Christian is not to say no to the good world, which God has made. It is, of course, to turn one's back on all the corruptions into which the world has fallen and into which each individual has fallen. Sometimes converts will need to say a firm no to things that are not evil in themselves (alcohol, for instance) in order to put a clear space between themselves and habits and patterns of life that previously held them in their grip. But to think in terms of a new creation avoids the problem of supposing for a moment that one could forget earth and concentrate on heaven.

Second, to see evangelism in terms of the announcement of God's kingdom, of Jesus's lordship and of the consequent new creation, avoids from the start any suggestion that the main or central thing that has happened is that the new Christian has entered into a private relationship with God or with Jesus and that this relationship is the main or only thing that matters. (Some currently popular Christian songs seem to suggest this rather too frequently, as though the main thing about the gospel were that Jesus could take the place of my girlfriend or boyfriend.) Seeing evangelism and any resulting conversions in terms of new creation means that the new convert knows from the start that he or she is part of God's kingdom project, which stretches out beyond "me and my salvation" to embrace, or rather to be embraced by, God's worldwide purposes. Along with conversion there will then go, at least in principle, the call to find out where in the total project one can make one's own contribution. (The fact that this vocation often takes time to emerge doesn't mean it isn't something one must expect from the outset.)

Third, putting evangelism and conversion within the context of new creation means that the convert, who has heard the message in terms of the sovereign and saving lordship of Jesus himself, will never be inclined to think that Christian behavior—saying no to the things that diminish human flourishing and God's glory and saying yes to the things that enhance them—is an optional extra or simply a matter of wrapping your head around some rather strange rules and regulations. Some kinds of evangelism in the past implied that the main thing is to sign on, to pray a particular prayer, which results in the assurance that one is safely on the way to heaven—and failed to mention, to the frustration of pastors and teachers who then tried to look after such converts, the fact that following Jesus means just that, *following Jesus,* not checking a box that says "Jesus" and then sitting back as though it's all done. To speak, rather, of Jesus's lordship and of the new creation, which results from his victory on Calvary and at Easter, implies at once that to confess him as Lord and to believe that God raised him from the dead is to allow one's entire life to be reshaped by him, knowing that though this will be painful from time to time, it will be the way not to a diminished or cramped human existence but to genuine human life in the present and to complete, glorious, resurrected human life in the future. As with every other aspect of new creation, there will be surprises on the way. But Christian ethics will only gain from being understood as one expression of Christian hope.

CONCLUSION

The mission of the church must therefore reflect, and be shaped by, the future hope as the New Testament presents it. I believe that if we take these three areas—justice, beauty, and evangelism—in terms of the anticipation of God's eventual setting to rights of the whole world, we will find that they dovetail together and in fact that they are all part of the same larger whole, which is the message of hope and new life that comes with the good news of Jesus's resurrection.

This is the foundation, I believe, for the work of hope in the day-to-day life of the church. My own vocation has taken me to an area of my country where, for many people, hope is in short supply. A nebulous sense of injustice hangs over many a community in the shape of the half-formed belief that the industrial collapse of the late twentieth century must be somebody's fault and that something should be done about it. This is very different from the sense that the world owes you a living. It is a reflection of the fact that when a large community has been built up over several generations around one or two key industries, and when those industries are then shut down not because they are unproductive or because the workers are incompetent or lazy but because they do not fit the larger strategic plans of people whose faces are never seen in the area, then there is a quiet anger, a sense that something has gone wrong at a structural level. Human societies should not work like that, and if they do then questions have to be asked. Part of the task of the church must be to take up that sense of injustice, to bring it to speech, to help people both articulate it and, when they are ready to do so, to turn it into prayer (it's surprising, until you find yourself in that position, how many of the Psalms suddenly become relevant!). And the task then continues with the church's work with the whole local community, to foster programs for better housing, schools, and community facilities, to encourage new job opportunities, to campaign and cajole and work with local government and councils, and, in short, to foster hope at any and every level. And part of the argument of this book is that when this is done, this is not something other than the surprising hope of the gospel, the hope for life after life after death. It is the direct result of that: the hope for life before death.

The second feature of many communities both in the postindustrial West and in many of the poorer parts of the world is ugliness. True, some communities manage to sustain levels of art and music, often rooted in folk culture, which bring a richness even to the most poverty-stricken areas. But the shoulder-shrugging functionalism of postwar architecture, coupled with the passivity born of decades of television, has meant that for many people the world appears to offer little but bleak urban landscapes, on the one hand, and tawdry entertainment, on the other. And when people cease to be surrounded by beauty, they cease to hope. They internalize the message of their eyes and ears, the message that whispers that they are not worth very much, that they are in effect less than fully human.

To communities in danger of going that route, the message of new creation, of the beauty of the present world taken up and transcended in the beauty of the world that is yet to be—with part of that beauty being precisely the healing of the present anguish—comes as a surprising hope. Part of the role of the church in the past was—and could and should be again—to foster and sustain lives of beauty and aesthetic meaning at every level, from music making in the village pub to drama in the local primary school, from artists' and photographers' workshops to still-life painting classes, from symphony concerts (well, they managed them in the concentration camps; how inventive might we be?) to driftwood sculptures. The church, because it is the family that believes in hope for new creation, should be the place in every town and village where new creativity bursts forth for the whole community, pointing to the hope that, like all beauty, always comes as a surprise.

And, of course, evangelism, which will flourish best if the church is giving itself to works of justice (putting things to rights in the community) and works of beauty (highlighting the glory of creation and the glory yet to be revealed): evangelism will always come as a surprise. You mean there is more? There is a new world, and it has already begun, and it works by healing and forgiveness and new starts and fresh energy? Yes, answers the church, and it comes about as people worship the God in whose image they are made, as they follow the Lord who bore their sins and rose from the dead, as they are indwelt by his Spirit and thereby given new life, a new way of life, a new zest for life. It is often pointed out that some of the places most lacking in hope are not the industrial wastelands or the bleak landscapes shorn of beauty but the places where there is too much money, too much high culture, too much of everything except faith, hope, and love. To such places, and to the sad people who live in them as well as to those who find themselves battered by circumstances beyond their control, the message of Jesus and his death and resurrection comes as good news from a far country, news of surprising hope.

This is the good news—of justice, beauty, and above all Jesus—that the church is called upon to live and to speak, to bring into reality, in each place and each generation. What might the life of the church look like if it was shaped, in turn, by this hope-shaped mission?

14. RESHAPING THE CHURCH FOR MISSION (1): BIBLICAL ROOTS

INTRODUCTION

If today's, and tomorrow's, church is to engage in this kind of mission, seeking both to implement the achievement of Jesus and his resurrection and thereby to anticipate the final renewal of all things, it must itself be renewed, resourced, and reshaped for this mission. What will this look like?

It is vital that we address this question in terms of the scriptural witness to the resurrection and the way in which, in the Bible itself, this witness is directly translated into mission and the life of the church. The present chapter will therefore examine briefly the gospels, Acts, and Paul with this in mind, and in the final chapter we shall apply this to specific issues in the life of the church.[1]

Much of the talk about mission-shaped church in recent days inevitably, and rightly, is about the practicalities of church life: about restructuring ministry and parishes, ways of working in order to better facilitate the mission to which we are called. I'm not going to address that in what follows. Instead, I want to undergird that necessary and vital task by setting out what seem to be the scriptural and spiritual priorities of a church refocused on a hope-shaped mission. Without this, there is always the danger of mere pragmatism. And with pragmatism there often comes opportunism—for the advancing of agendas that are driven not by the imperative to mission but by one or other of the old models of church life, which are now running out of steam. My task in this chapter and the final one will be, rather, to lay some foundations: first in the Bible and then in key areas of Christian living.

THE GOSPELS AND ACTS

The first and perhaps most obvious meaning of the resurrection of Jesus, which emerges strongly in all four gospels, is that God has vindicated the Jesus who proclaimed the kingdom and died as Israel's representative. This may sound obvious, but to judge from the reactions I often get when I say this sort of thing I think it is not sufficiently recognized. In Mark's short and probably truncated account there is no sense of "Jesus is raised, therefore there really is life after death"; rather, the point is, "Jesus is raised, therefore you'd better go to Galilee and see him there." For anyone who has read the whole gospel, the strong implication is, "Jesus is raised, just as he told you he would be; in other words, all that he said about the coming of the kingdom through his own work, through his death and resurrection, has come true." The resurrection completes the inauguration of God's kingdom. In Mark's perspective, it is at least part of what Jesus meant when he said that some standing with him would not taste death before they saw the kingdom of God come with power. This points us forward to the more detailed outworking in the other gospels. The resurrection is not an isolated supernatural oddity proving how powerful, if apparently arbitrary, God can be when he wants to. Nor is it at all a way of showing that there is indeed a heaven awaiting us after death. It is the decisive event demonstrating that God's kingdom really has been launched on earth as it is in heaven.

When we turn to Matthew, we find that he takes this further—and it is indeed quite possible that Mark's original text had something like this as well. When the disciples go to Galilee and see

Jesus there, they worship him (though some, interestingly, doubt); this is the culmination of the Christology that has been building up throughout the gospel. Jesus is vindicated as the Emmanuel, the man who is God-with-us. But there is no sense either that this is just a nice thing that's happened to him or that the point of it all is for him to say, "So if you go on behaving yourselves you'll be able to join me in heaven one day." On the contrary. Just as Jesus taught his followers to pray that God's kingdom would come on earth as in heaven, so now he claims that all authority in heaven and on earth has been given to him, and on that basis he commands the disciples to go and make it happen—to work, in other words, as agents of that authority. What remains implicit in Mark, at least as we have it, is made explicit in Matthew: resurrection doesn't mean *escaping from* the world; it means *mission to* the world based on Jesus's *lordship over* the world.

Already we begin to see how the watershed works. If the resurrection is an event that actually occurred (in some sense) in time and space as well as in the material reality of Jesus's body, it has implications for other events that must follow. If it's only a so-called spiritual event, either involving Jesus being alive now in some heavenly realm or simply involving a new sense of faith and hope in our minds and hearts, the only events that will follow are various forms of private spirituality. So Matthew gives us the clear message of what the resurrection means: Jesus is now enthroned as the Lord of heaven and earth. His kingdom has been established. And this kingdom is to be put into practice by his followers summoning all nations to obedient allegiance to him, marking them out in baptism. The closing line draws together the major themes of the gospel: the Emmanuel, the God-with-us, is now Jesus-with-us until the final end of the old age, the time when the new age, which has been inaugurated in the resurrection, has completed its transforming work in the world.

This brings us to Luke, and in particular to the marvelous story of the two disciples on the road to Emmaus. There is much that could be said about Luke 24, but for the moment I simply draw attention to the answer that this chapter gives to the question, So what if Jesus is raised bodily from the dead?[2] The biggest and most important answer is that with the resurrection of Jesus the entire story of God and Israel, and God and the world, must be told in a new way.

This, again, is watershed stuff. Without the resurrection there is one way of telling the story; with the resurrection there is a whole other way. Without the resurrection, the story is an unfinished and potentially tragic drama in which Israel can hold on to hope but with an increasing sense that the narrative is spinning out of control. Without the resurrection, even the story of Jesus is a tragedy, certainly in first-century Jewish terms, as the two on the road to Emmaus knew very well. But with the resurrection there is a new way of telling the entire story. The resurrection isn't just a surprise happy ending for one person; it is instead the turning point for everything else. It is the point at which all the old promises come true at last: the promises of David's unshakable kingdom; the promises of Israel's return from the greatest exile of them all; and behind that again, quite explicit in Matthew, Luke, and John, the promise that all the nations will now be blessed through the seed of Abraham.

If Jesus has not been raised, Luke is saying, all you have is hopes raised and dashed once more. The disciples would go on hoping, no doubt, because they were faithful Jews, but if Jesus is not raised, nothing has happened to show that their hopes might after all be fulfilled. But if Jesus has been raised, then this is how the Old Testament has to be read: as a story of suffering and vindication, of exile and restoration, a narrative that reaches its climax not in Israel becoming top nation and beating the rest of the world at its own game but in the suffering and vindication, the exile and restoration, of the Messiah—not for himself alone but because he is carrying the saving promises of God. If the messenger bringing vital news falls into the river and is then rescued, he is rescued not for himself alone but for the sake of those who are waiting in desperate hope for his life-giving message. If Jesus is raised, Luke is saying, he really was and is the Messiah; but if he's the Messiah, he is God's messenger, God's promise-bearer, carrying the promises made to Abraham, Moses, David, and the prophets—promises not only for Israel but also for the whole world.

That is why, incidentally, the Old Testament must be seen as part of Christian scripture. I respect those who call the Old Testament the Hebrew scriptures to acknowledge that they are still the scriptures of a living faith community different from Christianity. But Luke insists that since Jesus really was raised from the dead, the ancient scriptures of Israel must be read as a story that reaches its climax in Jesus and will then produce its proper fruit not only in Israel but also in Jesus's followers and, through them, in all the world. That's why, when Jesus appears to the disciples in the upper room in verses 36–49, his opening of their minds to understand the scriptures (verses 44–46) results directly in the new commission: that "repentance and forgiveness of sins is to be proclaimed in his name to all nations, beginning from Jerusalem." This is not something other than the Jewish hope. It is woven into the scriptures from very early on that when God finally does for Israel what he's going to do, then the nations of the world will come to share in the blessing. This, indeed, is one of the central keys to unlocking New Testament theology.

Of course, if Jesus is not raised from the dead, we might recognize two sorts of religion or faith: a Christian faith that believed it gained access to the divine through Jesus and a Jewish faith that believed it gained access to the divine apart from Jesus (and was perhaps still waiting for another Messiah). But both of these would be very different from real Christianity and real Judaism. If, out of a desire to be fair to Judaism, you turn both Christianity and Judaism into examples of a religion, a way of ordering your own spirituality, you may be more politically correct, but you will do violence to both actual households of faith. But if Jesus is raised from the dead, then the scriptures have reached their goal in him, and it's now time for the moment the psalmists and prophets longed to see, when the nations of the earth will bring their treasures in loyalty and obedience to God's anointed king, Israel's Messiah.

The further question, of how Christianity continues to relate to the Judaism that does not recognize Jesus as Messiah, is of course vital. It is addressed in the New Testament, not least by Paul. But we cannot allow our proper sensitivities on this subject to prevent us from speaking of Jesus's resurrection and from embracing the challenge that comes as a result. For Luke, the point of the resurrection is that the long story of Israel, the great overarching scriptural narrative, has reached its goal and climax and must now give birth, as it always intended, to the worldwide mission in which the nations are summoned to turn from their idolatry and find forgiveness of sins. And they are to do this, Luke implies, because in Jesus we see the true God in human form, the reality of which all idols are parodies, and the true forgiveness of sins through his cross, the reality before which all sacrifices are types and shadows. The resurrection, in other words, is for Luke neither an odd miracle that restored Jesus to life but has no other meaning nor a sign that we shall all go to heaven when we die but rather the fulfillment of the ancient scriptural promises and the beginning of God's worldwide mission.

All these themes reach their fullest statement in the gospel of John, where they are displayed in a sequence of scenes that are as moving as they are masterly.[3] John 20 and 21 present us with two main themes: the new day and the new commission.

John 20 stresses twice (in verses 1 and 19) that Easter is the first day of the new week. John has so ordered his gospel that the sequence of seven signs, climaxing in the cross of Jesus on the sixth day of the week and his resting in the tomb on the seventh, functions as the week of the old creation; and now Easter functions as the beginning of the new creation. The Word through whom all things were made is now the Word through whom all things are remade. So far from being an odd or isolated supernatural event, breaking in as a sign of what God could do if he chose but normally doesn't, Jesus's resurrection is to be seen as the beginning of the new world, the first day of the new week, the unveiling of the prototype of what God is now going to accomplish in the rest of the world.

Mary supposes Jesus is the gardener; that's the right mistake to make because, like Adam, he is charged with bringing God's new world to order. He has come to uproot the thorns and thistles and to plant myrtle and cypress instead, as Isaiah promised in his great picture of the new creation that would result from the Word of God coming like rain or snow into the world.[4]

This too has little to do with the resurrection showing that we "go to heaven when we die" and a great deal to do with the new commission of the disciples to be for the world what Jesus was for Israel: "As the father sent me," he says, "so I send you."[5] And, as in Luke, the commission is accompanied by the necessary equipment: to be Jesus's agents in the world, his followers need, and are given, his own Spirit. Easter and Pentecost belong together. Easter commissions Jesus's followers for a task; Pentecost gives them the necessary equipment to accomplish it.

In particular, as we began to see in an earlier chapter, Jesus calls his followers to a new mode of *knowing*.[6] I have written elsewhere about what I call an epistemology of love. We have traditionally thought of knowing in terms of subject and object and have struggled to attain objectivity by detaching our subjectivity. It can't be done, and one of the achievements of postmodernity is to demonstrate that. What we are called to, and what in the resurrection we are equipped for, is a knowing in which we are involved as subjects *but as self-giving, not as self-seeking, subjects:* in other words, a knowing that is a form of love. The story of Thomas encapsulates this transformation of knowing. He wants knowledge he can control, objective evidence and all that goes with it. But when Jesus confronts him and offers him the proof he asked for, his blustering turns to belief and confession: "My Lord," he says, "and my God!"[7] The story of Peter in John 21 then opens this up to a different level: the key question, echoing down the centuries in the ears of all who have struggled and failed in their discipleship, is the ultimate one: Do you love me?

This sends us back to Ludwig Wittgenstein, whom we met earlier in the book, and to his famous saying that "it is love that believes the resurrection." Wittgenstein's most famous book, the *Tractatus Logico-Philosophicus,* was first published in 1921 and remains one of the most original and provocative texts of philosophy not only of the modern period but also, some would say, ever. Wittgenstein orders his remarks with a severe and logical numbering: 1, 1.1, 1.11, 1.12, 1.13, 1.2, 1.21, then 2, and so on. Actually, number 1 takes only half a page, whereas 2 takes five pages, 3 takes nine, and so on. There are six sections in all, ending with a subsection numbered 6.54. Then, tellingly, section 7 consists of a single sentence: "What we cannot speak about, we must pass over in silence."[8]

Wittgenstein, of course, was Jewish, and a man of amazing cultural and aesthetic awareness. He had perfect musical pitch and a perfect architect's eye. He also had a strong mystical streak. I can't claim to understand all of the first six sections of the *Tractatus,* but I think I know what Wittgenstein was doing at this final point. I think he was consciously modeling Genesis 1: knowledge, like creation, starting small but pregnant, developing in complexity until the full height of the sixth day, the day when humans are created in God's image. Then, on the seventh day, a silence: a rest, a pregnant pause—in other words, a sabbath. Some things, Wittgenstein indicates, go beyond speech and philosophy, and about them one can and must remain silent. What I want to suggest, with great temerity, is that in the resurrection one is given the beginning of a new knowing, a new epistemology, a new coming-to-speech, the Word born afresh after the death of all human knowing and speech, all human hope and love, after the silent rest of the seventh-day sabbatical in the tomb. I don't know if any Christian philosophers have thought of writing a post-Wittgensteinian *Tractatus Resurrectio-Philosophicus,* starting with the number 8; but I suggest that to attempt such a thing would be to take seriously, in terms of the science of knowing itself, what John is saying in chapters 20 and 21.

Coming back to the text from that diversion, we find in John 21 (one of the most moving and profound chapters in the whole Bible) a multilayered statement of the new commission already announced in 20:19–23. The disciples go fishing but catch nothing. Jesus then helps them to an enormous catch but proceeds to commission Peter to be a shepherd rather than a fisherman. There are many things going on simultaneously here, but at the center is the challenge to a new way of life, a new forgiveness, a new fruitfulness, a new following of Jesus, which will be wider and more dangerous than what has gone before. This is a million miles from the hymns that speak of Jesus's resurrection in terms of our own assurance of a safe and happy rest in heaven. Quite the contrary. Jesus's resurrection summons us to dangerous and difficult tasks on earth.

In this story, fishing seems to stand for what the disciples, like the rest of the world, were doing anyway whereas shepherding seems to stand for the new tasks within the new creation. To develop that as a metaphor, it seems to me that a good deal of the church's work at the moment is concentrating on fishing, and helping others to fish, rather than on shepherding. Yes, there are tasks to be done in helping the present world to do better what it should be doing. Jesus will help us to do that. We are to be at work in partnership with the wider world. But if we only try to do alongside others what they are doing already, we will miss the really significant task. As with Isaiah's vision in the Temple, and many other scenes both biblical and modern, Peter's change from fisherman to shepherd comes through his facing of his own sin and his receiving of forgiveness, as Jesus with his three-times-repeated question goes back to Peter's triple denial and then offers him forgiveness precisely in the form of a transformed and newly commissioned life. Those who don't want to face that searching question and answer may remain content to help the world with its fishing. Those who find the risen Jesus going to the roots of their rebellion, denial, and sin and offering them love and forgiveness may well also find themselves sent off to be shepherds instead. Let those with ears listen.

All this comes out in a dozen ways in Acts. As Jesus was about to be taken from them for the last time, the disciples were still pressing the point that they thought was the center of his whole mission in the first place. "Lord, is this the time when you will restore the kingdom to Israel?"[9] Often, when that passage is read, people assume that Jesus's response means, "No, you've got the wrong end of the stick"; in other words, "We've left behind the categories of kingdom, Israel, and all that; instead, you've got quite a different job to do." But I suggest that if we understand what the kingdom and Israel mean, and what Jesus's reply is about, we can see that his answer is actually, "Yes!—but it won't look like you imagine; it will look like something very different instead."

The disciples are assuming that for the kingdom to be restored to Israel will mean some kind of national superiority, perhaps a military defeat of Israel's enemies. But what Jesus has in mind is every bit as much the fulfillment of God's long-delayed plan for Israel and the kingdom. Jesus has now been raised from the dead as Israel's Messiah, and Israel's Messiah, as the psalms and prophets insist, is the world's true Lord. "His dominion shall be from one sea to the other, from the River to the ends of the earth."[10] That, of course, is the true message of the ascension story that follows immediately: as every Roman knew, the one who ascends into heaven is enthroned as the divine Emperor.

And how is this Emperor going to take command of his worldwide empire? His messengers, his emissaries, are to go off into all the territories of which he is already enthroned as Lord and to bring the good news of his accession and his wise and just rule. "You are to be my witnesses," he says, "in Jerusalem, Judaea, Samaria and to the ends of the earth."[11] And that is of course exactly the pattern that follows in the whole book of Acts. The apostles are not offering people a new religious experience, though that will come as well. They are not telling them that they can now go to heaven when they die, though they will, if they believe, there to wait until the resurrection itself. Nor are they telling them that God has done an extraordinary miracle that shows how powerful he is, though he has. They are to go and tell the world that Jesus, the Jewish Messiah, is the world's true Lord and to summon them to believing obedience. And that is exactly what they do.

Notice how the shape of the book of Acts works this out in terms not of what we call religion so much as what we call politics. The first half of Acts, up to chapter 12, has Jesus being announced as the risen Messiah, King of the Jews, under the nose of the Jewish authorities and particularly the Herod family. Finally Herod Agrippa, who had James killed and tried to have Peter killed as well, gets a dose of megalomania and thinks he's become divine, like a Hellenistic princeling or a Roman emperor, and he dies on the spot. (The incident is recorded by Josephus as well and is clearly grounded in solid history.)[12] Then in the second half of the book, Paul is always traveling, confronting Caesar's empire with news of its new Lord, and he ends up in Rome, under Caesar's nose, proclaiming God's kingdom, says Luke, and teaching about King Jesus as Lord, openly and without hindrance.[13] There could not be a much clearer statement of intent: the kingdoms of the world are now claimed as the kingdom of Israel's God, and of his Messiah.

And the basis of this announcement is the resurrection of Jesus: not his parables, not his healings, not even his atoning death, important though all of those are and remain. It is the resurrection of Jesus that means he is now enthroned as Lord. (We note in passing that though this sequence of thought makes perfect though surprising sense within the world of first-century Judaism, the opposite movement doesn't work at all. Some people have suggested that the church first came to believe that Jesus was enthroned as Lord and then deduced from that that he had been raised from the dead. This would make no sense whatever within that world.) The whole point is that Israel and the world have turned a great corner, and people have to be told about it. In a telling phrase, Luke says that the Sadducees were annoyed because the apostles were "proclaiming in Jesus the resurrection of the dead."[14] Many modern translations tone this down to something like "announcing the resurrection of dead because of Jesus," implying that the apostles were saying that because of Jesus's resurrection other people could now be raised to life. They may have been saying that too, but that's not the point Luke is getting at. The point is that they were announcing that in Easter "the resurrection from the dead" had actually begun. Easter was the beginning of God's new world, the long-awaited new age, the resurrection of the dead.

Then, dramatically, Paul stands on the Areopagus in Athens, where, in Aeschylus's play six centuries earlier, Apollo had declared that "When a man dies, and his blood is shed on the ground, there is no resurrection." And on that spot, according to Acts 17, Paul declares that the speculations and puzzles of pagan theology and philosophy can now all be put on a different footing because the one true God has unveiled himself and his plan for the whole world by appointing a man to be judge of the whole world and has certified this by raising him from the dead.[15] This is what the resurrection does: it opens the new world, in which, under the saving and judging lordship of Jesus, the Jewish Messiah, everything else is to be seen in a new light.

All this, naturally and rightly, raises huge questions for us. They are put succinctly in a letter I received a year or two ago, after I protested about the way in which the notion of the kingdom of God was carefully and deliberately screened out—and I mean literally screened out!—from the BBC television series *Son of God*. My correspondent went straight to the point. "As there is clearly no trace of a new kingdom after 2,000 years," he wrote, "perhaps it is kinder to Jesus to leave it out." Well, it depends what you mean. People tend, in this conversation, to refer to the Crusades and the Spanish Inquisition and to imply that all the Christian church has ever done can be summed up by those two monstrosities. This is of course ridiculous, but the church has been on the back foot for so long that we've forgotten how to give the right answer. But we might just note two striking lessons from the last twenty-five years of world history.

Granted that Eastern European Communism was going to fall by its own weight sooner or later, it is highly significant that the thing that actually put the crowbar under it and toppled it over was the fearless witness of a Polish pope and those who took courage from his faith and hope. And granted that apartheid could not last forever, it is highly significant that at the center of the movement for its peaceful dismantling, instead of the bloodbath all commentators had been expecting and many on the ground were hoping for, was a black African archbishop who spent the first three hours of every day, and repeated moments thereafter, in devout and fervent prayer. Who would have thought, thirty years ago, that we would see a Commission of Truth and Reconciliation set up to bring healing to that troubled country?

Now of course there are still many running sores in the world, many of which, like Northern Ireland, have brought shame on the church. Of course it is open to anyone to give alternative explanations of these and other events and to ignore evidence suggesting that Jesus is Lord. His lordship is, after all, always exercised through, and visible to, faith. Even the striking occasional miracles that the early apostles performed didn't convince everybody at the time. This isn't just a cop-out. The difference between the kingdoms of the world and the kingdom of God lies exactly in this, that the kingdom of God comes through the death and resurrection of his Son, not through naked displays of brute force or wealth. But I rejoice that we don't have to talk only of St. Francis or Mother Teresa or even of William Wilberforce but that we can speak perfectly credibly in our own day too of the power of the kingdom of the risen Jesus to overthrow proud and oppressive regimes and to give hope to the humble and poor, and to do so with remarkable restraint, dignity, justice, and peace. And, on a smaller scale, there are of course hundreds and thousands of things being done by the church, in the name and power of the risen Jesus, every day. I was privileged to be in Southwark Cathedral one Saturday in 2001 to witness Nelson

Mandela opening a new suite of buildings, which have dramatically extended the cathedral's work with the homeless and with young people, including a room named after Bishop Desmond Tutu: a striking symbol, at the heart of multiracial South London, of the power of the resurrection in a community that has often been troubled and divided.

The gospels and Acts set the scene. But our main spokesman for the early church is St. Paul, and, as we now move to consider his writings, we shall see that he doesn't just agree with the gospel writers about the basic significance of the resurrection; he turns this into a bracing challenge to Christian living in the present.

PAUL

We have already studied Paul's robust hope for the resurrection of the body. We have seen too that he can speak movingly of the intermediate state between death and resurrection: his desire, he says, is "to depart and be with Christ, which is far better."[16] Clearly this belief is based not just on the beliefs of his Jewish upbringing, important though they were, but also on the resurrection of Jesus himself.

But, like the gospel writers, Paul does not see Jesus's resurrection as simply meaning that we are assured of being with Christ after death and of final resurrection beyond that. The meaning of Easter for him is by no means confined to hope beyond the grave. He, like the gospel writers, sees Jesus's resurrection as the start of a new world, a new creation, in which Jesus is already ruling and reigning as Lord. Nobody could accuse Paul of being unaware of the paradox of making such claims. Some of his most striking statements of the point are written from prison. And in that context, it is Paul who articulates most strikingly what the resurrection means not just for the world in particular, vital though that is as the overall context, but also for the ordinary life of every Christian, child, woman, and man.

We begin with Paul's great statement of the new world in 1 Corinthians 15:12–28. He is battling to get it into the heads of the ex-pagan Corinthians, many of whom clearly didn't fully grasp that the gospel meant what it said about Jesus's resurrection. The crunch comes in verse 17: if the Messiah isn't raised, then your faith is futile *and you are still in your sins.* In other words, with the resurrection of Jesus a new world has dawned in which forgiveness of sins is not simply a private experience; it is a fact about the cosmos. Sin is the root cause of death; if death has been defeated, it must mean that sin has been dealt with. But if the Messiah has not been raised, we are still in a world where sin reigns supreme and undefeated so that the foundational Christian belief, that God has dealt with our sins in Christ, is based on thin air and is reduced to whistling in the dark.

Paul then describes this new world in the striking passage in verses 20–28. The writing here is typically dense, but the central statements are strong and clear. The Jewish expectation of resurrection—the resurrection of all God's people at the end of time—has been split into two: first an advance foretaste, then the rest to follow. The Messiah has been raised as the start of the general resurrection; those who belong to him will be raised at his final appearing (verse 23). Then, and only then, will he complete the implementation of the victory he won at Calvary and Easter. That is the time when all enemies, including death itself, will be put under his feet, in fulfillment of scriptural promise (verses 24–26). But notice verse 25a: *he must reign until . . .* ; in other words, he is already reigning even though we do not yet see the full result of that reign.[17] And if we ask what on earth can possibly justify such an outrageous statement—that Jesus is already king of the world even though Caesar seems to be and death is still rampant—there can be only one answer: the resurrection.

Paul is thus firmly on the same page as the gospel writers. The main meaning of the resurrection of Jesus for him is that God's new world has been brought into being through this event, the long-promised new world in which the covenant will be renewed, sins will be forgiven, and death itself will be done away with. The resurrection is neither an isolated and out-of-character divine miracle nor simply the promise of eternal life beyond the grave. It is, rather, the decisive start of the worldwide rule of the Jewish Messiah, in which sins are already forgiven and the promise of the eventual new world of justice and incorruptible life are assured.

So what will this mean in practice for us? We may be prepared to grant that the resurrection of Jesus has opened a new era in world history. Even this, however, takes some doing. As we saw a moment ago, the anti-Christian rhetoric of the last two hundred years in the Western world has done its best to deny such a thing. Most of us have a Pavlovian reaction to the claim about the present kingdom that the New Testament makes. We instantly want to talk about the ambiguities of the Constantinian settlement, the connivance of many churches in twentieth-century atrocities, and much in between. But we shouldn't let a proper penitence for past wickedness turn into a false humility about the extraordinary achievements of the church in both the past and the present. The Wilberforces and the Tutus are real, and they matter, and so do a million others who are less well known but equally signs of the strange lordship of Jesus over the world. We are all called to live within the world where these things are possible and to be agents of such things insofar as they lie in our calling and sphere. But for Paul the resurrection is not just about large-scale or public work. It is about the personal and intimate life of resurrection to which each of us is called. It is, in other words, about baptism and holiness. This is where his bracing command comes home to us: it's time to wake up.

The first main passage in which this point is made is Romans 6. This chapter directly follows one of Paul's majestic overviews of the whole of God's saving purposes: "As sin reigned through death," he writes at the end of Romans 5, "so grace shall reign through righteousness to eternal life through Jesus the Messiah, our Lord." There is God's new world, and the question is, where do we belong in it?

He faces this question in 6:1: "What shall we say? Shall we continue in sin, that grace may abound?" Are we just spectators in God's great drama, sitting on the sidelines, unaffected by the big picture? If God delights to bring his grace to sinners, as Christian evangelists have always rightly insisted, should we go on being sinners in order to get more grace?

Paul's answer is clear: certainly not! We are committed, in our baptism, to being resurrection people. Verses 2–4 set out the groundwork: in baptism we died with the Messiah and were raised with him to new life. Then, in typical Pauline style, he explains further what he means in verses 5–7. We were planted with the Messiah in his death, with the result that our old identity, the old self, was crucified with him. And if that's true, it means that sin has no rights over you, no official hold over you. Instead (verses 8–10), if the Messiah has been raised from the dead, and if you are in the Messiah—by baptism a member of his people—then it means that you too, in him, have been raised from the dead. Many have supposed that Paul meant this in a purely future sense, but the point of verse 11 is that it is also a present experience: you must now calculate, do the sum, reckon it up, "consider yourself"[18] to be dead to sin and alive to God in the Messiah, Jesus. It is on this basis that he can go on in the following passage to instruct his hearers not to let sin rule in their present bodies.

We can sum this up in the following way. *The revolutionary new world, which began in the resurrection of Jesus—the world where Jesus reigns as Lord, having won the victory over sin and death—has its frontline outposts in those who in baptism have shared his death and resurrection.* The intermediate stage between the resurrection of Jesus and the renewal of the whole world is the renewal of human beings—you and me!—in our own lives of obedience here and now.

Before we comment further on this, we note that the same point is underlined in Colossians 2 and 3. We begin with 2:12: "In baptism—which corresponds to the Jewish circumcision [that is, it is the mark of entry into God's covenant people]—you were buried with the Messiah; and you were also raised with him through faith in the power of God who raised him from the dead." Paul assumes that baptism is coupled with faith in God's resurrection power because the basic baptismal confession is "Jesus is Lord," and the belief that grounds this confession is the gospel message that God raised Jesus from the dead.[19] He then continues to draw out the implications of having died with the Messiah: the Jewish laws and regulations no longer have any hold over you (2:16–23).

But at the start of Colossians 3 he focuses on what it actually means to share, here and now, in the resurrection of the Messiah. Paul insists that if you are already raised with Christ—in other words, if you through baptism and faith are a resurrection person, living in the new world begun at Easter, energized by the power that raised Jesus from the dead—then you have a responsibility to share in the present risen life of Jesus. "If, then, you are risen with the Messiah, seek the things that are above; set your thoughts on things above, not on things of the earth." It is no use simply saying, "I've been baptized; therefore God is happy with me the way I am." Paul's logic is: "You have been baptized; therefore God is challenging you to die to sin and live the resurrection life."

At this point we face a problem that is best dealt with head-on. It has two aspects, a street-level one and a more recondite one. To discuss them we shall have to think a bit harder about the meaning of the word *heaven* and similar ideas like "the things that are above."

The street-level problem is the old jibe about being "so heavenly minded that we are no earthly use." I say it's an old jibe; I haven't heard it so much recently, perhaps because these days many practicing Christians bend over backward in the other direction and are often so earthly minded, so concerned with practical details and nuts and bolts, that one wonders if they are any longer any *heavenly* use. However, that's not the point. The jibe only works in a world where heaven and earth are assumed to be detached from each other, having nothing to do with each other. But in the Bible heaven and earth are made for each other. They are the twin interlocking spheres of

God's single created reality. You really understand earth only when you are equally familiar with heaven. You really know God and share his life only when you understand that he is the creator and lover of earth just as much as of heaven. And the point of Jesus's resurrection, and the transformed body he now possesses, is that he is equally at home in earth and heaven and can pass appropriately between them, slipping through the thin curtain that separates us from God's blinding reality. That, as we saw in chapter 7, is part of the core meaning of the ascension.

The second-order problem is a kind of grown-up version of the street-level one, and it's this: doesn't this talk of resurrection in the present mean that we are reducing resurrection to a spiritual experience? Isn't that buying into a Gnostic system, which devalues the physical body, including the risen body of Jesus?

No. Our minds are so conditioned, I'm afraid, by Greek philosophy, whether or not we've ever read any of it, that we think of heaven as by definition nonmaterial and earth by definition as nonspiritual or nonheavenly. But that won't do. Part of the central achievement of the incarnation, which is then celebrated in the resurrection and ascension, is that heaven and earth are now joined together with an unbreakable bond and that we too are by rights citizens of both together. We can, if we choose, screen out the heavenly dimension and live as flatlanders, materialists. If we do that, we will be buying in to a system that will go bad, and will wither and die, because earth gets its vital life from heaven.[20]

But if we focus our attention on the heavenly dimension, all sorts of positive and practical results will follow. In Colossians 3:11 Paul sees the unity of the church across cultural and ethnic boundaries as one of the first of these results. In the passage that follows, he lists all kinds of other things that ought to appear in the life of anyone who really sets his or her mind on the world that is now Jesus's primary home, the world that is designed to heal and restore our present one. In each case what he's talking about *is actual current physical reality, shot through now with the life of heaven.* Part of getting used to living in the post-Easter world—part of getting used to letting Easter change your life, your attitudes, your thinking, your behavior—is getting used to the cosmology that is now unveiled. Heaven and earth, I repeat, are made for each other, and at certain points they intersect and interlock. Jesus is the ultimate such point. *We as Christians are meant to be such points, derived from him.* The Spirit, the sacraments, and the scriptures are given so that the double life of Jesus, both heavenly and earthly, can become ours as well, already in the present.

All of which brings us to our last Pauline passage. Ephesians is a companion letter to Colossians, and here we find the bracing instruction, taken perhaps from an early Christian poem or hymn: "Awake, sleeper, rise from the dead, and the Messiah will give you light!" (5:14).

In other words, it's time to wake up! Living at the level of the nonheavenly world around you is like being asleep; worse, it's like that for which sleep is a metaphor—being dead. Lying, stealing, sexual immorality, bad temper, and so on (Paul lists them all in a devastating short passage)[21] are forms of death, both for the person who commits them and for all whose lives are touched by their actions. They are ways of sleeping a deadly sleep. It's time to wake up, he says. Come alive to the real world, the world where Jesus is Lord, the world into which your baptism brings you, the world you claim to belong to when you say in the creed that Jesus is Lord and that God raised him from the dead. What we all need from time to time is for someone (a friend, a spiritual director, a stranger, a sermon, a verse of scripture, or simply the inner prompting of the Spirit) to say, "It's time to wake up! You've been asleep long enough! The sun is shining and there's a wonderful day out there! Wake up and get a life!"

The message of Easter, then, is neither that God once did a spectacular miracle but then decided not to do many others nor that there is a blissful life after death to look forward to. The message of Easter is that God's new world has been unveiled in Jesus Christ

SURPRISED BY HOPE

and that you're now invited to belong to it. And precisely because the resurrection was and is bodily, albeit with a transformed body, the power of Easter to transform and heal the present world must be put into effect both at the macrolevel, in applying the gospel to the major problems of the world—and if Soviet Communism and apartheid don't count on that scale I don't know what does—and to the intimate details of our daily lives. Christian holiness consists not of trying as hard as we can to be good but of learning to live in the new world created by Easter, the new world we publicly entered in our baptism. There are many parts of the world we can't do anything about except pray. But there is one part of the world, one part of physical reality, that we can do something about, and that is the creature each of us calls "myself." Personal holiness and global holiness belong together. Those who wake up to the one may well find themselves called to wake up to the other as well. And that leads us precisely into the next, and final, chapter.

15. RESHAPING THE CHURCH FOR MISSION (2): LIVING THE FUTURE

INTRODUCTION: CELEBRATING EASTER

So how can we learn to live as wide-awake people, as Easter people? Here I have some bracing suggestions to make. I have come to believe that many churches simply throw Easter away year by year; and I want to plead that we rethink how we do it so as to help each other, as a church and as individuals, to live what we profess. I am speaking here particularly from, and to, the church I know best. Those who celebrate in other ways will, I think, be able to make appropriate adjustments and take whatever they need to apply to their own situations.

For a start, consider Easter Day itself. It's a great step forward that many churches now hold Easter vigils, as the Orthodox church has always done, but in many cases they are still too tame by half. Easter is about the wild delight of God's creative power—not very Anglican, perhaps, but at least we ought to shout Alleluias instead of murmuring them; we should light every candle in the building instead of only some; we should give every man, woman, child, cat, dog, and mouse in the place a candle to hold; we should have a real bonfire; and we should splash water about as we renew our baptismal vows. Every step back from that is a step toward an ethereal or esoteric Easter experience, and the thing about Easter is that it is neither ethereal nor esoteric. It's about the real Jesus coming out of the real tomb and getting God's real new creation under way.

But my biggest problem starts on Easter Monday. I regard it as absurd and unjustifiable that we should spend forty days keeping Lent, pondering what it means, preaching about self-denial, being at least a little gloomy, and then bringing it all to a peak with Holy Week, which in turn climaxes in Maundy Thursday and Good Friday . . . and then, after a rather odd Holy Saturday, we have *a single day* of celebration.

All right, the Sundays after Easter still lie within the Easter season. We still have Easter readings and hymns during them. But Easter week itself ought not to be the time when all the clergy sigh with relief and go on holiday. It ought to be an eight-day festival, with champagne served after morning prayer or even before, with lots of alleluias and extra hymns and spectacular anthems. Is it any wonder people find it hard to believe in the resurrection of Jesus if we don't throw our hats in the air? Is it any wonder we find it hard to *live* the resurrection if we don't do it exuberantly in our liturgies? Is it any wonder the world doesn't take much notice if Easter is celebrated as simply the one-day happy ending tacked on to forty days of fasting and gloom? It's long overdue that we took a hard look at how we keep Easter in church, at home, in our personal lives, right through the system. And if it means rethinking some cherished habits, well, maybe it's time to wake up. That always comes as a surprise.

And while we're about it, we might write some more good Easter hymns and take care to choose the many good ones already written that celebrate what Easter really is rather than treating it as simply our ticket to a blissful life hereafter. Interestingly, most of the good Easter hymns turn out to be from the early church and most of the bad ones from the nineteenth century. But we should be taking steps to celebrate Easter in creative new ways: in art, literature, children's games, poetry, music, dance, festivals, bells, special concerts, anything that comes to mind. This is our greatest festival. Take Christmas away, and in biblical terms you lose two chapters at the front of Matthew and Luke, nothing else. Take Easter away, and you don't have a New Testament; you don't have a Christianity; as Paul says, you are still in your sins. We shouldn't allow the secular world, with its schedules and habits and parareligious events, its cute Easter bunnies, to blow us off course. This is our greatest day. We should put the flags out.

In particular, if Lent is a time to give things up, Easter ought to be a time to take things up. Champagne for breakfast again—well, of course. Christian holiness was never meant to be merely negative. Of course you have to weed the garden from time to time; sometimes the ground ivy may need serious digging before you can get it out. That's Lent for you. But you don't want simply to turn the garden back into a neat bed of blank earth. Easter is the time to sow new seeds and to plant out a few cuttings. If Calvary means putting to death things in your life that need killing off if you are to flourish as a Christian and as a truly human being, then Easter should mean planting, watering, and training up things in your life (personal and corporate) that ought to be blossoming, filling the garden with color and perfume, and in due course bearing fruit. The forty days of the Easter season, until the ascension, ought to be a time to balance out Lent by taking something up, some new task or venture, something wholesome and fruitful and outgoing and self-giving. You may be able to do it only for six weeks, just as you may be able to go without beer or tobacco only for the six weeks of Lent. But if you really make a start on it, it might give you a sniff of new possibilities, new hopes, new ventures you never dreamed of. It might bring something of Easter into your innermost life. It might help you wake up in a whole new way. And that's what Easter is all about.

SPACE, TIME, AND MATTER: CREATION REDEEMED

At this point we have to face a serious current problem. Many of the places within the Western churches where new life is erupting, with young people coming into the church and all kinds of new energy, music, and initiative, are also often places where people have deliberately abandoned most of the traditional practices of the mainstream churches—church buildings, liturgies, formal prayers, and even, in some places, the sacraments themselves (except in a rather occasional and halfhearted way). This, I think, stems from a kind of latent Protestantism in Western Christian culture, an implicit belief that buildings, liturgies, and so on are in their very nature unspiritual, uninspiring, and stultifying and that the less we have of them, the better. Many people in the newer churches that have gone this route, and in the newer expressions of this type within traditional denominations, have indeed found that their traditional churches were fairly lifeless. Such people, discovering the joy of new life in Christ for themselves, have gladly abandoned all that they now regard as boring, staid, and even unspiritual. For many people, in fact, fresh expressions of faith mean no church buildings, no services as such, certainly no liturgy, no fixed times or days, and no sacraments (at least, no formal Eucharist; there will be various kinds of homemade parasacraments, but that's another story.) It may be that some readers, coming at last to a chapter on shaping the church for mission, are expecting that I will agree with this relentless popular-level Protestantism (which is what it is).

If so, I am afraid I am going to disappoint them. Let me be clear. I am all for a mixed economy in worship. We live in a many-sided society both locally and globally, and it would be silly to suppose that any one size or shape will fit all the worshippers who, we hope, might think of joining us. But the logic of new creation compels me to what I hope are some salutary reflections, not to dampen the enthusiasm of new expressions of Christian life but to remind people that they must not throw the banana away with the skin. There is always the danger, as in one of Jesus's greatest parables, of a plant that grows up energetically but that has no root—just as, of course, there are plants that have very deep roots but allow other things to choke them. In other words, it won't do either to stick slavishly to old forms of church or, equally slavishly, to abandon all traditions and insist on perpetual innovation. We must keep our eyes fixed on the hope that is set before us and on the resurrection of Jesus, which is our launching pad, and we must reorder our worship and our work in the world accordingly.

Let us then remind ourselves of the starting point. The created order, which God has begun to redeem in the resurrection of Jesus, is a world in which heaven and earth are designed not to be separated but to come together. In that coming together, the "very good" that God spoke over creation at the beginning will be enhanced, not abolished. The New Testament never imagines that when the new heavens and new earth arrive, God will say, in effect, "Well, that first creation wasn't so good after all, was it? Aren't you glad we've got rid of all that space, time and matter?" Rather, we must envisage a world in which the present creation, which we think of in those three dimensions, is enhanced, taken up into God's larger purposes, no doubt, but certainly not abandoned.

What happens when we think of space, time, and matter as being renewed, not abandoned, within the life of the church?

The renewal and reclaiming of *space* has recently involved, among other things, a fresh grasp of the Celtic tradition of "thin places," places where the curtain between heaven and earth seems almost transparent. This is in fact just one aspect of a much wider theology of place, which has been under serious threat in the West since the Enlightenment.[1] We urgently need to recapture this theology before, to use an obvious metaphor, all the ancient trees are cut down to make room for a shopping center and parking lot just when people are starting to realize how much shade those trees provide in summer, how much fruit they bear in autumn, and how beautiful they look in spring. Jesus does indeed declare that God calls all people everywhere to worship him in spirit and truth rather than limiting worship to this or that holy mountain.[2] But this doesn't undercut a proper theology of God's reclaiming of the whole world, which is anticipated in the claiming of space for worship and prayer.

Church buildings and other places where, in Eliot's phrase, "prayer has been valid" *are not a retreat from the world but a bridgehead into the world,* a way of claiming part of God-given space for his glory, against the day when the whole world will thrill to his praise.

It is nothing short of dualistic folly, then, simply to declare without ado (as many try to do today, supposedly in the interest of mission but in fact in the interest of dualism—or a quick profit) that old church buildings and the like are irrelevant to the mission of God today and tomorrow. Of course in many cases a church building has served its purpose and can now be demolished or given over to alternative use. But many are rediscovering in our day that there are indeed such things as places sanctified by long usage for prayer and worship, places where, often without being able to explain it, people of all sorts find that prayer is more natural, that God can be known and felt more readily. We should reflect long and hard on a proper theology of place and space, thought through in terms of God's promise to renew the whole creation, before we abandon geography and territory. Yes, territorial claims can become idolatrous or abusive—as, for instance, when a church that has long since abandoned any pretense at orthodox Christianity tries to use its canonical powers to insist on some kind of territorial rights or when a few people cling to a building for sentimental reasons long after it has ceased to serve its local community. But the answer to abuse is not dualism but proper use.

The renewal and reclaiming of *time* takes at least three forms.

1. It was dramatically symbolized in the fourth century when Dionysus the Insignificant constructed a dating scheme for the whole world based on the (supposed) birth date of Jesus. The fact that this scheme is still in use more or less worldwide despite abortive attempts such as that of the French Revolutionaries to supplant it came briefly to notice a few years ago at the time of the millennium but is largely ignored.[3] Like a great church bell ringing out over a

sleepy town, every time someone puts a date on something it speaks of the lordship of Jesus, whether people listen or not.

2. More specifically, though, the *time* of the church, the long story of church history and the tradition that has accrued during it, must be taken seriously in any eschatologically based and mission-shaped view of the church. Once again, we must of course beware of idolatry, the hallowing of things that were once indifferent and are now irrelevant. One must be constantly aware that the church has done and said many foolish and wicked things as well as many wise and godly things. But the story of the church is the story of the ways in which, despite folly, failure, and downright sin, God's future has already burst in upon what, for our forebears, was the present time, leaving us a legacy of that bit of the past that is full not only of mistakes and culturally conditioned lifestyles but also of patterns of new creation, which have already, from our point of view, been woven into history—bits of God's future, so to speak, which are now already bits of our past.

It is of course all-important to discern what, in tradition, is to be seen as an example of this and what is to be seen as an example of the church getting it wrong. But jettisoning tradition just because it is tradition is to capitulate to postmodernity and to a kind of ultra-Protestantism that cuts the tree off at the root because it believes that trees should be entirely visible and obviously fruitful, no part of them buried in dirty soil.

3. In particular, the gospels (especially John) and the early practice of the church (as in Paul) reflect the very early understanding of the church that *the first day of the week,* the day of Easter, has become a sign within the present world and its temporal sequence that the life of the age to come has already broken in. Sunday, kept as a commemoration of Easter ever since that event itself (a quite remarkable phenomenon when you come to think about it), is not simply a legacy

of Victorian values but a perpetual sign, joyfully renewed week by week, that all time belongs to God and stands under the renewing lordship of Jesus Christ.[4]

Of course, worship should be "seven whole days, not one in seven." Many Christians will find, for all kinds of reasons, that Sunday is a difficult day to attend long church services. But we should remind ourselves that the earliest Christians lived in a world where Sunday was the first day of the working week, much like our Monday, and that they valued its symbolism so highly that they were prepared to get up extra early both to celebrate Easter once again and to anticipate the final Eighth Day of Creation, the start of the new week, the day when God will renew all things.

The most contentious of the space-time-matter trio is of course matter itself, the stuff of which (as the Protestant tradition has always rightly warned) idols are made. Yet again, however, if we are not to collapse into Platonism, denying the goodness of creation itself, it is crucial to recapture both the bodily incarnation and resurrection of Jesus and the promise that creation itself will be renewed, liberated from death and decay (and therefore presumably, as in C. S. Lewis's remarkable imaginative world in *The Great Divorce,* more solid, more real, than the present one). It is within this framework of thought that the classic Christian sacraments of baptism and Eucharist make sense.

Of course, the sacraments can degenerate into mere superstition and idolatry. But we should never forget what happened when the Israelites allowed that to happen with the Ark of the Covenant, treating it simply as a magic talisman to be taken note of only when they were doing badly in battle (1 Samuel 4–5). The ark was captured, and the Israelites lost the battle. But when the Philistines put the ark into the temple of Dagon their god, Dagon fell flat on his face before it. Abuse of the sacrament does not nullify the proper use.

Successive Christian generations have struggled to find language to do justice to the reality of what happens in baptism and of what happens in the Eucharist. It is perhaps not surprising that they have largely failed because in fact the sacraments are designed to be their own language, ultimately untranslatable, even though we can describe what is going on from various angles, themselves all inadequate. (Remember the ballerina who, asked to say what a particular dance meant, replied, "If I could have said it, I wouldn't have needed to dance it.") But to reject, marginalize, trivialize, or be suspicious of the sacraments (and quasi-sacramental acts such as lighting a candle, bowing, washing feet, raising hands in the air, crossing oneself, and so forth) on the grounds that such things *can* be superstitious or idolatrous or that some people might suppose that by doing them they are putting God in their debt, is like rejecting sexual relations in marriage on the grounds that it's the same act that in other circumstances constitutes immorality. (I am always amused, on this point, when I visit churches that carefully abandoned all signs of professional worship from a former age—robed choirs, processions, organists, and the like—and then invented new forms of worship that demand just as much professionalism in terms of competent people managing sound systems, lighting, overhead projection and PowerPoint, and so on. There is nothing wrong with either. All can and should be done to the glory of God. But the implication that older styles of worship are somehow less spiritual and the modern electronic worship is somehow more worthy is sheer cultural prejudice and should be happily laughed at whenever it emerges.)

Try looking at it like this (shortening, for the moment, a much longer case that could be argued). In the Eucharist, the bread and the wine come to us as part of God's new creation, the creation in whose reality Jesus already participates through the resurrection. They speak powerfully, as only encoded actions can speak (whether a handshake, a kiss, the tearing up of a contract, or whatever), both of the death he suffered, through which idolatry and sin have been defeated, and of his future arrival in which creation is to be renewed (1 Corinthians 11:26). We feed on that reality even though we may find it difficult to conceptualize what *sort* of reality it is. Knowing that we are thereby renewed as the people of Jesus who live and work in the tension between Easter and the final renewal enables us at least to relax and enjoy all that the sacrament has to offer.

If, then, the church is to be renewed in its mission precisely in and for the world of space, time, and matter, we cannot ignore or marginalize that same world. We must, rather, claim it for the kingdom of God, for the lordship of Jesus, and in the power of the Spirit *so that we can then go out and work for that kingdom, announce that lordship, and effect change through that power.* You do not teach people to sing by first carefully throwing away your musical instruments. The mission of the church must therefore include, at a structural level, the recognition that our present space, time, and matter are all subject not to rejection but to redemption. Living between the resurrection of Jesus and the final coming together of all things in heaven and earth means celebrating God's healing of his world not his abandoning of it; God's reclaiming of space as heaven and earth intersect once more; God's redeeming of time as years, weeks, and days speak the language of renewal; and God's redeeming of matter itself, in the sacraments, which point in turn to the renewal of the lives that are washed in baptism and fed with the Eucharist. Despite the tendency in some parts of the emerging church to marginalize space, time, and matter, I remain convinced that the way forward is to rediscover a true eschatology, to rediscover a true mission rooted in anticipating that eschatology, and to rediscover forms of church that embody that anticipation.

RESURRECTION AND MISSION

What then will the church look like as it moves from renewed worship into renewed mission?

I hope I have said enough to make it clear that the mission of the church is nothing more or less than the outworking, in the power of the Spirit, of Jesus's bodily resurrection and thus the anticipation of the time when God will fill the earth with his glory, transform the old heavens and earth into the new, and raise his children from the dead to populate and rule over the redeemed world he has made.

If that is so, mission must urgently recover from its long-term schizophrenia. As I have said before, the split between saving souls and doing good in the world is a product not of the Bible or the gospel but of the cultural captivity of both within the Western world. We return to the themes of two chapters ago (justice, beauty, evangelism) with hope renewed precisely because of the promise of space, time, and matter renewed. The world of space, time, and matter is where real people live, where real communities happen, where difficult decisions are taken, where schools and hospitals bear witness to the "now, already" of the gospel while police and prisons bear witness to the "not yet." The world of space, time, and matter is where parliaments, city councils, neighborhood watch groups, and everything in between are set up and run for the benefit of the wider community, the community where anarchy means that bullies (economic or social as well as physical) will always win, where the weak and vulnerable will always need protecting, and where therefore the social and political structures of society are part of the Creator's design.

And the church that is renewed by the message of Jesus's resurrection must be the church that goes to work precisely in that space, time, and matter and claims it in advance as the place of God's kingdom, of Jesus's lordship, of the power of the Spirit. Councils and parliaments can and often do act wisely (the "already" of the gospel, which the church must seek to foster) though, because they may in turn become agents of bullying and corruption, they will always need scrutiny and accountability (the "not yet" of the gospel, in which the church must be active and watchful).

Thus the church that takes sacred *space* seriously not as a retreat from the world but as a bridgehead into it will go straight from worshipping in the sanctuary to debating in the council chamber—discussing matters of town planning, of harmonizing and humanizing beauty in architecture, in green spaces, in road traffic schemes, and (not least in the rural areas, which are every bit as needy) in environmental work, creative and healthy farming methods, and proper use of resources. If it is true, as I have argued, that the whole world is now God's holy land, we must not rest as long as that land is spoiled and defaced. This is not an extra to the church's mission. It is central.

The church that takes seriously the fact that Jesus is Lord of all *time* will not just celebrate quietly every time we write the date on a letter or document, will not just set aside Sunday as far as humanly and socially possible as a celebration of God's new creation (and will point out the human folly of a seven-day working week), will not just seek to order its own life in an appropriate rhythm of worship and work. Such a church will also seek to bring wisdom, and freshly humanizing order, to the rhythms of work in offices and shops, in local government, in civic holidays, and in the shaping of public life. These things cannot be taken for granted. The enormous shifts during my own lifetime, from the whole town observing Good Friday and Easter to those great days being simply more occasions for football matches and yet more televised reruns of old movies (with, often enough, no sign in the television schedules of anything remotely to do with Jesus or the gospel!) are an index of what happens when a society loses its roots and drifts with prevailing social currents. The reclaiming of time as God's good gift (as opposed to time as simply a commodity to be spent for one's own benefit, which often means fresh forms of slavery for others) is not an extra to the church's mission. It is central.

And, of course, the church that take seriously the fact that in and through Jesus the Creator God has grasped the world of *matter* once more and has transformed it by his own person and presence, and will one day fill it with his knowledge and glory as the waters cover the sea, not only will seek to celebrate the coming of God in Christ in and through the sacramental elements but also will go straight from baptism and the Eucharist to make God's healing, transforming presence a reality in the physical matter of real life. One of the things I have most enjoyed about being a bishop is watching ordinary Christians (not that there are any "ordinary" Christians, but you know what I mean) going straight from worshipping Jesus in church to making a radical difference in the material lives of people down the street by running playgroups for children of single working moms; by organizing credit unions to help people at the bottom of the financial ladder find their way to responsible solvency; by campaigning for better housing, against dangerous roads, for drug rehab centers, for wise laws relating to alcohol, for decent library and sporting facilities, for a thousand other things in which God's sovereign rule extends to hard, concrete reality. Once again, all this is not an extra to the mission of the church. It is central.

It should be clear that this way of coming at the tasks of the church in terms of space, time, and matter plays straight into the categories I used before, of justice and beauty. But it also leads directly into evangelism. When the church is seen to move straight from worship of the God we see in Jesus to making a difference and effecting much-needed change in the real world; when it becomes clear that the people who feast at Jesus's table are the ones in the forefront of work to eliminate hunger and famine; when people realize that those who pray for the Spirit to work in and through them are the people who seem to have extra resources of love and patience in caring for those whose lives are damaged, bruised, and shamed, then it is not only natural to speak of Jesus himself and to encourage others to worship him for themselves and find out what belonging to his family is all about but it is also natural for people, however irreligious they may think of themselves as being, to recognize that something is going on that they want to be part of. In terms that the author of Acts might have used, when the church is living out the kingdom of God, the word of God will spread powerfully and do its own work.

Of course, no one individual can attempt more than a fraction of this mission. That's why mission is the work of the whole church, the whole time. Some will find God nudging them to work with handicapped children. Some will sense a call to local government. Others will discover a quiet satisfaction in artistic or educational projects. All will need one another for support and encouragement. All will need to be nourished by the central, worshipping life of the church, and that central life will itself be nourished and renewed as the friends of Jesus come back to worship from their mission in the world.[5]

A good deal of this activity will cheerfully and rightly overlap with work being done, and often done very well, by those of other faiths or none. That is what we should expect and welcome, if indeed it is true that (over against all dualisms) the one true God is the creator of all, who has not left himself without witness in the world. Paul's advice to the Philippians—even though he and they knew they were suffering for their faith and might be tempted to retreat from the world into a dualistic, sectarian mentality—was up-beat. "These are the things you should think through," he wrote: "whatever is true, whatever is holy, whatever is upright, whatever is pure, whatever is attractive, whatever has a good reputation; anything virtuous, anything praiseworthy."[6] And in thinking through these things, we will discover more and more about the same creator God whom we know in and through Jesus Christ and will be better equipped to work effectively not over against the world but with the grain of all goodwill, of all that seeks to bring and enhance life.

The same letter, of course, also urges us not to be naive. There are plenty of places and situations where vested interests, corrupt policies and politicians, tyrants, bullies, and communities that have turned in on themselves racially and culturally will find the church's witness in any of the ways I have described threatening and offensive. This will be no surprise to those churches who find themselves facing, in today's Western world, the politically correct banning of Christian symbols and festivals. Nor will it be a surprise to those who have tried to campaign for better housing, for better conditions for farm or factory workers, and found implacable anger from those who were quietly but ruthlessly exploiting others.

But note what such people will then say. They will tell the church, again and again, to get back to its proper business of saving souls. *That radical distortion of Christian hope belongs exactly with a quietism that leaves the world as it is and thus allows evil to proceed unchecked.* This is where the surprise of hope catches people unawares, and they react by telling us Christians what *they* think our hope ought to be—a hope that will cut the nerve of, and the need for, any attempt to make things better in the present world of space, time, and matter.

It is at this point that the church must learn the arts of collaboration without compromise and of opposition without dualism. There are good things going on in the wider world, and we must join in while always remaining on the lookout for the point where we will be asked to do something that goes against the grain of the gospel. There are wicked things going on in the wider world, and we must stand out against them while always remaining on the lookout for the point where we become mere dualists, retreating from the world, which is already charged with the grandeur of God. All this is difficult enough at the best of times and all the more so now because we in the West have simply not thought in these terms for a couple of hundred years. Once again, William Wilberforce and others like him have something to teach us. And suddenly all those shrewd remarks of Jesus come home to roost. It is time to figure out what it will mean, in the real world of the twenty-first century, to be wise as serpents and innocent as doves.

I have argued that a mission-shaped church must have its mission shaped by its hope; that the genuine Christian hope, rooted in Jesus's resurrection, is the hope for God's renewal of all things, for his overcoming of corruption, decay, and death, for his filling of the whole cosmos with his love and grace, his power and glory. I have argued that to be truly effective in this kind of mission, one must be genuinely and cheerfully rooted in God's renewal of space, time, and matter within the life of the church. There is no use (to adapt once more a metaphor I have used more than once) trying to get fruit from a tree whose roots you have systematically dug up.

I am not, of course, saying, "Do traditional church well and mission will follow." Far too much traditional church has consisted of too much tradition and not enough church. What I am saying is, think through the hope that is ours in the gospel; recognize the renewal of creation as both the goal of all things in Christ and the achievement that has already been accomplished in the resurrection; and go to the work of justice, beauty, evangelism, the renewal of space, time, and matter as the anticipation of the eventual goal and the implementation of what Jesus achieved in his death and resurrection. That is the way both to the genuine mission of God and to the shaping of the church by and for that mission.

All of this means, of course, that the people who work at and for this mission in the wider world must themselves be living, modeling, and experiencing the same thing in their own lives. There is ultimately no justification for a private piety that doesn't work out in actual mission, just as there is ultimately no justification for people who use their activism in the social, cultural, or political sphere as a screen to prevent them from facing the same challenges within their own lives—the challenge, that is, of God's kingdom, of Jesus's lordship, and of the Spirit's empowering. If the gospel isn't transforming you, how do you know that it will transform anything else?

From one point of view, this might seem to lead back to some rather ordinary topics. But I now want to suggest, in the final section of this concluding chapter, that the basic disciplines of Christian spirituality, the disciplines through which the church is nourished for this space-time-matter mission of justice, beauty, and evangelism, are themselves best understood in the context of the surprising hope, the hope that is rooted in Jesus's resurrection and that reaches out to anticipate God's new creation in all its fullness.

Space forbids more than a brief outline of six central aspects of Christian spirituality that appear in a new light when we see them as part of God's surprising hope, the Easter call to us to wake up and come alive within his new world.

New Birth and Baptism

One of the most striking mentions of the new birth is found in the great opening of 1 Peter. God in his great mercy has given us a new birth to a living hope by the resurrection of Jesus Christ from the dead.[7] Jesus's resurrection is directly instrumental in bringing about this new birth and its consequences. It is all because of what happened at Easter: a new reality has opened up in the world, a new kind of life both inward and, importantly, outward in holiness and in the hope of our own resurrection. The preaching for, and experience of, the new birth has of course been central to some movements within Christianity, notably evangelicalism, down the years. Though often mocked and caricatured (one recalls the snide remarks journalists used to make about President Jimmy Carter "having been born a bit too often"), it rightfully retains that place.

But what has proved much harder to do, in those movements that have stressed the new birth as a vital spiritual experience, is to articulate a theology of baptism that goes with it, as it obviously does in the New Testament. Evangelicalism's inability to do this left the door wide open to the various theologies of Spirit baptism that have characterized Pentecostalism, but that's another story. Baptism too, of course, is closely allied with the resurrection of Jesus in two passages in particular: Romans 6 and Colossians 2.

In order to understand baptism, here and elsewhere, we have to say something about sacramental theology. I have come to believe that the sacraments are best understood within the theology of creation and new creation, and of the overlapping of heaven and earth, that I have been exploring throughout this book. The resurrection of Jesus has brought about a new state of affairs in cosmic history and reality. God's future has burst into the present, and (as happens sometimes in dreams, when the words we are saying or the music we are hearing are also *happening* in the events in which we are taking part) somehow the sacraments are not just signs of the reality of new creation but actually part of it. Thus the event of baptism—the action, the water, the going down and the coming up again, the new clothes—is not just a signpost to the reality of the new birth, the membership (as all birth gives membership) in the new family. It really is the gateway to that membership.

Of course, as all pastors in all traditions know only too well, many who have shared in baptism now seem to want nothing to do with the new family or the new life to which it should have introduced them. But this is not an argument against Paul's very realistic language about baptism. (Nor is it an argument against baptizing young children; the problem of people "falling away" is just as real with adult baptisms.) In fact, Paul himself seems to have faced the same problem in 1 Corinthians 10, where some who had been baptized were refusing to live in the appropriate way. In addressing this problem, he doesn't deny the validity of their entry into the people of God but rather presupposes it. The consequence is a severe warning: God will judge those who presume upon his kindness, upon their privilege of membership.

The important thing, then, is that in the simple but powerful action of plunging someone into the water in the name of the triune God, there is a real dying to the old creation and a real rising into the new—with all the dangerous privileges and responsibilities that then accompany the new life as it sets out in the as-yet-unredeemed world. Baptism is not magic, a conjuring trick with water. But neither is it simply a visual aid. It is one of the points, established by Jesus himself, where heaven and earth interlock, where new creation, resurrection life, appears within the midst of the old.

The idea of associating baptism with Easter always was, and still is, a proper Christian instinct. Just as for many Christians the truth of Easter is something they glimpse occasionally rather than grasp and act on, so, for many, baptism remains in the background, out of sight, whereas it should be the foundational event for all serious Christian living, all dying to sin and coming alive with Christ.

Eucharist

From baptism we move naturally to the Eucharist. Let me sketch three views of the Eucharist and show how the theology of new creation, coming forward to meet us in the present, enables us to see more clearly what's going on.

For many Christians, the sacraments have been all too close to the performance of sympathetic magic. A holy person, a shamanlike figure, mumbles the magic words and does the magic deeds; a wonderful conjuring trick is performed in which ordinary food is turned into the actual body and blood of Jesus Christ; once again evil is warded off, atonement is made, God is appeased, prayers are offered with special efficacy, social power and control are reinforced, everyone is happy. A caricature, of course, of what real theologians actually believed, but this is how things have often appeared to many ordinary folk. And at that level the church's sacraments are little better than pagan ritual.

Until, of course, the Reformation, at which point the entire system was challenged. One extreme of Reformation theology, determined to resist anything that smacked of magic or paganism or that confirmed the power of the priestly class, insisted on denying everything that Rome taught. Thus the radical Swiss Reformers regarded the Eucharist as a bare sign, a simple reminder, of the historic fact that Christ had died for our sins. Meditate on that fact, they said, and you would get just as much spiritual benefit as you would from eating the bread—indeed, much more than if you ate it without such meditation.

In between the quasi-magic ritual, on the one hand, and the bare memory, on the other, a more historically grounded view reminds us of how the Jewish sacred meals (not least the Passover, from which the Eucharist takes its point of origin) were thought to function. To this day, when Jews celebrate Passover they don't suppose they are essentially doing something *different from* the original event. "This is the night," they say, "when God brought us out of Egypt." The people sitting around the table become not the distant heirs of the wilderness generation but the same people. Time and space telescope together. Within the sacramental world, past and present are one. Together they point forward to the still-future liberation.

What happens in the Eucharist is that through the death and resurrection of Jesus Christ, this future dimension is brought sharply into play. We break this bread to share in the body of Christ; we do it in remembrance of him; we become for a moment the disciples sitting around the table at the Last Supper. Yet if we stop there we've only said the half of it. To make any headway in understanding the Eucharist, we must see it as the arrival of God's future in the present, not just the extension of God's past (or of Jesus's past) into our present. We do not simply remember a long-since dead Jesus; we celebrate the presence of the living Lord. And he lives, through the resurrection, precisely as the one who has gone on ahead *into the new creation,* the transformed new world, as the one who is himself its prototype. The Jesus who gives himself to us as food and drink is himself the beginning of God's new world. At communion we are like the children of Israel in the wilderness, tasting fruit plucked from the promised land. It is the future coming to meet us in the present.

This perspective is a far more helpful way to talk about the presence of Christ in the Eucharist than trying to redefine the old language of transubstantiation. The problem with the old language was not that it was the wrong answer but that it was the right answer to the wrong question. It was right to insist on the true presence of Christ but wrong to explain that presence in terms of the philosophies of the time, the Aristotelian distinction between substance and accident, and the supposed power of the priest to alter the "substance" (the inner, invisible reality of an object like a piece of bread) while leaving the "accidents" (its outward properties like weight, color, chemical makeup) apparently untouched. That was one way of saying what needed to be said in language that some people in the Middle Ages could understand, but it has produced all kinds of misunderstandings and abuses.

A far better way is provided by the New Testament's language about new creation. Take Romans 8 as a good starting point: creation is groaning in travail as it waits for redemption. But one part of the old creation has already been transformed, is already liberated from bondage to decay, namely, the body of Christ, the body that died on the cross and is now alive with a life that death can't touch. Jesus has gone ahead into God's new creation, and as we look back to his death through the lens he himself provided—that is, the meal he shared on the night he was betrayed—we find that he comes to meet us in and through the symbols of creation, the bread and the wine, which are thus taken up into the Christ story, the event of new creation itself, and become vessels, carriers, of God's new world and the saving events that enable us to share it.

Within this framework, that of a true Easter understanding of creation and new creation, we can understand the Eucharist most fully as the anticipation of the banquet when heaven and earth are made new, the marriage supper of the Lamb. (Some liturgies have tried to express this but sadly have often collapsed back into mere talk of heaven, which is precisely not the point.) It is the breaking in of God's future, the Advent future, into our present time. Every Eucharist is a little Christmas as well as a little Easter.

This is not magic. Magic seeks to gain by cunning, and for personal power or pleasure, what God gives by grace, to faith, to promote holiness and love. The resurrection of Jesus and the promise of a world made new provide the ontological, epistemological, and above all eschatological framework within which we can understand the Eucharist afresh. Let us not rob ourselves of the hope that comes forward from God's future to sustain us in the present. God's new world has begun. If we don't see it breaking into the present world, we are denying the energizing foundation of Christian life.

Prayer

The third area is prayer. There is something about prayer which says: we are open to someone, something, beyond; we are, at least in principle, aware of a power beyond our own power, a presence, perhaps even a person, beyond and probably higher than our own person. All prayer is like that. It is at least a start.

But because of the death and resurrection of Jesus and the bursting into our present world of God's future reality, the New Testament writers do not want to leave our praying in the rather crude, vague, and unformed state implied by that lowest-common-denominator description. We may again outline three different ways of looking at prayer and then show how an authentically Christian view retains the strong point of each while going beyond, called by the God of the future, who has burst into the present.[8]

The first way of understanding prayer is as a kind of nature mysticism: being open to the beauty, joy, and power of the world around us. It is what happens, unaided and unbidden, as we gasp at a vision of snowcapped mountains or as we stand on a summer's night away from the city lights and are overwhelmed with awe at the starry heavens. It's what happens when we fall deeply in love and discover a previously unimagined wholeness, a fulfillment of self in giving self away. Each of these is, as people often say, a profoundly religious experience. Each of them, if we hold them in our minds and hearts, can be described as a sort of prayer, celebrating something beyond ourselves and feeling part of it, caught up in it, in a kind of union way beyond humdrum daily life. Such a sense of nature mysticism can be extremely powerful and moving, indeed life changing. Some people describe such experiences glowingly and expect the church to approve. But this is not, yet, what the New Testament understands by Christian prayer.

At the other extreme we find that kind of prayer, common in ancient paganism, for example, which sees it as the making of petitions to a deity or deities who are distant, not well known, certainly capricious, and possibly malevolent. Here is a sailor going off to sea. He visits Poseidon's temple and offers a sacrifice to pray for a safe voyage. He is still secretly afraid that someone else may have bribed Poseidon more successfully to create a wind going in the wrong direction. Or he may have got some of the magic formulae wrong. Or the sacrifice may be blemished in some way despite his best efforts. Many people approach prayer like that, even in church: a distant appeal to a faceless bureaucrat who may or may not be interested or kindly disposed.

In between the two, with elements of both but going way beyond, we find the prayer life of ancient Israel. Though the Psalms do have some pagan parallels here and there, nothing like this collection exists anywhere else. It celebrates the goodness of creation ("The earth is the Lord's, and all that therein is") and recognizes that the heavens declare the glory of God. Yet the Psalms celebrate their intimate union not with creation as such but with the creator God, whose love and power are made known in creation. The Psalmists often feel that God has become distant and remote, perhaps even that he has turned to fight against them. Yet they refuse to believe, when they call and nothing happens, that the boss has gone fishing or is away playing golf. They go on battering on his door until they can remind him of his personal promises, his great acts of old on Israel's behalf, and above all his personal love. And even when they find no way to turn the corner toward resolution (Psalms 88, 89), they are eventually if sorrowfully content to leave the dire situation in front of God's door. "*You* have put lover and friend away from me." Like Job, though God should slay them, yet will they trust in him.[9] And of course, along with the Psalms, the thrice-daily prayer of the Jew from early times to the present was and is the great Shema prayer: "Hear, O Israel: the Lord our God, the Lord is One." There is one God, and he is *our* God. Transcendence, intimacy, celebration, covenant: those are the roots of biblical prayer.

Now notice what happens when we move into the New Testament, particularly in the light of Jesus's death and resurrection. We find, as with everything else, that the Jewish theory and practice of prayer have been refocused and drawn further forward by the climactic and decisive events concerning Jesus. And through this, the twin poles of nature mysticism and petitionary prayer, particularly prayer in trouble or danger, are drawn together into a new configuration.

Among the great passages on prayer, the Farewell Discourses of John 13–17 stand out, culminating of course in Jesus's own astonishing prayer to the Father. There is much to ponder here for which there isn't space, but I want to note that in these chapters Jesus speaks repeatedly of the new relationship that the disciples will have with the Father as a result of his own "going away"—more or less a shorthand for his death and resurrection—and as a result of his sending of the Spirit, his own Spirit, to be with them and in them. In this intimacy of relationship they are encouraged to ask for whatever they want—anything at all—in Jesus's name. "The Father himself loves you," explains Jesus.[10]

Gradually we realize what is happening. The extraordinary, unique, intimate relationship that Jesus himself had enjoyed with the Father is now open to all his followers. John finally explains why and how this comes about, in the first of his resurrection chapters. The risen Jesus tells Mary Magdalene to go and say to "my brothers," "I am going up to my Father *and your Father,* to my God *and your God.*"[11] Jesus, as himself the fulfillment and goal of Israel's vocation to be God's son, his beloved one, now shares this status and its benefits with all his followers. God's intention for the end, to draw humans freely into intimate fellowship with himself, has come forward to meet us in Jesus of Nazareth. This is yet one more meaning of the resurrection.

But if this new intimacy stands at the heart of the New Testament's view of prayer, it doesn't mean that we've left behind that sense of oneness with the created order that we find in so many religions and indeed in our own experience. The great heavenly scene of Revelation 4 and 5 stands out as a moment when the church is gathering up the praises of all creation and presenting them before God's throne. But within these chapters, again, the central problem of nature mysticism is named and dealt with. The world is out of joint. If we bring ourselves simply into harmony with the created order as it is at present, we are embracing death: not only nature red in tooth and claw but also the cosmos running down into the cold night of entropy. Yes, says Revelation 5: the problem with the good creation is, how can God's purposes for it be fulfilled? How can the scroll of God's will be unrolled and read so that it comes to pass? No one is worthy to do it. The answer, through which the prayer and worship of the church and creation are taken through into a new dimension, is that the Lion who is also the Lamb has conquered, and through him God's purposes are going forward. And, with that, prayer and worship break out in a new way. Heaven and earth come together in a new way. Future and present are joined in a new way. In the death and resurrection of Jesus the new creation has begun, and with it the new song, "Worthy is the Lamb," the song that lies at the heart of Christian adoration.[12]

Nor have we thereby abandoned the Psalmist's sense of frustration, of battering at God's door. Paul, at one of the most climactic moments in all his writings (Romans 8), pauses to comment that we Christians are caught in between creation and new creation, and this shows in how we pray and what we pray for. Or rather in the fact that much of the time we don't know what to pray for. We have glimpsed in Jesus the new creation coming to birth. We have felt something of its power, by the Spirit, in our own lives. But this hasn't given us a simplistic, easy answer to the puzzles and problems of prayer. Rather, it has given us the immense privilege of sharing the intimate life of the triune God himself. The Spirit calls from deep within us, calls to the Father, calls from the pain of the world, the pain of the church, the pain of our hearts. And with that call, and with the answering love of the Father, we are, as Paul says, conformed to the image of the Messiah, God's son (Romans 8:26–30), the one who shared the suffering of the world so that he might be the true intercessor for the world. The connections between Romans 8 and the Johannine Farewell Discourses are many and deep, and never more so than when they speak of the way in which the inner life of God himself, Father, Son, and Spirit, comes to meet us, comes forward from God's future to where we are in the present.

Notice what happens with all this. If we were to say, "Well, that's all a bit complex and high-flown; I'm not sure I really grasp it; I'll rest content to feel a oneness with the sea and the sky, the leaves and the loves of this world, and that will be enough to keep me from collapsing into a one-dimensional secular world," the New Testament writers would be horrified. "What," they'd say, "God's future has come forward to meet you in the present, to transform your present muddled praying into the sharing of his own intimate life, and you're going to be happy with living in the unredeemed world, untouched by the future that burst into our world at Easter?"

It will, of course, be costly. You don't get to share God's life and escape without wounds. Look what happened to Jesus himself. But see what happens when the central Jewish prayer, the Shema, comes forward into Christianity and turns into the Lord's Prayer. Thy kingdom come *on earth as in heaven*. Is that not what we've been talking about throughout this book? Are we going to refuse, at the final hurdle, to finish the course and translate our theology into prayer?

Scripture

Fourth, scripture. This may seem a strange topic to bring in as a way of reflecting on how the themes of resurrection and new creation are reflected in Christian spirituality and practice and of how our future hope, which shapes our mission, must also shape our common Christian life. But I am convinced that unless we think something like this, we will misunderstand scripture and perhaps also misuse it.[13]

Scripture—the Old and New Testaments—is the story of creation and new creation. Within that, it is the story of covenant and new covenant. When we read scripture as Christians, we read it precisely as people of the new covenant and of the new creation. We do not read it, in other words, as a flat, uniform list of regulations or doctrines. We read it as the narrative in which we ourselves are now called to take part. We read it to discover "the story so far" and also "how it's supposed to end." To put it another way, we live somewhere between the end of Acts and the closing scene of Revelation. If we want to understand scripture and to find it doing its proper work in and through us, we must learn to read and understand it in the light of that overall story.

As we do this—as groups, churches, and individuals—we must allow the power of God's promised future to have its way with us. As we read the gospels, we must remind ourselves again and again—because the pull of prevailing Western culture is so strong that if we don't it will suck us back down into dualism—that this is the story of how God's kingdom was established on earth as in heaven in and through the work of Jesus, fulfilling Israel's great story, defeating the power of evil, and launching God's new world. As we read the letters, we must remind ourselves that these are the documents designed to shape and direct the community of the new covenant, the people who were called to take forward the work of new creation. As we read Revelation, we must not allow the wonderful heavenly vision in chapters 4 and 5 to lull us into imagining that this is the *final* scene in the story, as though the narrative were simply to conclude (as in Charles Wesley's hymn) with the redeemed casting their crowns before the throne. This is a vision of *present* reality, seen in its heavenly dimension. We must read on to the end, to the final vision of Revelation 21 and 22, the chapters that give final meaning to all that has gone before and indeed to the entire canon.

Likewise, when we read the Old Testament, we must read it—as it manifestly asks to be read—as the long and winding story of how God chose a people to take forward his plan to rescue his creation, not the story of how God had a shot at calling a people whom he would save from the world and how this was aborted, forcing him to try something else (a caricature, I know, but one many will recognize). And this means that though the Old Testament must be read as part of "our story" as Christians, we must not imagine that we are still living within that moment in the story. The story itself points beyond itself, like a set of parallel lines meeting in the infinitely rich narrative of the gospels and the sudden outburst of new life in Acts and the letters.[14]

The Bible as a whole thus does what it does best when read from the perspective of new creation. And it is designed not only to tell us *about* that work of new creation, as though from a detached perspective, not only to provide us with true information about God's fresh, resurrection life, but also to *foster* that work of new creation in the churches, groups, and individuals who read it, who define themselves in terms of the Jesus they meet in it, who allow it to shape their lives. The Bible is thus the *story of* creation and new creation, and it is itself, through the continuing work of the Spirit who inspired it, an *instrument of* new creation in human lives and communities.

The Bible is not, in other words, simply a list of true doctrines or a collection of proper moral commands—though it includes plenty of both. The Bible is not simply the record of what various people thought as they struggled to know God and follow him, though it is that as well. It is not simply the record of past revelations, as though what mattered were to study such things in the hopes that one might have one for oneself. It is the book whose whole narrative is about new creation, that is, about resurrection, so that when each of the gospels ends with the raising of Jesus from the dead, and when Revelation ends with new heavens and new earth populated by God's people risen from the dead, this should come not as a surprise but as the ultimate fulfillment of what the story had been about all along. (This, by the way, is the deep-level reason why the other gospels were not included in the canon. It isn't that they were the really exciting or subversive bits that the early church excluded in the interests of power and control. They were the books that had stopped talking about new creation and were offering a private, detached spirituality instead. The sudden enthusiasm for these other gospels in certain quarters of the Western world in our own day is a token not of the rediscovery of genuine Christianity but of the desperate attempts to avoid it. New creation is far more demanding— though ultimately, of course, far more exhilarating—than Gnostic escapism.)

Thus, just as the proclamation of Jesus as Lord results in men, women, and children coming to trust and obey him in the power of the Spirit and to find their lives transformed by his saving lordship, so the telling of the story of creation and new creation, of covenant and new covenant, doesn't just *inform* the hearers *about* this narrative. It *invites them into it,* enfolds them within it, assures them of their membership in it, and equips them for their tasks in pursuit of its goal.

All of which leads us to one of the greatest challenges of our day.

Holiness

Fifth, holiness. This is what Paul hammers away at in the early chapters of 1 Corinthians, and it's because they don't understand the resurrection that the Corinthians are having difficulty with it. What you do with your body in the present matters, he insists, because God raised the Lord and will also raise us by his power. Glorify God in your body because one day God will glorify the body itself. What is to be true in the future must begin to be true in the present, or it will be called into question whether you are really on track in the first place. Here we are building once more on passages like Romans 6 and Colossians 3 and working out what it means to live as part of God's new creation.

It is Romans that provides the key to so much of this, the key that seems to have been thrown away in some recent debates. The letter works in a complex but coherent symphonic development. It is not simply a string of points one after another, with some doctrines here and some ethics there. In particular, the analysis of the human plight in 1:18–2:16 is not at all meant as a throwaway bit of polemic against rent-a-crowd stage villains, as is often suggested. It is carefully calibrated and integrated into the flow of the letter. When Paul reflects on the behavior that had become standard among pagans, he speaks of God "giving them up" to an unfit *mind,* and the worst thing he can say about pagan immorality in chapter 1 is the last verse, that "they not only do such things, but approve those who practice them."[15] It's one thing to be lured into sin, quite another to change the moral compass and call good evil and evil good. And this cast of the mind links directly to the major command of 12:1: do not be conformed to this world, but be transformed by the renewal of your minds. This is inaugurated eschatology; this is what the resurrection looks like when it comes forward into the moral life of the person of faith. For Paul, holiness is never a matter of simply finding out the way you seem to be made and trusting that that's the way God intends you to remain. Neither is it a matter of blind obedience to arbitrary and out-of-date rules. It's a matter of *transformation,* starting with the mind.

That is why, to return to 1 Corinthians, it is the resurrection—both that of Jesus and that of ourselves—that provides, in passages like chapters 5 and 6, the ultimate rationale for Christian behavior. It isn't the case that Christian ethics consists of a few odd regulations and restrictions that Christians are supposed to follow while still living in exactly the same world as everyone else, just as it isn't the case that the resurrection of Jesus was simply a very strange miracle within the world of old creation. The resurrection was the full bursting in to this world of the life of God's new creation; Christian ethics is the lifestyle that celebrates and embodies that new creation. Living out a life of Christian holiness makes sense, perfect sense, *within God's new world,* the world into which we are brought at baptism, the world where we are nourished by the Eucharist. Of course, if you try to live a Christian lifestyle outside this framework, you will find it as difficult, indeed nonsensical, as it would be for an orchestral performer to play his or her part separated from the rest of the players amid the crashes and metallic screeching of an automobile factory. Not that we aren't called, of course, to practice our discipleship in the hard, outside world, which rumbles on as though Easter had never happened. But if we are to be true to our risen Lord, we will need, again and again, to retune our instruments and practice once more alongside our fellow musicians.

All of which brings us, in Paul's words, to the most excellent way of all.

Love

Finally, and climactically, we come to love. Think of the wonderful poem that we call 1 Corinthians 13, which looks forward to the exposition of the resurrection in 1 Corinthians 15. The poem itself is complete, and exquisite. But it speaks of something that is incomplete, frustratingly so:

> Our knowledge is incomplete; our prophecy is incomplete; but when completion arrives, the incomplete is done away. When I was a child, I spoke as a child, I thought as a child, I reasoned like a child; but when I became a man, I put away childish things. For now we see in a mirror, dimly, but then face to face; now I know in part, but then shall I know, even as also I am known.[16]

This passage is the bit we don't expect in this wonderful chapter. The poem doesn't just celebrate the fact that love is the greatest thing in God's world. It doesn't just explain what love will mean in hard-edged practice (patient, kind, not jealous or boastful, and so on). It isn't, in other words, a poetic way of giving us simply a rule of life, another goal in the struggle for obedience or even Christlikeness.

The poem does much, much more: it yearns over the fact that our experience of love, as of everything else that matters, is decidedly incomplete. The way we are now, seen against the way we shall be in God's design, is only partly what it is meant to be and is emphatically partly not what it is meant to be. But Paul is urging that *we should live in the present as people who are to be made complete in the future.* And the sign of that completeness, that future wholeness, the bridge from one reality to the other, is love.

Remember what the letter as a whole is about. The young church was in a mess. They were ridden with personality cults. They were socially divided, rich against poor. They were spiritually divided, jealous of one another's gifts. They tolerated immorality. Their worship was chaotic; their grasp of the gospel was shaky. Oh, they had an energy, a drive; they were going somewhere, even if they weren't sure in which direction. I'd rather have a live church with problems than a dead church offering the spurious peace of the tombstone, though let me quickly add that I'd rather not have all the problems of Corinth at once, thank you very much.

Paul goes through the problems one by one, almost as though they form a kind of shopping list. Great discussions, each one hammered out on the anvil of scripture and serious Christian thinking. And then, in the middle of it all, like Mozart's *Ave Verum* making its way through the noise of a factory until the machinery falls silent, is the still music of chapter 13. Listen to it in the old language of the King James version:

> Though I speak with the tongues of men and of angels, and have not charity, I am become as sounding brass, or a tinkling cymbal. And though I have the gift of prophecy, and understand all mysteries, and all knowledge; and though I have all faith, so that I could remove mountains, and have not charity, I am nothing. . . .
>
> Charity suffereth long, and is kind; charity envieth not; charity vaunteth not itself, is not puffed up; doth not behave itself unseemly,

seeketh not her own, is not easily provoked, thinketh no evil; rejoiceth not in iniquity, but rejoiceth in the truth; beareth all things, believeth all things, hopeth all things, endureth all things. . . .

For now we see through a glass, darkly; but then face to face: now I know in part; but then shall I know even as also I am known. And now abideth faith, hope, charity, these three; but the greatest of these is charity.

This isn't simply a wonderful poem stuck in to the letter at this point to change the mood. This poem, both in tone and content, is the still, quietly beating heart that makes sense of everything else. Everything Paul says in the rest of the letter is drawn together at this point.

But he's not done yet. That last stanza of the poem, insisting on the incompleteness of our present experience, points on to the final great discussion of the letter, namely chapter 15, in which Paul gives the fullest exposition in all early Christian writing of Jesus's resurrection and what it means. It means that a new world order has opened up in the midst of the present one. God's future has arrived in the present in the person of the risen Jesus, summoning everybody to become people of the future, people in Christ, people remade in the present to share the life of God's future. Our present experience, even our present Christian experience, is incomplete. But in Christ we have heard the complete tune; we know now what it sounds like and that we shall one day sing it in tune with him. Our present experience, with all its incompleteness, is meant to point us to the fact that we will one day wake up and arise from sleep. That, after all, is what resurrection is all about.

It is this future emphasis, the stress that what we are at the moment is incomplete, that turns Paul's poem on love away from being mere moralism ("please try harder to behave like this!") and into something altogether stranger and more powerful. We all know that it's no good simply telling people to love one another. One more exhortation to love, to patience, to forgiveness, may remind us of our duty. But as long as we think of it as duty we aren't very likely to do it.

The point of 1 Corinthians 13 is that love is not our duty; it is our *destiny.* It is the language Jesus spoke, and we are called to speak it so that we can converse with him. It is the food they eat in God's new world, and we must acquire the taste for it here and now. It is the music God has written for all his creatures to sing, and we are called to learn it and practice it now so as to be ready when the conductor brings down his baton. It is the resurrection life, and the resurrected Jesus calls us to begin living it with him and for him right now. Love is at the very heart of the surprise of hope: people who truly hope as the resurrection encourages us to hope will be people enabled to love in a new way. Conversely, people who are living by this rule of love will be people who are learning more deeply how to hope.

This is the message that underlies the gospel command to forgiveness—which is also, of course, the command to remit debts, about which I spoke earlier. But forgiveness is not a moral rule that comes with sanctions attached. God doesn't deal with us on the basis of abstract codes and rules like that. Forgiveness is a way of life, God's way of life, God's way *to* life; and if you close your heart to forgiveness, why, then you close your heart to forgiveness. That is the point of the terrifying parable in Matthew 18, about the slave who had been forgiven millions but then dragged a colleague into court to settle a debt of a few pence. If you lock up the piano because you don't want to play to somebody else, how can God play to you?

That is why we pray, "Forgive us our trespasses, *as we forgive those who trespass against us.*" That isn't a bargain we make with God. It's a fact of human life. Not to forgive is to shut down a faculty in the innermost person, which happens to be the same faculty that can receive God's forgiveness. It also happens to be the same faculty that can experience real joy and real grief. Love bears all things, believes all things, hopes all things, endures all things.

Of course, in our incomplete world God's gentle offer and demand press upon us as fearful things, almost threatening. But God's offer and demand are neither fearful nor threatening. God in his gentle love longs to set us free from the prison we have stumbled into—the loveless prison where we refuse both the offer and the demand of forgiveness. We are like a frightened bird before him, shrinking away lest this demand crush us completely. But when we eventually yield—when he corners us and finally takes us in his hand—we find to our astonishment that he is infinitely gentle and that his only aim is to release us from our prison, to set us free to be the people he made us to be. But when we fly out into the sunshine, how can we not then offer the same gentle gift of freedom, of forgiveness, to those around us? That is the truth of the resurrection, turned into prayer, turned into forgiveness and remission of debts, turned into love. It is constantly surprising, constantly full of hope, constantly coming to us from God's future to shape us into the people through whom God can carry out his work in the world.

APPENDIX: TWO EASTER SERMONS[1]

If I were a betting man, I would lay good money on two basic messages going out from pulpits this Easter.

Pastor Frank Gospelman believes passionately in the bodily resurrection of Jesus, the empty tomb, the angels, the whole supernatural shebang. Every Easter he denounces the wicked liberals, not least the Reverend Jeremy Smoothtongue up the road, for their unwillingness to acknowledge that the Bible is true, that God really does do miracles, and that—as the demonstration of those two points—Jesus really did rise again. Pastor Gospelman may try a few stunts to show that eyewitnesses can tell strange stories and still be speaking the truth: watch him eat a daffodil in the pulpit. He may quote the old chorus: "You ask me how I know he lives? He lives within my heart!" Yes, Jesus is risen from the dead, and he is therefore alive and we can get to know him for ourselves.

When it comes to the "so what," the pastor is equally emphatic. There really is a life after death! Jesus has gone to prepare a place for us in heaven! Salvation awaits, in a glorious, blissful world beyond this one. We are, after all, "citizens of heaven," as Paul says, so when we're done with this wicked world our souls will be snatched away to be there forever. We shall be reunited with our loved ones (don't you wish there was a better phrase, even a better cliché, for saying that?). We shall share the life of the New Jerusalem. "Here for a season, then above, O Lamb of God, I come." "Till we cast our crowns before thee, lost in wonder, love and praise."

Alas, Pastor Gospelman has missed the point. Much of what he says is true, but most of it isn't the truth that the Easter stories were written to convey.

Down the road, fortified by champagne in the rectory after the midnight Easter vigil (why not break the Lenten fast in style, even if your fasting has been, well, somewhat sporadic), Mr. Smoothtongue is in full flow. We know of course that the crude, surface meaning of the story can't be what the writers really meant. Modern science has shown that miracles don't happen, that dead people don't rise. Anyway, what kind of a God would break into history just this once to rescue one favored person while standing back and doing nothing during the Holocaust? To believe in something so obvious, so blatant, so . . . *unspiritual* as the empty tomb and the bodily resurrection—it's offensive to all one's finer instincts. In particular, it might be taken to mean (as his good friend Pastor Gospelman up the road would no doubt imagine, bless his fundamentalist socks) that Christianity is therefore superior to all other faiths, whereas we know that God is radically inclusive and that all religions, all faiths, all worldviews can be equally valid pathways to the Divine.

So, the stories of the empty tomb were probably made up many years later. The learned rector wants to make this quite clear: they are a remythologization of the primal eschatological drama, which caught up the disciples in a moment of sociomorphic, possibly even sociopathic, empathy with the apocalyptic denouement of the Beatific Vision. Hmm. No, the congregation didn't quite get that either. But then they too had ended the Lenten fast in style.

When it comes to the "so what," Mr. Smoothtongue is emphatic. Now that we've got away from that crude supernatural nonsense, the way is clear to "True Resurrection." This, it turns out, is a new way of construing the human project, breaking through the old taboos (he has traditional sexual ethics in mind but is much too delicate to mention it) and discovering a new kind of life: a welcoming, yes, "inclusive" approach. The "stone" of legalism has been rolled away, and the "risen body," the true spark of life and identity hidden

SURPRISED BY HOPE

inside each of us, can burst forth. And, well, of course, this new life must now infect all our relationships. All our social policies. Resurrection must become not a one-time event, imagined by premodern minds and insisted on by backward-looking conservatives, but an ongoing event in the liberation of humans and the world.

Mr. Smoothtongue is on to something here at last, but he doesn't know what it is. Or why.

What Pastor Gospelman never notices is that the resurrection stories in the gospels *aren't about going to heaven when you die.* In fact, there is almost nothing about "going to heaven when you die" in the whole New Testament. Being "citizens of heaven" (Philippians 3:20) doesn't mean you're supposed to end up there. Many of the Philippians were Roman citizens, but Rome didn't want them back when they retired. Their job was to bring Roman culture to Philippi.

That's the point that all the gospels actually make, in their own ways. Jesus is risen, therefore God's new world has begun. Jesus is risen, therefore Israel and the world have been redeemed. Jesus is risen, therefore his followers have a new job to do.

And what is that new job? To bring the life of heaven to birth in actual, physical, earthly reality. This is what Pastor Gospelman never imagines (though his preaching does, accidentally, often have this result). The bodily resurrection of Jesus is more than a proof that God performs miracles or that the Bible is true. It is more than the Christians' knowing of Jesus in our own experience (that is the truth of Pentecost, not of Easter). It is much, much more than the assurance of heaven after death (Paul speaks of "going away and being with Christ," but his main emphasis is on *coming back again* in a risen body, to live in God's newborn creation). Jesus's resurrection is the beginning of God's new project not to snatch people away from earth to heaven but to colonize earth with the life of heaven. That, after all, is what the Lord's Prayer is about.

That's why Mr. Smoothtongue's final point has a grain of truth in it though all his previous denials make it impossible for him to see why it's true or what its proper shape is. The resurrection is indeed the foundation for a renewed way of life in and for the world. But to get that social, political, and cultural result, you really do need the bodily resurrection, not just a "spiritual" event that might have happened to Jesus or perhaps simply to the disciples. And his insistence on "modern science" (not that he's read any physics recently) is pure Enlightenment rhetoric. We didn't need Galileo and Einstein to tell us that dead people don't come back to life.

When Paul wrote his great resurrection chapter, 1 Corinthians 15, he didn't end by saying, "So let's celebrate the great future life that awaits us." He ended by saying, "So get on with your work because you know that in the Lord it won't go to waste." When the final resurrection occurs, as the centerpiece of God's new creation, we will discover that everything done in the present world in the power of Jesus's own resurrection will be celebrated and included, appropriately transformed.

Of course, when the muddled rector tries to make Easter mean "liberation from moral constraint" and "discovering the true spark within each of us," he is standing genuine Christianity on its head and making it perform tricks like a circus lion, turning it into just another form of Gnosticism. Easter is about new creation, a huge and stunning fresh gift of transforming grace, not about discovering that the old world has been misunderstood and needs simply to be allowed to be truly itself. Romans 6, 1 Corinthians 6, and Colossians 3 stand firmly in his way at this point.

Hands up, all those who have heard one or other of those sermons. Thank you. How much did I win?

Now hands up, those who have heard a sermon that reflects what Paul is talking about in Romans 8 or the evangelists in their final chapters or John the Seer in Revelation 21 and 22: that with Easter, God's new creation is launched upon a surprised world, pointing ahead to the renewal, the redemption, the rebirth of the entire creation. Hands up, those who have heard the message that every act of love, every deed done in Christ and by the Spirit, every work of true creativity—doing justice, making peace, healing families, resisting temptation, seeking and winning true freedom—is an earthly event in a long history of things that *implement* Jesus's own resurrection and *anticipate* the final new creation and act as signposts of hope, pointing back to the first and on to the second. . . .

I thought so. Thank you.

NOTES

PREFACE

1. See, in particular, my books *The New Testament and the People of God* (1992); *Jesus and the Victory of God* (1996); *The Resurrection of the Son of God* (2003); and *Paul: Fresh Perspectives* (2005), the first three forming part of the series *Christian Origins and the Question of God*. All are published by SPCK in London and Fortress Press in Minneapolis; the American title given to the last is *Paul in Fresh Perspective*. In subsequent references these works are referred to as *NTPG, JVG, RSG,* and *Paul.*

1. ALL DRESSED UP AND NO PLACE TO GO?

1. See my *The Cross and the Colliery* (London: SPCK, 2007).

2. David Edwards describes a modern version of this in his *After Death? Past Beliefs and Real Possibilities* (London: Cassell, 1999), 101f.

3. Nigel Barley, *Grave Matters: A Lively History of Death Around the World* (New York: Holt, 1997), 97.

4. Margaret Edson, *Wit: A Play* (London: Faber & Faber, 1999).

5. See the comments of Pat Jalland, "Victorian Death and Its Decline, 1850–1918," in *Death in England: An Illustrated History,* ed. P. C. Jupp and C. Gittings (New Brunswick, NJ: Rutgers University Press, 1999), 245, referring to Thomas Huxley.

6. Dylan Thomas, "Do Not Go Gentle into That Good Night" (1952), *The New Oxford Book of English Verse,* chosen and edited by Helen Gardner (Oxford: Oxford University Press, 1972), 942.

7. Will Self, *How the Dead Live* (London: Bloomsbury, 2000), 390.

8. The poem is often attributed to Mary Elizabeth Frye (1904–2004), but its origin is sometimes disputed.

9. Quoted in Ted Harrison, *Beyond Dying: The Mystery of Eternity* (Oxford: Lion, 2000), 68, 72.

10. Philip Pullman, *His Dark Materials,* a trilogy consisting of *Northern Lights, The Subtle Knife,* and *The Amber Spyglass* (London: Scholastic, 1997, 2000).

11. See, for example, Harrison, *Beyond Dying,* 17.

12. Barley, *Grave Matters,* 84.

2. PUZZLED ABOUT PARADISE?

1. Henry Scott Holland, "The King of Terrors," in *Facts of the Faith: Being a Collection of Sermons Not Hitherto Published in Book Form,* ed. Christopher Cheshire (London: Longmans, Green, 1919), 125–34.

2. "Death, Be Not Proud," in *The New Oxford Book of English Verse,* chosen and edited by Helen Gardner (Oxford: Oxford University Press, 1972), 197. The punctuation of the last line becomes a major theme in Edson's play *Wit* (see discussion of *Wit* in previous chapter).

3. Compare Donne's famous prayer, "Bring us, O Lord, *at our last awakening,* into the house and gate of heaven" (emphasis added). We might want to clarify the use of *heaven* for the risen life, as we shall see, but the point I am making is that Donne was clear about a two-stage postmortem existence, with the relation between the first and second stages being conceived in terms of sleeping and waking.

4. That is why I find it extraordinary that so good a scholar as Douglas J. Davies can say that "Christianity glorified death" and that "the very existence of Easter" led people "to speak of human life as a journey through life to the heavenly city"; see *A Brief History of Death* (Oxford: Blackwell, 2005), 7. Davies's book is remarkable for the way it either marginalizes resurrection altogether or collapses it into a heavenly life after death.

5. Brian Innes, *Death and the Afterlife* (New York: St. Martin's Press, 1999).

6. Shakespeare, *Hamlet,* act 3, scene 1.

7. Maria Shriver, *What's Heaven?* (New York: St. Martin's Press, 1999).

8. The pages are not numbered; these extracts comprise the main message of the whole, short book.

9. A healthy corrective is found in a series of books by Randy Alcorn, principally *Heaven* (Carol Stream, IL: Tyndale House, 2004). Alcorn comes from a tradition that might easily have lapsed into Shriver-type platitudes, but his study of scripture has led him to a far more robust and biblical view—even

though he still uses the word *heaven* when what he emphatically talks about throughout is the new heavens and new earth.

10. I have set this out at length in *JVG* and *The Challenge of Jesus* (Downers Grove, IL: InterVarsity Press, 2000).

11. "Till we cast our crowns before thee / Lost in wonder, love and praise," from "Love Divine, All Loves Excelling."

12. It is fascinating to see how, even when faced with the clear and unambiguous teaching of Rev. 21 about "new heavens and new earth" and about the New Jerusalem *coming down from heaven,* some writers continue to refer to all this as simply "heaven": for example, Roland Chia, *Hope for the World: A Christian Vision of the Last Things* (Downers Grove, IL: InterVarsity Press, 2005), 102, contrasted with his later brief treatment at 129–33.

13. Cf., for example, Peter Stanford, *Heaven: A Traveller's Guide to the Undiscovered Country* (London: HarperCollins, 2003); and even Alister E. McGrath, *A Brief History of Heaven* (Oxford: Blackwell, 2003). Considerably more thorough and nuanced, but with several of the same weaknesses, are Colleen McDannell and Bernhard Lang, *Heaven: A History,* 2nd ed. (New Haven, CT: Yale University Press, 2001), and Jeffrey Burton Russell, *A History of Heaven* (Princeton, NJ: Princeton University Press, 1997). Ulrich Simon's older work, *Heaven in the Christian Tradition* (London: Rockliff, 1958), does its best to combine traditional visions of heaven with the solidity of the resurrection ("The Bible views Heaven and Earth as one world. If the earth is spatial, so is Heaven," 126), but, though pregnant and thoughtful, the book never quite resolves matters in the way the New Testament itself does.

14. See the remarkable statement of this in David Edwards, *After Death? Past Beliefs and Real Possibilities* (London: Cassell, 1999), 78. For fuller discussion of this point, see chap. 8 below.

15. A classic statement of this position is found in John Hick, *Evil and the God of Love* (London: Fontana, 1974).

16. John Keble, "Sun of My Soul, Thou Saviour Dear."

17. J. H. Newman, "Lead, Kindly Light."

18. I am grateful to the Reverend Peter Tyreus for pointing out to me the difference between the hymn as English speakers know it and the original Swedish.

19. This point seems to be missed by Stephen Smalley, *Hope for Ever: The Christian View of Life and Death* (Milton Keynes, UK: Paternoster, 2005), 79, who treats the "rest" and the "calm" as part of an undifferentiated final heavenly state. This is consonant with his view that a "spiritual resurrection"

awaits us after death (17, 78); cf. 65: resurrection will be "spiritual and relational, rather than physical."

20. See my book *For All the Saints? Remembering the Christian Departed*
(Harrisburg, PA: Morehouse, 2003).

21. See my book *The Last Word: Scripture and Authority of God—Getting
Beyond the Bible Wars* (San Francisco: HarperSanFrancisco, 2006).

22. Wright, *For All the Saints?*

3. EARLY CHRISTIAN HOPE IN ITS HISTORICAL SETTING

1. K. R. Popper, *The Open Society and Its Enemies,* rev. ed. (Princeton, NJ:
Princeton University Press, 1971).

2. David Edmonds and John Eidinow, *Wittgenstein's Poker: The Story of
a Ten-Minute Argument Between Two Great Philosophers* (London: Faber &
Faber, 2001).

3. For all this, and much besides, see *RSG.* The speculation by Herod
Antipas that Jesus might be John the Baptist risen from the dead (Mark 6:16)
is an exception that proves the rule.

4. Mark 6:14–16 and parallels.

5. John 11:24.

6. On this whole area, see the important study of J. D. Levenson, *Resurrection and the Restoration of Israel: The Ultimate Victory of the God of Life* (New
Haven, CT: Yale University Press, 2006).

7. Mark 12:18–27; Matt. 22:23–33; Luke 20:27–40.

8. Mark 9:10; interestingly, reported in Mark only.

9. Nor did anybody say of Jesus what Johanan ben Zakkai is reported to
have said about the destruction of the Temple in A.D. 70: Don't worry about
its destruction; we've got something just as good—Torah!

10. David Lawrence, *Heaven: It's Not the End of the World! The Biblical
Promise of a New Earth* (London: Scripture Union, 1995).

11. Luke 23:43; John 14:2; Phil. 1:23 with 3:9–11, 3:20–21.

12. 1 Cor. 15:12.

13. 2 Tim. 2:18.

14. See *RSG,* 534–51.

15. Stephen Patterson, in his review of *RSG* in the *Journal of Religion* 84
(2004): 636ff., suggests that this is a "novel view" of 1 Cor. 15:44. It isn't; and the
argument I presented in *RSG,* 347–60, ought to demonstrate it beyond cavil.

16. Matt. 13:43.

17. Phil. 2:15.

18. Gen. 5:25; 2 Kings 2:11–12.

19. Note the way Jesus can speak of "in the resurrection," parallel to "in the new world": Matt. 19:28, 22:30.

20. Acts 1:6; see too Rom. 11:15.

21. Josephus, *Antiquities* 20.200–203, on which, see *NTPG,* 353f. For the various resistance movements, see *NTPG,* 170–81.

22. See Josephus, *Jewish War* 7.153–57.

23. See *Paul,* chap. 4.

24. See my *Judas and the Gospel of Jesus* (Grand Rapids, MI: Baker, 2006), especially chap. 5. Note particularly the rationale given by the pagans for the persecutions at Lyons in A.D. 177. Note too the way in which "resurrection" is diminished in importance during the medieval period as the church itself becomes increasingly imperial.

4. THE STRANGE STORY OF EASTER

1. I leave out of consideration the very different account in the so-called Gospel of Peter: see *RSG,* 592–96.

2. I here summarize *RSG,* 599–608.

3. One reviewer of *RSG* suggested that I had not sufficiently demonstrated that the four narratives are independent. Close study of the Greek text should make the point well enough: even when the writers are telling the same story, they manage to find quite different phraseology.

4. *Docetism* comes from the Greek word for "seem" or "appear."

5. On all this, see *RSG,* 697–701.

6. On this, see *RSG,* 701–6.

7. John Updike, "Seven Stanzas at Easter," *Telephone Poles and Other Poems* (New York: Knopf, 1964), 72f.

8. This argument, which appears ridiculous even to many skeptics, has been seriously proposed by S. J. Patterson, *The God of Jesus: The Historical Jesus and the Search for Meaning* (Harrisburg, PA: Trinity Press International, 1998), chap. 7. Patterson repeats it in his review in *Journal of Religion* 84 (2004): 637: "Those who did accept Jesus' resurrection as a fact might well have done so out of sheer devotion to their slain martyr and the conviction held by many pious Jews, that God in his righteousness would not give the enemy the final word." The short answer to this is that we know of a good many pious Jews who were faced with just this kind of situation and that in

no other case did they ever say that their slain, righteous martyr *had already been* raised from the dead.

9. Cf. Acts 12:15, with *RSG,* 134.

10. Two writers who have devoted a great deal of attention to these questions, and whose numerous works have done a great deal to advance the apologetic argument, are William Lane Craig, *Assessing the New Testament Evidence for the Historicity of the Resurrection of Jesus* (New York: Edwin Mellen Press, 1989), and Gary Habermas, *The Case for the Resurrection of Jesus* (Grand Rapids, MI: Kregel, 2004). I regret that I did not cite Craig or Habermas in *RSG.*

11. I did once actually watch the sun *set* twice in a day; one winter's afternoon I took off from Aberdeen shortly after sunset, and the sun rose again, in the west, as we climbed, only then to set, gloriously, a second time shortly afterward. That was, of course, cheating.

12. So, for instance, Lesslie Newbigin, *Living Hope in a Changing World* (London: Alpha International, 2003), 36.

13. Though some have gone that route and have found their way thereby to full faith, for example, Frank Morison, *Who Moved the Stone?* (London: Faber & Faber, 1930).

14. *Easter Oratorio,* music by Paul Spicer, words by Tom Wright, is recorded by the Birmingham Bach Choir and available from Farringdon Records: see www.easteroratorio.com.

15. See particularly Gerald O'Collins, *Easter Faith: Believing in the Risen Jesus* (London: Darton, Longman & Todd, 2003), 32f., 106f.

16. L. Wittgenstein, *Culture and Value: A Selection from the Posthumous Remains,* rev. ed., ed. G. H. von Wright et al., trans. Peter Winch (Oxford: Blackwell, 1998), 39. The whole passage is truly remarkable and deserves close attention.

17. Once more, Wittgenstein has some extremely suggestive reflections on this issue. See, for example, L. Wittgenstein, *Lectures and Conversations on Aesthetics, Psychology, and Religious Belief,* ed. C. Barrett (Berkeley and Los Angeles: University of California Press, 1966).

18. Patterson, in his review already referred to, *Journal of Religion* 84 (2004): 637, suggests that this line of thought is ironic, meaning presumably that it is my own view that is trying to bully opponents into submission. Those who have chafed under the tyranny of being told that because we are children of the Enlightenment we cannot believe in these ancient superstitions will understand what I am talking about.

19. Oscar Wilde, *Salome,* in *Complete Works of Oscar Wilde* (London and Glasgow: Collins, 1966), 565.

5. COSMIC FUTURE: PROGRESS OR DESPAIR?

1. Theologians will recognize that I am in implicit dialogue throughout this part of the book with two of the great German theologians of the last generation: Wolfhart Pannenberg in, for example, his *Systematic Theology,* vol. 3 (Grand Rapids, MI: Eerdmans, 1993), chap. 15 and many other places; and Jürgen Moltmann in, for example, *Theology of Hope* (London: SCM, 1967), and *The Coming of God: Christian Eschatology* (Minneapolis: Fortress Press, 1996). There is an entire book to be written as part of this ongoing conversation, but this is not it. On Moltmann, see particularly R. J. Bauckham, *God Will Be All in All: The Eschatology of Jürgen Moltmann* (Edinburgh: T & T Clark, 2005).

2. Sources I have found helpful in this chapter include John Polkinghorne and Michael Welker, ed., *The End of the World and the Ends of God: Science and Theology on Eschatology* (Harrisburg, PA: Trinity Press International, 2000); John Colwell, ed., *Called to One Hope: Perspectives on Life to Come* (Carlisle, UK: Paternoster, 2000). The latter includes my lecture "New Heavens, New Earth," originally given in 1993, which anticipates several aspects of the present book, not least this chapter. See too my *The Myth of the Millennium* (London: SPCK, 1999), published in the United States as *The Millennium Myth* (Louisville, KY: WJKP, 1999). Among other recent writers, Richard Bauckham is prolific and, in my view, largely on the right lines: see, for example, his book with Trevor Hart, *Hope Against Hope: Christian Eschatology in Contemporary Context* (Grand Rapids, MI: Eerdmans, 1999).

3. See R. J. Bauckham, "The Year 2000 and the End of Secular Eschatology" in Colwell, ed., *Called to One Hope,* 240–51.

4. On the reasons for the uncritical acceptance of Darwin see, interestingly, L. Wittgenstein, *Lectures and Conversations on Aesthetics, Psychology, and Religious Belief,* ed. C. Barrett (Berkeley and Los Angeles: University of California Press, 1966), 26f.

5. Ursula King, "Teilhard de Chardin, Pierre," in *The Oxford Companion to Christian Thought,* ed. A. Hastings (Oxford: Oxford University Press, 2000), 695.

6. King, "Teilhard de Chardin," 696.

7. The prayer (which begins, "O God of unchangeable power and eternal light") appears to originate in the 1912 Scottish Book of Common Prayer.

8. See my *Evil and the Justice of God* (Downers Grove, IL: InterVarsity Press, 2006).

9. On all this, see Polkinghorne and Welker, "Science and Theology on the End of the World and the Ends of God" in Polkinghorne and Welker, eds., *End of the World*, 1–13; W. R. Stoeger, "Scientific Accounts of Ultimate Catastrophes in Our Life-Bearing Universe," in the same book, chap. 1 (19–28); and Polkinghorne, "Eschatology: Some Questions and Insights from Science," in the same book, chap. 2 (29–41). Polkinghorne begins his chapter by questioning the "scientific" side of Teilhard de Chardin's theory.

10. See too my *Judas and the Gospel of Jesus* (Grand Rapids, MI: Baker, 2006) and other works referred to there.

11. Joni Mitchell, "Woodstock" (1970).

12. See Stuart Holroyd, *The Elements of Gnosticism* (Shaftesbury, UK: Element, 1994), especially chaps. 1 and 7.

13. On Phil. 3:20f.; 1 Pet. 1; etc., discussed below.

6. WHAT THE WHOLE WORLD'S WAITING FOR

1. See Hag. 2:6f.; cf. Rom. 8:18–26.

2. On Colossians 1, cf. my *The Climax of the Covenant: Christ and the Law in Pauline Theology* (Minneapolis: Fortress Press, 1992), chap. 5. The relevant passage is set out in full at the end of the present chapter.

3. 1 Cor. 15:20, 23; cf. Rom. 8:23, 11:16, 16:5; 1 Cor. 16:15; 2 Thess. 2:13; James 1:18.

4. There are attempts from time to time to imply that even Jesus's resurrection might be evidence of a new strand in some sort of evolutionary process: Jesus had "developed" further than the rest of us so that he was able, by "natural" means, to pass through death and on into a new life: for example, Stephen Holt, in *Resurrection*, ed. S. E. Porter, M. A. Hayes, and D. Tombs, JSNT Supplement Series 186 (Sheffield, UK: Sheffield Academic Press, 1999), 11.

5. Contra Kathryn Tanner, "Eschatology Without a Future?" in *The End of the World and the Ends of God: Science and Theology on Eschatology*, ed. John Polkinghorne and Michael Welker (Harrisburg, PA: Trinity Press International, 2000), 232.

6. This is taken for granted by, for instance, Alister McGrath in *A Brief History of Heaven* (Oxford: Blackwell, 2003), 12f. McGrath goes so far as to

suggest that this (mis)interpretation is "one of the leading themes of Paul's theology."

7. On Phil. 3:20f., see *RSG*, 229–36.

8. See, for example, J. Moltmann, *God in Creation: An Ecological Doctrine of Creation* (London: SCM Press, 1985), 86–93.

9. Isa. 11:9; Hab. 2:14.

10. Paul of course also knows this idea: Gal. 4:26. Cf. too Heb. 12:22–24.

11. This translation is taken from my *Paul for Everyone: The Prison Letters* (Louisville, KY: WJKP, 2002), 148.

7. JESUS, HEAVEN, AND NEW CREATION

1. Ps. 110:1, a favorite text of the early Christians: cf. Matt. 22:44 and pars.; Mark 16:19 (in the "longer ending," of course); Acts 2:34f.; Eph. 1:20; Col. 3:1; Heb. 1:13, 10:12; 1 Pet. 3:22; Rev. 3:21; cf. Luke 19:27; 1 Cor. 15:25.

2. For example, Rom. 8:34; Eph. 1:20, 2:6.

3. Douglas Farrow, *Ascension and Ecclesia: On the Significance of the Doctrine of the Ascension for Ecclesiology and Christian Cosmology* (Grand Rapids, MI: Eerdmans, 1999). See too G. S. Dawson, *Jesus Ascended: The Meaning of Christ's Continuing Incarnation* (London: T. & T. Clark International, 2004.)

4. See particularly T. F. Torrance, *Space, Time and Resurrection* (Edinburgh: Handsel Press, 1976), 110, 123–26; also his *Space, Time and Incarnation* (London: Oxford University Press, 1969).

5. Matt. 28:19.

6. 2 Cor. 4:5.

7. On the continuing human work of Jesus, see particularly, of course, the letter to the Hebrews (for example, 7:25, 9:24); and cf., for example, Torrance, *Space, Time and Resurrection*, 130, 133.

8. Farrow, *Ascension and Ecclesia*, 130–32, 153f. More detail in J. Pelikan, *The Christian Tradition: A History of the Development of Doctrine*, 5 vols. (Chicago and London: University of Chicago Press, 1971–1989), 3:160ff.

9. Likewise, finally, only when we grasp that Jesus is *already* Lord of the world and that at his final appearing every knee will eventually bow to him do we realize that the proper Feast of Christ the King is either Ascension Day itself or Advent Sunday, and to have a feast by that name at any other time is not just a category mistake but indicative of muddled, and actually damaging, theological thinking. Jesus does not become king of the world gradually, and his kingdom can never be *identified,* one for one, with the extension of the

church's witness and influence, as is all too easily implied by the very recent innovation, in Roman Catholic and Anglican circles, of having such a "feast" on the last Sunday before Advent. See my *For All the Saints? Remembering the Christian Departed* (Harrisburg, PA: Morehouse, 2003), 63–70.

10. See again T. F. Torrance, *Space, Time and Resurrection* (Edinburgh: Handsel Press, 1976), 133f.

11. Hal Lindsey, *The Late Great Planet Earth* (Grand Rapids, MI: Zondervan, 1971).

12. A very helpful summary and critique of the movement is one of the many virtues of Craig C. Hill's book *In God's Time: The Bible and the Future* (Grand Rapids, MI: Eerdmans, 2002), 199–209.

13. See, not least, Pss. 96 and 98.

14. See my *Simply Christian: Why Christianity Makes Sense* (San Francisco: HarperSanFrancisco, 2005), chap. 2.

15. For a full discussion, see *NTPG*, chap. 10, and especially *JVG*, 207–9. A radically different usage, and historical proposal, can be found in J. D. Crossan, *The Birth of Christianity* (San Francisco: HarperSanFrancisco, 1998), especially chaps. 15–18. A very helpful study can be found in Richard Bauckham's article "Eschatoloy," in *The Oxford Companion to Christian Thought*, ed. A. Hastings (Oxford: Oxford University Press, 2000), 206–9.

8. WHEN HE APPEARS

1. And another thing, while we're deconstructing that lovely hymn: in neither the Bible nor Christian tradition (Heb. 2:13, quoting Isa. 8:18, is the only possible exception) are Jesus's followers described as his *children.* "His brethren" would be better, or today perhaps "his siblings." This may be the implicit Docetism of the hymn peeping through, not for the only time, collapsing the vital distinction between Jesus and the Father.

2. See *JVG*, chaps. 8, 13; *The Challenge of Jesus* (Downers Grove, IL: InterVarsity Press, 2000), chaps. 2, 5.

3. Mark 13:26, 14:62 (and parallels).

4. For example, Matt. 25:14–30; Luke 19:11–27; and the small scenarios in 12:35–48 and elsewhere. On these, see *JVG*, 632–39.

5. For example, Mal. 3:1; cf. Zech. 14:5; other texts in *JVG*, 615–24.

6. Acts 1:11.

7. See especially, for example, Acts 3:19–21.

8. See especially *Paul,* chap. 7.

9. See, for example, Josephus, *Antiquities* 3.80, 203.

10. 1 Thess. 5:2; 1 Cor. 1:8, 5:5; 2 Cor. 1:14; Phil. 1:6 and 10, 2:16; 2 Pet. 3:10.

11. See C. J. Setzer, "The Parousia of Jesus and Jewsish Messianic Hopes," in J. T. Carroll et al., *The Return of Jesus in Early Christianity* (Peabody, MA: Hendrickson, 2000), 169–83.

12. See further *Paul,* chap. 4, and other material referred to there.

13. For the persecution of the Thessalonians, cf., for example, 1:6, 2:14, 3:3f.

14. 1 Cor. 16:22.

15. Col. 3:4.

16. Rev. 1:7, 2:25, 3:11, 16:15, 22:7, 12, 20.

17. James 5:7–8 is important, as is Heb. 9:28. 1 Pet. 1:20f. and 5:4 use the word *appear* both for the first and the second coming of Jesus.

18. See C. H. Talbert in *Vigilae Christianae* 20 (1966): 142, quoted by Jeffrey S. Siker, "The Parousia of Jesus in Second- and Third-Century Christianity," in Carroll et al., *Return of Jesus,* 148. And for all these passages, see the relevant places in *RSG;* in particular, for 2 Pet. 3:5–13, see *RSG,* 462f.

19. See Siker, "Parousia," in Carroll et al., *Return of Jesus,* and especially *NTPG,* 459–64.

9. JESUS, THE COMING JUDGE

1. Ps. 98:8; the whole psalm is relevant, as are several others in that section of the Psalter.

2. See particularly Miroslav Volf, *Exclusion and Embrace: A Theological Exploration of Identity, Otherness, and Reconciliation* (Nashville: Abingdon Press, 1994).

3. Acts 17:31; cf. 10:42.

4. On all this, see my *What Saint Paul Really Said* (Grand Rapids: Eerdmans, 1997), chap. 7, and *Paul,* chap. 6. See also my "Redemption from the New Perspective," in *Redemption,* ed. S. T. Davis, D. Kendall, and G. O'Collins (Oxford: Oxford University Press, 2004), 69–100; "4QMMT and Paul: Justification, 'Works,' and Eschatology," in *History and Exegesis: New Testament Essays in Honor of Dr. E. Earle Ellis on His 80th Birthday,* ed. Sang-Won (Aaron) Son (New York and London: T & T Clark, 2006), 104–32; and "New Perspectives on Paul," in *Justification in Perspective: Historical Developments and Contemporary Challenges,* ed. Bruce L. McCormack (Grand Rapids, MI: Baker Academic, 2006), 243–64.

5. See my "Romans," in the *New Interpreter's Bible* (Nashville: Abingdon, 2002), 10:393–770; the various volumes of *Paul for Everyone,* published jointly in London by SPCK and Louisville, KY, by WJKP: *Galatians and Thessalonians* (2002); *The Prison Letters* (2002); *1 Corinthians* and *2 Corinthians* (2003); *Romans,* 2 vols. (2004); and *The Climax of the Covenant* (Minneapolis: Fortress Press, 1992), especially chaps. 7, 8, 10, and 13.

6. Cf., for example, 2 Tim. 4:1; 1 Pet. 4:5.

7. John 5:22–30.

8. For example, John 16:8–11, about which there is no space to say more at this point.

9. See Douglas Farrow, *Ascension and Ecclesia: On the Significance of the Doctrine of the Ascension for Ecclesiology and Christian Cosmology* (Grand Rapids, MI: Eerdmans, 1999), 271.

10. 1 Cor. 11:27–34.

11. See especially T. F. Torrance, *Space, Time and Resurrection* (Edinburgh: Handsel Press, 1976), 158.

12. 2 Cor. 4:5.

13. This is the logic behind, for example, 1 Cor. 15:58; see my *The Way of the Lord* (Grand Rapids, MI: Eerdmans, 1999), chap. 9, and in this book, chap. 13.

10. THE REDEMPTION OF OUR BODIES

1. See, obviously, *RSG*.

2. 1 John 3:1f.

3. John 5:25–29.

4. John 14:2.

5. Luke 23:43.

6. Those interested in exploring the background to the word *Paradise* will find a detailed and fascinating account in J. N. Bremmer, *The Rise and Fall of the Afterlife* (London and New York: Routledge, 2002), 109–27. I regret that this work appeared too late for me to interact with it in *RSG*.

7. Phil. 1:23.

8. Matt. 6:20, 19:21; Luke 12:21; cf. 1 Tim. 6:19.

9. 1 Pet. 1:3.

10. Cf. *RSG,* chaps. 6, 7.

11. Cf. 2 Cor. 5:17.

12. From "Light's Abode, Celestial Salem," attributed to Thomas à Kempis, trans. J. M. Neale. Unfortunately, Neale published this in a collec-

tion called *The Celestial Country: Hymns on the Joys and Glories of Paradise* (London: Seeley & Co., 1866), which our earlier argument shows to be a typically misleading nineteenth-century way of putting it.

13. 1 Cor. 15:44.

14. 1 Cor. 15:50. See, for example, Irenaeus, *Against Heresies* 5.9.1–4, discussed in *RSG*, 515.

15. Details in *RSG*, chap. 11.

16. C. S. Lewis, *Miracles* (London: Fontana, 1960), 155. Lewis's chapter "Miracles of the New Creation," from which this is taken, remains one of the clearest succinct statements of the biblical picture.

17. Jeffrey Burton Russell, *A History of Heaven,* new ed. (Princeton, NJ: Princeton University Press, 1998), 119f.

18. C. S. Lewis, *The Great Divorce* (London: Macmillan, 1946).

19. 1 Tim. 6:16.

20. For example, Rom. 5:17; 1 Cor. 6:2, 3; 2 Tim. 2:12; Rev. 1:6, 5:10, 20:4, 22:5. Perhaps also (depending on its interpretation) Luke 19:17, 19.

21. This seems to be the position of, for instance, Douglas J. Davies, *Death, Ritual and Belief: The Rhetoric of Funerary Rites* (New York: Continuum, 2002), 128: "For Christians, resurrection would be the mode of entry into a heavenly domain where salvation would be fully known." This combines several misunderstandings.

22. Rev. 6:9–11.

23. To be fair, the song in question, "When the Trumpet of the Lord Shall Sound," by James M. Black (1893), deconstructs its own incipient Platonism with the next line: "And the morning breaks eternal, bright and fair." If morning is breaking, it can hardly be true that time has stopped.

24. Lewis, *Miracles,* 153.

25. See the whole discussion in J. Polkinghorne, *The God of Hope and the End of the World* (London: SPCK, 2002), especially 107–12.

11. PURGATORY, PARADISE, HELL

1. 1 Tim. 1:18, 6:12; see too 2 Tim. 4:7.

2. The best and most fascinating treatment I have come across of this whole development is in Stephen Greenblatt, *Hamlet in Purgatory* (Princeton: Princeton University Press, 2001), especially chap. 2. Greenblatt's eventual thesis—that *Hamlet* has as its subtext an implicitly Protestant son (Hamlet has been studying at Wittenberg) confronted by an implicitly Catholic

paternal ghost still suffering postmortem anguish—is spectacular, but so, equally, is his historical and cultural treatment of the rise and development of purgatory and its hold on late-medieval culture. See also the very helpful study of J. N. Bremmer, *The Rise and Fall of the Afterlife* (London and New York: Routledge, 2002), chap. 5.

3. See K. Rahner, *On the Theology of Death* (New York: Herder & Herder, 1961). Rahner's teaching is helpfully summarized in William J. La Due, *The Trinity Guide to Eschatology* (New York and London: Continuum, 2004), 51–57.

4. See Joseph Ratzinger, *Eschatology: Death and Eternal Life,* vol. 9 of *Dogmatic Theology,* ed. Johann Auer and Joseph Ratzinger (Washington, DC: Catholic University of America Press, 1988), 218–33. See too, for example, the wise exposition of Dermot A. Lane, *Keeping Hope Alive: Stirrings in Christian Theology* (Eugene, OR: Wipf & Stock, 2005), 143–48. Lane describes a shift among theologians "from seeing Purgatory as a place to a moment of personal and transforming encounter with the love of God" (148).

5. It seems that this was the preferred option in the famous sermon by Scott Holland we discussed in chapter 2 above.

6. Phil. 1:26.

7. Rom. 8:1.

8. Rom. 8:38f.

9. Luke 13:3, 5. On the whole topic, cf. *JVG,* chap. 8.

10. Luke 12:35–59, 16:19–31.

11. Matt. 25:31–46.

12. Miroslav Volf, *Exclusion and Embrace: A Theological Exploration of Identity, Otherness, and Reconciliation* (Nashville: Abingdon Press, 1994); Desmond Tutu, *No Future Without Forgiveness: A Personal Overview of South Africa's Truth and Reconciliation Commission* (London: Rider, 2000).

13. See 1 Tim. 6:16.

14. Rom. 2:8, 11:31.

12. RETHINKING SALVATION: HEAVEN, EARTH, AND THE KINGDOM OF GOD

1. For my recent debates with J. D. Crossan, see particularly Robert B. Stewart, ed., *The Resurrection of Jesus: John Dominic Crossan and N. T. Wright in Dialogue* (Minneapolis: Fortress Press, 2006).

2. A good deal of what follows is in parallel to the work of Richard Bauck-

ham and Trevor Hart, *Hope against Hope: Christian Eschatology at the Turn of the Millennium* (Grand Rapids, MI: Eerdmans, 1999), though it was developed independently. The work of Bauckham here and in many other places—for example, *Bible and Mission: Christian Witness in a Postmodern World* (Grand Rapids: Baker Academic, 2004)—remains powerful and seminal.

3. 1 Cor. 15:19.

4. *Mission-Shaped Church* (London: Church House Publishing, 2004).

5. Adrian Plass, *Bacon Sandwiches and Salvation: An A–Z of the Christian Life* (London: Authentic Media, 2007).

6. Plass, *Bacon Sandwiches,* 163.

7. Plass, *Bacon Sandwiches,* 164f., emphasis added.

8. Mark 5:23, 28, 34.

9. Matt. 9:22.

10. There is abundant material to follow up this point: see, for example, Matt. 8:25, 14:30; Mark 6:56, 10:52; Luke 8:36, 50, 17:19, 18:42; Acts 4:9, 14:9, 16:30, 31, 23:24, 27:20, 31, 34, 43, 44, 28:1, 4.

11. See, for a start, my book *Evil and the Justice of God* (Downers Grove, IL: InterVarsity Press, 2006), chap. 3.

12. Rom. 8:19.

13. Matt. 28:18; Rev. 11:15.

14. I have explored this most fully in *JVG.*

15. See particularly *Paul,* chap. 2.

16. See, for example, my *Evil and the Justice of God,* chap. 3; *The Challenge of Jesus* (Downers Grove, IL: InterVarsity Press, 2000), chap. 4; *JVG,* chap. 12; N. T. Wright and Marcus Borg, *The Meaning of Jesus: Two Visions* (San Francisco: HarperSanFrancisco, 1999), chap. 6.

17. The so-called other gospels—Thomas and the rest—are distinguished by this: that they neither want to see God's kingdom inaugurated on earth as in heaven nor want to know anything about Jesus's saving death. That is why they are so attractive to those who today prefer, as some did at the time they were written, an escapist philosophy and a spirituality of self-discovery. On all this see, for example, Nicholas Perrin, *Thomas, the Other Gospel* (London: SPCK, 2007); Darrell L. Bock, *The Missing Gospels: Unearthing the Truth Behind Alternative Christianities* (Nashville, TN: Thomas Nelson, 2006).

13. BUILDING FOR THE KINGDOM

1. Mark 12:18–27 and parallels, referring to Exod. 3:6; see *RSG,* 416–29.

2. See Eric Metaxas, *Amazing Grace: William Wilberforce and the Heroic Campaign to End Slavery* (San Francisco: HarperSanFrancisco, 2007).

3. For example, F. A. Hayek, *The Road to Serfdom: Text and Documents,* ed. Bruce Caldwell (Chicago: University of Chicago Press, 2007).

4. On the use of *Sadducee* as a title for an intellectual movement within the German Enlightenment, following the line of Spinoza into an atheism that left the way clear for humans to do what they liked, see Jonathan I. Israel, *Radical Enlightenment: Philosophy and the Making of Modernity, 1650–1750* (Oxford: Oxford University Press, 2001), 154, 367, and elsewhere.

5. On this theme, see my *Simply Christian: Why Christianity Makes Sense* (San Francisco: HarperSanFrancisco, 2006), part 1.

6. 2 Cor. 5:17.

14. RESHAPING THE CHURCH FOR MISSION (1): BIBLICAL ROOTS

1. This chapter was drafted before I read C. J. H. Wright, *The Mission of God: Unlocking the Bible's Grand Narrative* (Downers Grove, IL: InterVarsity Press Academic, 2006). With this work, Christopher Wright (no relation) continues to establish himself as one of the leading biblical missiologists in the world today.

2. For other reflections on Luke 24, see, for example, my *The Challenge of Jesus* (Downers Grove, IL: InterVarsity Press, 2000), chap. 7.

3. For more detail here, see my *Challenge of Jesus,* chap. 8; *RSG,* chap. 17; and, in a different genre, *Easter Oratorio,* music by Paul Spicer, words by Tom Wright, recorded by the Birmingham Bach Choir and available from Farringdon Records: see www.easteroratorio.com.

4. Isa. 55:11–13.

5. John 20:21.

6. For an interesting statement of a similar set of questions, see J. L. Martyn, "Epistemology at the Turn of the Ages," in *Christian History and Interpretation: Studies Presented to John Knox,* ed. W. R. Farmer, C. F. D. Moule, and R. R. Niebuhr (Cambridge: Cambridge University Press, 1967), 269–87.

7. John 20:28.

8. Ludwig Wittgenstein, *Tractatus Logico-Philosophicus* (London: Routledge & Kegan Paul, 1974), 74.

9. Acts 1:6. On Acts, see my *Acts for Everyone* (Louisville, KY: WJKP, 2008).

10. Ps. 72:8; cf. the visions of worldwide Davidic kingship in, for example, Isa. 9, 11, 42, etc.

11. Acts 1:8.

12. Josephus, *Antiquities* 19.434–50.

13. Acts 28:31.

14. Acts 4:2.

15. Acts 17:31. See Aeschylus, *Eumenides* 647f. (discussed in *RSG*, 32).

16. Phil. 1:23.

17. Cf. Heb. 2:8f., also using Ps. 8.

18. NRSV; but this could sound as though it's just an opinion that might yet be false whereas Paul intends it emphatically as something that is necessarily true of all those in Christ. It needs "calculating" because it is not an *obvious* truth, but once the sum has been reckoned up, it will appear to be clearly the case.

19. Cf. Rom. 10:9–10.

20. Col. 3:5–9.

21. Eph. 4:21–5:20.

15. RESHAPING THE CHURCH FOR MISSION (2): LIVING THE FUTURE

1. See particularly John Inge, *A Christian Theology of Place* (London: Ashgate, 2003).

2. John 4:24.

3. See my book *The Millennium Myth* (Louisville, KY: WJKP, 1999).

4. See John 20:1, 19; 1 Cor. 16:2.

5. A spectacular and deeply moving account of Christian life in these terms is offered by Samuel Wells, *God's Companions: Reimagining Christian Ethics* (Malden, MA, and Oxford: Blackwell, 2006).

6. Phil. 4:8.

7. 1 Pet. 1:3.

8. I am here following through some of the lines I began to explore in *Simply Christian: Why Christianity Makes Sense* (San Francisco: HarperSanFrancisco, 2005), chap. 12.

9. Job 13:15.

10. John 16:27.

11. John 20:17.

12. Rev. 5:12.

13. See my book *Scripture and Authority of God—Getting Beyond the Bible Wars* (San Francisco: HarperSanFrancisco, 2006).

14. After writing this I came across the verdict of Wittgenstein (himself of course a Jew): "The Old Testament [should be] seen as the body without its head; the New T[estament]: the head; the Epistles of the Apostles: the crown on the head. If I think of the Jewish Bible, the Old Testament on its own, I should like to say: the head is (still) missing from this body. The solution to these problems is missing. The fulfilment of these hopes is missing. But I do not necessarily think of a head as having a *crown*"; see *Culture and Value: A Selection from the Posthumous Remains,* rev. ed., ed. G. H. von Wright et al., trans. Peter Winch (Oxford: Blackwell, 1998), 40e.

15. Rom. 1:32.

16. 1 Cor. 13:9–12.

APPENDIX: TWO EASTER SERMONS

1. Slightly adapted from the original, published at Easter 2003 on the Ship of Fools Web site, http://shipoffools.com/Features/frameit.htm?0403/wright _wrong.html.

INDEX

Atonement, 204
Augustus Caesar, 100
Auschwitz, 180
Ave Verum, 286
"Away in a Manger" (hymn), 22

Bach, Johann Sebastian, 209
Bacon Sandwiches and Salvation (Plass), 195–196
Baptism, 46–47, 56, 228, 248–249, 255, 285; and entering new world, 253; and new creation, 271–273; and participation with Jesus, 249–250; and sacraments of matter, 262, 264, 266
Barley, Nigel, 7, 8, 12
Barth, Karl, 85, 178
Bauckman, Richard, 310–311n.1
Bearing, Vivian, 9
Beauty, 222–225, 231–232, 267
Begbie, Jeremy, 223
Benedict XVI, Pope, 167
Bernard of Clairvaux, 158
Birth, new, 103–104. *See also* New creation
Blake, William, 89
Bodies, as shameful, 18; transformed in resurrection, 43–44; valuing of and resurrection, 26. *See also* Body of resurrected Christians
Body of resurrected Christians, 43–44; appearance of, 160; given as reward, 161; given to reign and do God's work, 161; as immortal, 160; as incorruptible and undying, 44, 155, 160; may be created from mere scattered ashes, 163; model of Jesus for Paul, 149; more real or bodily than present humans, 154, 159; not spiritual but physical body, 149; and Paul's description of new mode of physicality, 154; vs. present body, in Paul's letter to Corinthians, 155–156. *See also* Resurrection
Braithwate, Richard, 32
Buddha, 121

Buddhism, 7, 11, 20, 24, 143, 152
Burial ancient Jewish rites of, 58; in churchyard, 24; facing east to meet Lord, 16. *See also* Funeral practices

Caesar, 26, 50, 129
Calvary, 247, 257
Cambridge Moral Science Club, 31
Cambridge University, 31
Carter, Jimmy, 271
Cathedrals, 209–210
Celtic tradition, 259
Chad, 7–8
Charity, 286–287
Children and heaven, 17–18
Christian Aid, 197
Christians, early, belief in Jesus as Messiah, 216; belief in resurrection for all, 93; believed neither in progress nor otherworldliness, 93; expectation that Jesus would soon return, 120, 121–122, 136; and hell, 177; and hope in future resurrection, 79; and Jesus in charge of heaven and earth, 111–112; and judgment by Jesus, 137; and modifications to Jewish beliefs in life after death, 41–51; Paul addressing problems of, 286; and salvation as God's new world presently, 198–199; unanimous on topic of death, 148; and use of word *parousia,* 129–130; views of regarding death and resurrection, 34–51; and work for those waiting for resurrection, 173
Christian year, 23
Christmas, 23, 256–257, 275
Christmas carols, 21–22
"Christ-Omega," 84
Church, Christian, abandoning traditional forms within, 258; beliefs regarding death in, 16–20, 147; buildings of, 116, 260; and evangelism, 227–228; existence of poses question, 69; expectant, 166, 174; history of, 261; hymns and prayers of

and death, 8; as identical or not with Jesus, 112–113; militant, 166; misdeeds of and supposed new era, 248; mission-shaped is truly hope-shaped, 193–194; need to return to what New Testament teaches, 25; and prayers before God's throne, 279; task of in light of judgment, 143; three parts of prior to sixteenth century, 165; triumphant, 165, 174; and uncertainty regarding death, 6; and use of space, time, and matter, 257–264, 265, 270. *See also* Mission of Christian Church

Euripides, 223

Evangelicalism, 225, 271

Evangelism, 225–230, 267; always comes as surprise, 232; distinguished from evangelicalism, 225; and God as king and Jesus is Lord, 227–228; and heaven-and-hell and Jesus, 226, 227; and individuals accepting gospel, 228; many ways of performing, 227; and new creation, 228, 229-30; and personal relationship to God or Jesus, 229; and prayer, 226; and turning back on creation, 228–229

Evil, 101, 215; and arts, 223; biblical analysis of and reality, 138; God's condemnation of in judgment, 181; and humankind not same as divinity, 94; and Jesus' death and resurrection, 204; moral problem of, 86–87; and myth of progress, 85–87; nature of, 94–95

Evolution, 83, 220, 304n.4

Evolutionary optimism, 101, 102

Exile, 95

Exodus, 214, 222

Ezekiel, 46, 105

Faith, 68; justification by, 139–140, 142; and resurrection, 70, 250; and science and history, 71; Thomas as epistemology of, 72

Farewell Discourses of John, 278, 280

Farrow, Douglas, 110

Feast of Christ the King, 305–306n.9

Final day, 30, 38

Firstfruits, 98, 122, 155, 162

Fishing, 241

Flesh and blood, 156

"For All the Saints" (hymn), 22–23

Forgiveness, 241, 247, 248, 288

Forms, eternal, 88

Four Weddings and a Funeral (motion picture), 9

Frye, Mary Elizabeth, 297n.8

Fundamentalism, 118, 213, 220

Funeral practices, 13, 23–25, 170; and confusion regarding death, 11–12; and cremation, 4, 23–24

Future, after death two-step process, 41; of entire cosmos, 29; language regarding, xiii, 132; and negative view of world, 87–91; and Paul and risen Jesus, 287; and view of progress, 81–87

Galen, 43

Galilee, 234

Galilei, Galileo, 294

Garden, 210, 239

Geach, Peter, 32

Gehenna, 175–176

Genesis, 95

Gentile nations, 138

Ghosts, 12, 36

Gifts for dead, 11–12

Glory, 43, 44

Gnosticism, 36, 42, 104, 133, 283, 294; and Christianity, 89–90; dualism of, 102; and evil material world, 97, 197; and real world elsewhere, 88–89; and resurrection, 44, 47, 50, 156; thinkers and writers influenced by, 89

God, announcing he is becoming king, 227; as bearded man in clouds, 175; being rich toward, 151; and creation of world, 94, 101–102; as creator and good, 27, 71–72, 179; and the Enlightenment, 75; and evil, 86, 87; glory of and resurrection, 168; image of, 105–106, 207; intimacy with, 277–278, 279; and Jesus' resurrection, 236; love of and the world, 102; and marriage of heaven and earth, 105; offerings to those in afterlife, 20; and power to effect change, 218; presuming upon kindness of, 272; Psalms and intimate union with, 277–278; purposes of and death, 6; setting world right via judgment, 137; space of, 116; and transformation of world, 91; will be "all in all," 101–102

God of Israel (YHWH), 126, 129

God's kingdom. *See* Kingdom of God

Goethe, Johann, 89

Golden age, 21–22

Golding, William, 9

Good Friday, 150, 256, 266

Goodness of creation, 94, 95, 96, 194

Gospelman, Pastor Frank, 291–293

Gospel of Thomas, 50

Gospels, four, and mission, 234–246

Gothic architecture, 116

Grace, 60

Grave robbery, 59

Great Divorce, The (Lewis), 159, 262

Greek philosophy, 80. *See also* Plato and Platonism

Gregory the Great, 158

Grieving, 29

Gulag, Soviet, 86

Hamartia, 180

Hamlet (Shakespeare), 16, 309–310n.11

Harvest, 98–100

Hayek, F. A., 218–219

Heaven, 199; ancients' view of, 41; belief one will simply go to, 150; in Bible, 18, 19; conventional view of, 17–18; and Easter hymns, 190; focusing attention on, 251–252; geographical/spatial aspects of, 111, 115, 134; going to as Christians' purpose, 19, 90, 168, 194–197, 198, 239, 293; Jesus taken into, 109, 111, 151; Jesus taking his people to, 22, 291; and kingdom of God, 203; not simply nonspiritual, 251; one who goes also returns, 117; as present reality, 19; saints in heaven upon death, 165; and salvation, 194; as waiting afterlife, 172; "we are citizens of," 100–101, 148–149, 291; where God's purposes are stored, 151–152

Heaven and earth, and baptism, 272; and church buildings, 116; Jesus or followers at home in either, 251; made single by resurrection, 104–105, 208, 250–251, 252, 279; not physical localities, 115; "shaking" of, 95

Heaven and hell, 17, 18, 158, 184

Heavenly minded people, 250

Hegel, Friedrich, 6, 82

Hell, 17, 18, 158, 175–183, 184; and annihilationism, 181; conventional views of, 175, 176; denial of, 8, 19; and endless punishment, 180; and merciful God of universalists, 181; and parables regarding afterlife, 176–177

Herod, 36, 39, 75, 243, 300n.3

Hezekiah, King, 129

Hinduism, 4, 10, 24, 88, 143

Hiroshima atomic bomb, 86, 180

Historical argument, 64, 66, 68, 69, 74

History, 69–70, 71

Hoddle, Greg, 3–4, 10

Holbein, Hans, 57

Holiness, 253, 283–285

Holland, Canon Henry Scott, 13, 14, 15

Holocaust, 292

Holroyd, Stuart, 89

Holy Sonnets (Donne), 9

Holy Spirit, 47, 114, 117, 140, 210–211; resurrection done by, 163; and split with matter, 153–154

Homer, 69, 75, 162

Homer's shades, 35–36

Hope, Christian, come forward via Jesus, 151; confusion regarding, 13–16; and early beliefs and resurrection, 40–41; and easing suffering of world, 191–192; and evangelism, 225–226; false offered by Scott Holland sermon, 14; future leads to present, 191–192; and genuine political discourse, 81; given by resurrection, 75, 147, 190–191; ignorance of what it ultimately is, xi; learning through rule of love, 288; as mode of knowing and new creation, 72; must shape Christian mission, 269; Paul as epistemology of, 72; for renewal of world, 118; for salvation in Jesus' resurrection, xi, 152; two themes of, xi, 5; we are saved in, 198

Hope, Jewish fulfilled by Jesus' resurrection, 237; modern realities and scarcity of, 230

House of Lords, British, xiii

"How Great Thou Art" (hymn), 22

How the Dead Live (Self), 10

Hugh of Saint Victor, 158

Humans, and building of kingdom of God, 207; created as reflection of God, 94; as God's stewards over creation, 96, 199, 202; Jesus as embodied, 114; renewing of creation through, 185

Hume, David, 69

Hurricanes, 4

Hymns, 8, 20–23, 241; Easter, 190, 256

Idolatry, 179, 180, 181, 182, 261; proper response to, 212; and sacraments, 262, 263

Ignatius of Antioch, 43, 157

Image of God, 105–106, 182, 207; and artistic creation, 223; being conformed to, 280

Immortality, 28, 160, 181

Inaugurated eschatology, 221–222

Incarnation, 96, 251

Incorruptibility of body, 44

Individualism, 80, 114

Indulgences, 166

Intercession of Jesus, 114

Intermediate place after death before resurrection, 190, 246; and paradise, 22–23, 41, 150; picture in Judaism and Christianity, 162

Intermediate state between Jesus' and others' resurrection, 249

Intimacy, 277–279

Irenaeus, 41, 43, 157

Isaiah, 102, 105, 106, 239, 241

Israel, 54; and Ark of the Covenant, 262; to be light to nations, 202; and

coming out of Egypt, 98, 103, 274; and God becoming king at last, 202; God coming to rescue, 129, 185, 214; God leaving and returning, 126; God's covenant with, 202; Jesus as climax of history of, 71, 236–238, 243, 281, 293; Jesus' restoring kingdom to, 242; as means of redemption in Old Testament, 96; restoration of, 46, 47, 130, 138

Israeli soldiers, 7

"It Came Upon the Midnight Clear" (hymn), 21

Jairus, 198

James (brother of Jesus), 48, 61, 243

Japanese scientist, and ancestor worship, 7–8

Jenkins, Bishop David, 189–190

Jenkins, David, 33

Jenkins, Jerry, 119

Jerusalem, 175, 242; conquering of in A.D. 70, 49, 64, 127

Jerusalem, New, 19, 29, 104, 105, 184, 299n.12

"Jerusalem the Golden" (hymn), 22

Jesus of Nazareth, already reigning, 247; asking Simon if he loves him, 72–73; authenticity of, 33; and baptism, 272; been to hell and back, 183; being within paradise after death, 150; in charge of heaven and earth, 111–112; and conception of soul, 28; crucifixion of and disciples' hopes, 39–40; declares authority on heaven and earth, 201; and disciples as witnesses, 242; as everywhere vs. standing over against, 112–113; and fishing trip, 241; and Gehenna, 176; and handing over rule of kingdom to God, 100; and heaven, 18, 22, 151; hope come to life in, 5; as human being in charge of world, 114, 173; human work in life and after death, 113, 204; as identical or not with church, 112–113; and

Jesus of Nazareth *(continued)*
    Jewish focus on rescue of Israel, 185;
    and judgment at hand, 140–141,
    149–150; and kingdom of God on
    earth and afterlife, 201, 203; as king
    of new creation, 63, 68, 99; as Lord,
    50; meeting someone who looked
    like, 61; as Messiah and resurrection,
    47–48; obedient to the death of the
    cross, 142; personal relationship to,
    229; and prediction of his own death,
    38–39; presence of now vs. second
    coming, 123–124; received attentions
    for doings, 192; return of, 116, 125,
    126–127; said little of future life, 177;
    and salvation in present world, 198;
    seated at right hand of God, 109; sent
    by God for redemption, 96–97; and
    sharing intimacy with God with oth-
    ers, 278; and "son of man coming on
    clouds," 125–126; and story of king
    going away for a while, 126; teach-
    ing about resurrection, 37–39; and
    Thomas' doubt, 70–71; vindication
    of, 125–126, 234. *See also* Ascension
    of Jesus; Judgment by Jesus; Resurrec-
    tion of Jesus
Jews and Judaism, and already inau-
    gurated eschatology, 45; Christian
    modifications of resurrection beliefs
    of, 41–51; early views regarding resur-
    rection and afterlife, 7, 34, 37–38, 41,
    43, 247; and Jesus as Messiah, 237–
    238; laws and regulations of, 250; and
    messianic movements in centuries
    around Jesus, 48; prayers of, 277–278;
    and resurrection and creation and
    judgment, 157; sacred meals of, 274;
    and story line of second coming, 130;
    story of fulfilled by Jesus' resurrection,
    237, 238. *See also* Old Testament
Job, 277
Johanan ben Zakkai, 300n.9
John, 238–241; and Docetism, 56; fare-
    well address of, 278, 280; and grave

robbery of Jesus, 59; and resurrection,
    43, 54, 149; and second coming, 135
John the Baptist, 39, 300n.3
John the Seer, 41
Josephus, 48, 129, 243
Judaea, 242
Judas and the Gospel of Jesus (Knight),
    196
Judgment by Jesus of Nazareth, 29,
    120; anticipation of, 141–142; and
    Christian worldview, 143; downplayed
    in many churches, 177–178; and God
    as creator and good, 179; John's de-
    scription of, 140–141; a joyous event,
    137, 141; necessity of, 150, 178–179,
    180; Paul's description of, 139–140;
    and political discourse, 144; purga-
    tory in according to Ratzinger, 167;
    and second coming, 142–145; will set
    world right, 121
Jung, Carl, 89
Justice, 113, 213–222, 231, 232, 267;
    and Lord's Prayer, 215; nothing can
    be done until Jesus returns, 213,
    215–216; and social gospel, 215
Justification by faith, 139–140, 142
Justification by works, 139
Justin Martyr, 41, 43, 157

Kashmir, 5
Keble, John, 20
Kennedy, John F., 17
Kingdom of God, 37, 112, 201–205;
    breaking in to present world, 201,
    213; building for by individual, 193,
    208; built by God through humans,
    207; church building for, 143; church
    living and spreading word of God,
    267; created via resurrection not
    force, 245; creating through actions,
    208–209; final vs. present anticipa-
    tions of, 208; and following Jesus' way
    of cross, 204–205; inauguration of
    and Jesus' resurrection, 234, 235; and
    Jesus' public ministry, 204; and king-

dom theology, 203–204; "on earth as in heaven," 280; in present world, xiii, 19, 176; rendered as Kingdom of Heaven, 18, 201; seen by disciples before their death, 234; and *Son of God* television series, 244; term used in different ways, 203–204; works will be part of, 209–210

Kingdom theology, 203–204

Knowledge and knowing, challenge of resurrection to, 67–70; and epistemologies of love, 73, 74; as gift from God, 74; historic and scientific, 64–66; Jesus calls followers to new form of, 239; logic cannot comprehend love, 101; means for determining, 34; questioning current paradigms of, 69; source of, 27–28

Krishna, 121

Kyoto protocol, 219

LaHaye, Tim, 119

Last Supper, 274

Late Great Planet Earth, The (Lindsey), 119

Lazarus, 37, 177

Left Behind (LaHaye and Jenkins), 119

Lent, 256, 257, 292

Lewis, C. S., 115, 157, 159, 160, 180, 262

Liberalism, English, 112

Liberal modernism, 213

Liberal theology, 178, 219

Life after death. *See* Afterlife

Life before death, 197–198

Lindsey, Hal, 118

Lion and Lamb, 279

Literalism vs. skepticism, 110–111

Lonergan, Bernard, 72

Lord, Jesus as, 71, 242, 243, 252; and baptism, 250; by virtue of resurrection, 243; instead of Caesar, 50, 74, 129, 130–131

Lord's Prayer, 29, 104, 201, 215, 293

Love, 285–289; and agape, 73; and creation, 101; as destiny, 288; episte-

mology of, 72, 73, 239; of God and the world, 102; and Paul's Letter to Corinthians, 287–288; and prayer for dead, 172; and resurrection, 72

Luke, and Christmas, 257; and Docetism, 56; and Jesus' resurrection, 235–238, 243–244; and Jesus taken into heaven, 109; and paradise, 150–151; and Paul in Rome, 243

Luther, Martin, 166, 209

Lyons, persecutions at, 43, 301n.24

Maccabean martyrs, 43

Male and female, 105–106

Mandela, Nelson, 245–246

Manicheans, 88, 102

Marana tha, 134

Mark, 234

Marriage of heaven and earth, 104–106

Martha, 37

Martyrs, 50, 174

Marx, Karl and Marxism, 26, 83, 85, 224

Mary, 59, 214, 239

Mary Magdalene, 113, 278

Matter, 262–264, 266–267

Matthew, and biblical scriptures and resurrection, 54, 57; and Christmas, 257; and heaven, 18; and Jesus' appearance after death, 201; and Jesus entering kingdom of heaven, 151; and mission to world, 235; and salvation here and now, 198

Measure for Measure (Shakespeare), 181

Melville, Herman, 89

Messiah, to appear on earth not in heaven, 40; association with resurrection, 47–48; being conformed to image of, 280; death of not envisioned in Jesus' time, 130; early Christians' belief in Jesus as, 216; as God's agent to restore justice, 138–139; Jesus as Israel's, 237, 238, 242; Jesus is by virtue of resurrection, 236–237; Jesus' not believed to be at time of his death, 61; and Jesus'

Messiah *(continued)*
ruling over new creation, 99; physical things expected of, 47–48; and raising of Jesus, 56, 57, 247
Millenarian movements, 118
Miracles, 33
Mission of Christian Church, 264–270; and arts of collaboration, 269; to entire world, 239; and fostering beauty and aesthetic meaning, 232; and Jesus' lordship over the world, 235; living of in activism and private lives, 270; and making difference in world, 267; and new creation, 193; and postindustrial communities, 230–232; practical realities of, 233; present search to find, 211; and reactions from world, 268–269; and resurrection of Jesus and humankind, 264–265; and saving souls vs. good in world, 265; shaped by hope, 230, 269–270; and social gospel, 215; and use of space, time, and matter, 257–264, 265, 270; working now for time of kingdom of God, 211; work of whole church, 267–268
Mission of God, 208
Mission-shaped church, 193–194
Mitchell, Joni, 89
Moltmann, Jürgen, 102
Moral, objection to resurrection of Jesus, 189–190; problem of economic debt, 217; problem of evil, 86
Moses, 132, 141, 214
Mother Teresa, 245

Nag Hammadi scrolls, 89–90
Narnia stories, 115
Natural disasters of 2004 and 2005, 4
Nature mysticism, 276–277
Nazism, 217
Near-death experiences, 28
Nero, 37
New Age culture, 10, 84, 115
Newbigin, Bishop Leslie, 107–108
New birth, 103–104, 271–273

New creation, 44, 67, 71, 106; and beauty and artistic creativity, 222–225; Christianity ushering in, 67; continuous with present and not yet arrived, 162; converted Christian as bit of, 228; creates program for change on earth, 221; and Easter, 294; and the Eucharist, 273–276; evangelical announcement of, 229–230; and gospels not included in New Testament, 283; Jesus as ruler over, 99; and Jesus' resurrection, 76, 246, 279, 293; Paul's theology of, 154; and poem from Colossians, I, 107; promise of about mission of Church, 193; rather than personal heaven or hell, 185; resurrection occurs on new earth and new heaven, 159; and sacraments, 262–264, 271–272; and scripture, 281–283; and shepherding, 241; and unity of heaven and earth, 208; works done will be part of, 208. *See also* Creation
New Jerusalem, 19, 29, 104, 105, 184, 200n.12, 291
Newman, John Henry Cardinal, 20–21, 166, 167
New Orleans, 4
New Testament, 14, 22, 314n.14; and accounts of resurrection, 34, 53; authenticity of, 33, 57; and awfulnesses, 179, 180; and centrality of resurrection, 43; and Christian hope through Jesus, 56, 93, 107; and Christmas vs. Easter, 23; and Church practices, 25; and conception of soul, 28; and defeat of death, 15; and direct access to God, 173; Easter essential to, 257; Gospels not included in, 283; and heaven and hell, 18, 175, 184; and incorruptible resurrected body, 44; independence of our narratives, 54, 301n.3; and judgment, 141–142; kingdom of God already begun, 201; in light of overall Christian story,

281; marginalizing of, 219; and new creation, 106; one who goes to heaven also returns, 117; and Paul's letter to Corinthians, 155; and prayer, 276, 277, 278, 279, 280; and purpose of Gospels, 202–203; and rest period previous to resurrection, 190; and salvation here and now, 198; and "second coming," 125, 127–128; and sin, 179–180; and what happens after death, 147

New Testament and the People of God, The (Wright), 122

New world. *See* New creation

North American Christianity, 118, 125

Northern Ireland, 245

Objective knowledge, 73–74

Oklahoma City bombing, 3

Old Testament, as body without head, 314n.14; and death as exile, 95; and evolution, 83; and God's coming judgment, 137; and heaven and hell, 18, 19; as Hebrew scriptures, 237; and Jesus' resurrection, 53–54, 236–237, 238; and journey after death, 19; reading as story pointing to new creation, 282

Open Society and Its Enemies, The (Popper), 31

Origen, 40, 156, 157

Ossuary, 58

Oxford movement, 20

Pagan world, ancient, 35–37

Pakistan, 5

Palestinians, 7

Pantheism, 94, 97, 102, 105, 223

Paradigms, questioning of current, 69

Paradise, 171–174; church both triumphant and expectant, 174; as intermediate place of joy, 22–23, 41, 150, 171–172; love of God and presence of Jesus in, 172; and prayers for living, 172–173; and work for good of others, 173

Parapsychology, 27–28

Parousia, 128–132, 135

Passover, 98, 274

Paul, 33, 61, 74, 243, 246, 268; and ascension vs. raising from dead, 109; and baptism, 249, 272; and "citizens of heaven," 100–101, 148–149, 291; and Corinthians poem about completeness, 285–286; and creation, 97, 224; desire to be with Jesus, 41; and early Christian hope, 40; and "fellow workers with God," 184; and hope, 72, 93, 191; and humans as cracked earthenware vessels, 112; and Jesus as Lord and Messiah, 50, 238, 243; and Jesus' judgment, 139, 154, 244; and Jesus' resurrection, 43, 46, 56, 98, 287; and Jewish focus on God's rescue of Israel, 185; and justification by works and faith, 139–140; and life in world filled with life of heaven, 251–252; and living the resurrection life, 250, 286; and mechanism for going to heaven, 203; and mercy and conversion for all, 183–184; and mission of church, 112, 246–252; and new birth, 103–104; and new creation, 72, 122, 228; and no condemnation for those in Christ, 170; and no split between spirit and matter, 153–154; and *parousia,* 128, 129–130, 131–132; and present life as purgatory, 170–171; and the rapture, 121; and redemption of body, 147; and resurrection and Bible, 54; and resurrection and letters to Corinth, 152–156; and resurrection and treatment of body, 26, 283; and resurrection and work, 192–193; and resurrection body, 43–44; and second coming, 128, 131–135; seeing through glass darkly, xiii, 287; and waking up in Jesus, 248, 252; and "we were saved in hope," 198; and works not done in vain, 193, 208–209, 210, 216, 294

Pentecost, 98, 239, 293

Pentecostalism, 271

Perchance to Dream (motion picture), 9

Persecution, 50

Persuasion, 81

Peter, 72, 73, 74, 151, 152, 243; called by Jesus to be shepherd, 241; questioning by Jesus, 241; and sin and forgiveness, 241

Pharaoh, 68, 70

Pharisees, 38, 42, 50, 214, 215

Phenomenon of Man, The (Teilhard de Chardin), 84

Philippi, 100

Philippians, 268, 293

Philo, 37, 42

Physics, 107

Pincher Martin (Golding), 9

Place, theology of, 259

Plant without roots, 258

Plass, Adrian, 195–196

Plato and Platonism, 6, 21, 62, 69, 143, 154, 262; and abandoning of creation, 44; and Christianity, 90; and downgrading of body and created order, 26; and incarnation as mistake, 96; and rejection of matter and transience, 88, 153; and disembodied immortal soul, 36, 80, 160; and views of heaven, 18; world as illusory, 87

Plymouth Brethren, 118

Pneuma, 156

Political theology, xiii

Politics, and art as expression, 224; confrontation with and early Christian theology, 133–134; and disbelief of tyrants, 75–76, 302n.18; and final judgment, 144; and Jesus' message regarding Gehenna, 176; and myth of progress, 81–82, 85, 87, 144; and second coming, 120; and shape of Acts, 243

Polkinghorne, John, 107, 163

Popper, Karl, 31–32, 33, 35

Poseidon, 277

Practical theology, xiii

Pragmatism, 233

Prayer, 8, 276–280; of ancient Israel, 277; of departed for living, 172–173; and intimacy with God, 277–279; and nature mysticism, 276–277; and petition to deities, 277; places sanctified by, 260; and preaching, 226; for those in afterlife, 172

Presence, 124

Progress, myth of, 81–87, 98; cannot deal with evil, 84, 85–87; championed by politicians, 81–82; and evolution, 83; Jesus' evolution as sign of, 304n.4; not believed by early Christians, 93; parody of Christian vision, 82; and Teilhard de Chardin, 84–85

Prometheus, 82

Protestantism, 211, 258, 261, 262

Psalmists, 121

Psalms, 137, 231, 277–278, 279

Psychê, 152, 156

Purgatory, 19, 158, 166–171; all in same situation within, 169–170; and Cardinal Newman, 166; medieval focus upon, 166; modern quasi version of, 167–168, 171; and non-Christians, 167; not geographical place, 170; and praying for dead, 172; as preparation for judgment by all, 167–168; present life as, 170–171; and Rahner and sin, 167; and Ratzinger and judgment, 167

Quietism, 269

Rahner, Karl, 166–167, 171

Rapture theology, 119, 121, 128, 133–134; so who cares about world, 219

Ratzinger, Cardinal, 167, 171

Rebellion, world in, 102, 137, 199, 202, 207

Redemption, 96, 107, 123, 185, 204; of body according to Paul, 147; Christ as means of, 96–97; of created world and

celebration, 212; of creation, 211; on
last day, 19

Red Sea, 68, 70

Reflection of God, human beings as,
105–106, 182, 207, 280

Reformation and reformers, 172, 173,
273

Regeneration, 228

Reincarnation, 3–4, 10

Religion as opiate of people, 26

Religious right in America, 120

Rembrandt van Rijn, 57

Renaissance, 82

Resurrection, xi; acceptance of bodily
by early Christians/Church fathers,
41–42, 156–157; according to biblical
scriptures, 53–54; actual transformed
body of, 36, 43–44; for all but special
Christian case, 159; ancient views
toward bodily, 34, 35–37, 300n.3;
association with Messiah, 47–48;
belief in physical vs. eternal existence
of soul, 16; and Christian and Jewish
valuing of world, 26; of the dead with
parousia, 131; and defeat of death, 50,
62, 99–100, 143, 247; done by Spirit,
163; and early Christian hopes, 41;
and funeral services, 24–25; future,
according to Paul, 72; and glory of
God, 168; happening to all God's
people at once, 45; and heaven as ultimate place, 19; "hour for is at hand,"
140–141, 149–150; ignorance relative
to Christian belief in, xii, 12; and Judaism, 7, 157; later debates regarding,
156–158; as life *after* life after death,
151, 169, 197; love that believes,
72; necessary for wicked so may be
judged, 150, 154; as new bodily life
after interim, xii, 36, 66; not divinization for ancient pagans, 37; occur-
ring to one person ahead of others,
44–45; Paul's description of first Jesus
and then all, 247; and Paul's letters
to Corinth, 152–156; as rational for

Christian behavior, 148, 284–285;
rest time before, 190; revisionist
positions on, 48–50; revolutionary
doctrine in first-century world, 214;
takes place on new earth, 159; term as
metaphor and as metonymy, 46–47;
and Tertullian, 157; and treating
bodies well and good action, 26, 156,
162, 192; view that it occurs upon
death, 162, 309n.21. *See also* Body of
resurrected Christians

Resurrection of Jesus of Nazareth, 28,
108, 125; accuracy of event of, 33; and
artistic expression, 224; and biblical
accounts, 53–54; cannot be collapsed
with ascension, 109; cannot be proved
by historical argument, 64; Christianity began because of, 43, 63–64, 66;
created by devotion and convictions
only, 62, 301–302n.8; creates program
for change on earth, 221; as defeat of
death, 99–100, 143, 247; and disciples
meeting with Jesus and empty tomb,
58–59; disciples would only champion
if factual, 62–63; as evolutionary process, 304n.4; eyewitnesses to, 34, 55; as
first fruits, 98; and future hope, 56–57,
107, 152; and goodness of creation,
210; happened within our own world,
191; his description of his own, 38–39;
idea of derived from surrounding
culture, 48; importance of acceptance
of, 191; and Jesus as God's messenger,
236–237; Jesus' speaking of by quoting
Exodus, 214; lack of explanation for,
63; life of Jesus tragedy without, 236;
and mission of Jesus' lordship over
world, 235; moral objection to, 190;
and new birth, 103; new experience of
grace causing story of, 60; not cognitive dissonance, 60; participation with
in transforming the present, 45–46;
and poem in Colossians I, 106–107;
question of what difference it makes,
189–190, 291, 292; revisionist positions

Resurrection of Jesus of Nazareth
(continued)
regarding, 48–50, 59–60; rival explanations of, 59–62; and sharing intimacy
with God with others, 278; small-scale
arguments to support, 62–63; as "spiritual" experience, not physical, 62, 110;
and transformation of physical body,
55–56, 63; witness to, 233; wounds
visible on body of, 160, 224
Resurrection of the Son of God, The
(Wright), 106
Resurrection people, 30, 249, 250
Returning master or king story, 126, 127
Revelation, book of, 22, 172, 185; and
earth as kingdom of God, 201; and
healing of nations, 184; and hell, 177;
and large-scale Christian hope, 93;
and pictures of heaven, 18–19
Revelation of Saint John the Divine, 135
Reward, 161–162
Rich man, parable of, 177
Roman Catholicism and purgatory, 166
Romantic movement, 89
Rome and Romans, 49, 213, 243, 293;
and creation of colonies, 100; and
departed emperors, 37; Jesus' warning
vs., 176
Royal presence, 129, 131
Russell, Bertrand, 31–33

Sacramental theology, 271
Sacraments, 262–264, 266; close to
sympathetic magic, 273; as means by
which Jesus is present, 114; as part of
new creation, 272. See also Baptism;
Eucharist
Sadducees, 37, 38, 214; denial of resurrection of Jesus, 213–214, 218, 219, 243
Saints, 165, 169, 170, 173–174
Salome (Wilde), 75–76
Salvation, 194–201, 204; about relationship with God, 195–196; being raised
to life in God's new heaven and earth,
198; and going to heaven when you

die, 19, 90, 168, 194–197, 198, 239,
293; as having nothing to do with
world, 26; here and now, 198–199,
200; as life after life after death, 197;
and life before death, 197–198; not
just soul but whole human being, 199,
200; not simply personal but part of
God's plan, 200; past, present, and future, 199; in present vs. ultimate, 199;
through Jesus, 152; through putting
in practice God's rule in world, 205;
typical belief about, 195–196
Samaria, 242
Schubert, 66
Schwarzenegger, Arnold, 17
Scientific knowledge, 64, 65–66; as gift
from God, 74; and Jesus as Lord, 71;
use of love in, 73
Scripture, 27, 173, 281–283
"Second coming" of Jesus of Nazareth,
117–122; and verses in Thessalonians, 131–133; American obsession
with, 118–119, 120; and appearance
between Jesus and followers, 123,
134–135; confusion over use of term,
125; and delay, 135, 136; as events of
A.D. 70, 127; and hymnals, 22; and
Jesus descending and followers rising,
125; Jesus does not speak of, 125,
126–127; and Jesus taking people to
heaven, 22; Jewish background for,
130; and judgment, 142–145; margin-
alizing of, 120; and New Testament,
127–128, 136; not yet occurred, 127;
Paul's descriptions of, 131–135; and
word eschatology, 121
Seedtime and harvest, 98–100
Self, Will, 10
September 11, 2001, 4
Sex issues, 217, 219, 263, 292
Shakespeare, William, 113
"Shaking" of heaven and earth, 95
Shelley, Percy, 11, 20
Shema, 277–278, 280
Shepherding, 241

Ship of Fools Web site, xiv
Silence, 240
Simon, 72
Simon bar Giora, 49–50
Sin, forgiveness of and Jesus' resur-
  rection, 247, 248–249; as missing
  the mark, 179–180; and Peter, 241;
  punished by disabilities in future life,
  4; and purgatory, 166, 167; redemp-
  tion from, 96; reigning through death,
  248; removed at death, 170; victory
  over through baptism in Jesus, 249
Sinai, 98
Sistine Chapel, 141
Skepticism, 74
Slavery, 216, 217, 218, 219, 222
Sleep, 177, 252, 287
Smalley, Stephen, 299–300n.19
Smoothtongue, Reverend Jeremy,
  291–293
Social Darwinism, 83, 220, 221
Social gospel, 83, 215, 219
Son of God television series, 244
"Son of man" sayings, 125–126
Sophocles, 223
Souls, 152, 158, 202; disembodied
  future for, 37; eternal existence of, 16;
  immortality of, 28, 37; and Rahner's
  version of purgatory, 166–167; whole
  person vs. interior soul, 28, 199, 200
South African Commission for Truth and
  Reconciliation, 179, 245
Southwark Cathedral, 245–246
Soviet Communism, 253
Space, 115, 116, 211, 212; church using
  in mission, 265–266; renewal and
  reclaiming of, 259–260
Spanish Inquisition, 244
Spinoza, Baruch, 312n.4
Spirit. See Holy Spirit
Spirit baptism, 271
Spirits, 36
Spiritualism, and contact with dead, 12
Spirituality, 271–289; baptism, 271–
  273; Eucharist, 273–276; holiness,

283–285; love, 285–289; and prayer,
  276–280; and scripture, 280–283
Star, Jesus shining like, 55
St. Francis, 16, 245
Stoic philosophy, 143, 153
Stonemason, 209–210
Sunday, 238, 261–262, 266

Teilhard de Chardin, Pierre, 84–85, 86,
  101, 106, 107
Temple, William, 33, 222
Temple of Israel, 96, 105, 125, 126
Tennyson, Alfred, 20
Tertullian, 40, 157
Theology Through the Arts, 223
Thomas, 50, 56, 61, 74; and doubt and
  touching Jesus, 70–71, 239; as episte-
  mology of faith, 72
Thomas, Dylan, 10
Time, 115, 162–163, 168, 211, 212;
  and church using in mission, 266;
  and dating based on birth of Jesus,
  260–261, 266; renewal and reclaiming
  of, 260–262
Tombs, veneration of Jewish, 62
Torah, 98
Totalitarianisms, 75
Toulmin, Stephen, 32
Tractatus Logico-Philosophicus
  (Wittgenstein), 240
Transformation, 100, 142, 162, 284
Transience, 88, 94–95
Transubstantiation, 274–275
Trinity, 113–114
Triumphalism, 143, 216
Tsunami, Asian of 2004, 4
Tutu, Desmond, 179, 246, 248
Tyrants, 75–76
Tyreus, Reverend Peter, 299n.18

Ugliness, 231
United States, 118, 125; and resurrection and improving world, 27; what is
  good for is good for God, 219
Universalists, 175, 177–178, 181

Updike, John, 60–61
Utopian dream, 82, 144

Visions, 58, 62
Volf, Miroslav, 179

Waking up, 248, 252
War, 221
Waters, 102
Wesley, Charles, 299n.11
Wesley, John, 116
Westminister Abbey, xiv, 12
What's Heaven? (Shriver), 17
Wilberforce, William, 27, 216, 245, 248, 269
Wilde, Oscar, 75–76
Wit (Edson), 9, 298n.2
Witness to resurrection, 55, 233
Wittenstein, Ludwig, 31–33, 35, 53; and love and resurrection, 72, 239–240; and Old and New Testaments, 314n.14; and silence, 240; and *Tractatus Logico-Philosophicus,* 240
Women, 55, 105–106
Woolman, John, 217
Word, 238, 239
Work, idea that nothing can be done until Jesus returns, 213, 216, 221–222; justification by, 139–140; public not enough, must wake up, 248, 253; resurrection leads to, 192–193, 214; what is done is not done in vain, 193, 208–209, 210, 216, 294–295
World, applying gospel to problems of, 253; beauty of and God, 102; Christian/Jewish valuing of and resurrection, 26; Christian partnership with, 241; created by God but not different, 94; God intends transformation of as for Jesus, 91; God's reclaiming of

whole, 259; God's re-creation of and Bible, 184; improving and belief in resurrection, 27; as negative place, 87–91; setting right via judgment, 137; transformation of through Jesus, 142–143. *See also* New creation
World history, 113
Worldview issues, 64, 65, 69; Christian vs. other, 143; and Gnostic influences on Western Christianity, 90; and hope through resurrection, 75
World War I, 8, 85, 178
World War II, and attitudes regarding death, 8
Worship, becoming like what one worships, 182; returning to after action in world, 268; in spirit and truth, 259
"Worthy is the Lamb" (hymn), 279
Wright, N. T., and area of country where hope in short supply, 230; attacked for apparently not teaching second coming, 126; and Church of England, 24; and course on resurrection at Harvard, 160; and ecological questions in Thunder Bay, Ontario, 119; inexperience in politics of, xiii; lack of bereavement in life of, xii, xiii; and Oxford tutorial and hell, 178; preaching and praying of, 226; response to his bringing up economic issues, 217, 218; and silence about death in 1950s, 8; study of early Christianity, xii; and those who turn from God, 182–183; visit to Jerusalem of, 175–176; and watching Christians do good works, 267

Yeats, William Butler, 89

Zimzum, 102
Zoroastrianism, 36

Biblical Passages